# Hinds' Feet on High Places

*by Hannah Hurnard*

—— with a ——

# *Woman's Devotional*

*by Darien B. Cooper*

**Destiny Image Publishers**
**P.O. Box 310**
**Shippensburg, PA 17257**

"Speaking to the Purposes of God for this Generation"

ISBN 1-56043-116-4

For Worldwide Distribution
Printed in the U.S.A.

# The Author of the Devotionals

Darien B. Cooper has written books and min-
istered personally to women for nearly 20 years,
but her work on the *Woman's Devotional* for
*Hinds' Feet on High Places* realizes her heart's
desire of many years. "I have long desired to help
women enjoy their full inheritance in God," she
says. "The powerful allegory of 'Much-Afraid's'
journey helps us identify with life's struggles
and transform them into personal victories."

Darien lives in Georgia with her husband, Dewitt. From
1974 to 1979, she wrote *You Can Be the Wife of a Happy Husband*, *We Became Wives of Happy Husbands*, and *How to Be
Happy Though Young*, a book for teenagers. All three books
are currently out of print. In 1989, she wrote *The Beauty of
Beholding God*, published by Destiny Image Publishers. Their
three sons have all married, and the Coopers now have seven
grandchildren.

Destiny Image books are available through these fine distributors outside the United States:

| | |
|---|---|
| Christian Growth, Inc.<br>Jalan Kilang-Timor, Singapore 0315 | Successful Christian Living<br>Capetown, Rep. of South Africa |
| Lifestream<br>Nottingham, England | Vision Resources<br>Ponsonby, Auckland, New Zealand |
| Rhema Ministries Trading<br>Randburg, South Africa | WA Buchanan Company<br>Geebung, Queensland, Australia |
| Salvation Book Centre<br>Petaling, Jaya, Malaysia | Word Alive<br>Niverville, Manitoba, Canada |

# Dedicated to:

my sister
*Jan Bruner*
who has added
to my collection
of precious stones
as we have journeyed
together to the High Places.

# Contents

# Introduction

All of us are traveling on our life's journey. It is my desire that the devotions in this book be used by our Lord to enhance and enrich your journey.

Most of these devotions are "quiet time" meditations, ones which you can use to draw nearer to Jesus. As you do, you will be renewed from within—knowing who you are "in Him"; knowing the truth about who you are; and no longer believing the enemy's lie that defeats and discourages you. You also will learn who He is, how much He loves you, and how to love Him in return. It is to be a resting, establishing, and bonding time between you and your Lord which results in stabilization, security, strength, dignity, and peace in your inner being.

If spending time with the Lord as instructed here is new and different to you, you may feel foolish or that you are wasting your time and nothing is really happening. Know that such thoughts and feelings are from your enemy, who is trying to rob you of the greatest relationship in life: a love walk with Jesus Christ. Even when nothing seems to be happening, you are *not* wasting your time. It has been wisely said, "Not to wait on God is the only great idleness." The psalmist admonishes us to wait before Him: *"Be still and rest in the Lord; wait for Him, and patiently stay yourself upon Him"* (Ps. 37:7a AMP), as well as James: *"Come close to God and He will come close to you"* (Jas. 4:8 AMP). God's Word also promises that those who seek Him will find Him: *"I love those who love me* [wisdom], *and those who seek me early and diligently shall find me"* (Prov. 8:17 AMP).

When your thoughts wander during your devotional time, don't feel guilty. Just quietly focus on Him again. If you are faithful and persistent, you will be rewarded by tasting of the Lord and seeing that He is good. It will become the best and the most cherished time of your day. This time should also spill over into the rest of your day, influencing and guiding your thoughts. Gradually, you will learn to dwell in His presence *all day long*!

Whether the devotion is for a quiet time, an instructional time, or a time of examining your ways with Him, carefully follow through with the directions. Each devotional builds upon the previous one. They are carefully designed to firmly establish you in Him and to strengthen your daily walk.

You may want to read through the allegory first, enjoying the delightful flow of the story. Then take one devotional per day, comparing your own pilgrimage with Much-Afraid's. Using a special notebook, record your own journey. Take time to read each Scripture from your own Bible. Do not rush through these times with the Lord. A love relationship cannot and will not be developed unless quality time is spent with Him. Carefully meditate upon the areas that He makes personal to you. Cherish each nugget of truth as He brings it from His heart to your heart!

I'm looking forward to comparing our life's journey notes— whether here in time or there in eternity!

Darien Cooper

# Preface to the Allegory

One morning during the daily Bible reading on our mission compound in Palestine, our little Arab nurse read from *Daily Light* a quotation from the Song of Songs, "The voice of my Beloved! behold, he cometh leaping upon the mountains, skipping upon the hills" (Song of Solomon 2:8). When asked what the verse meant, she looked up with a happy smile of understanding and said, "It means there are no obstacles which our Savior's love cannot overcome, and that to Him, mountains of difficulty are as easy as an asphalt road!"

From the garden at the back of the mission house at the foot of Mount Gerizim we could often watch the gazelles bounding up the mountainside, leaping from rock to rock with extraordinary grace and agility. Their motion was one of the most beautiful examples of exultant and apparently effortless ease in surmounting obstacles which I have ever seen.

How deeply we who love the Lord of Love and desire to follow Him long for the power to surmount all difficulties and tests and conflicts in life in the same exultant and triumphant way. To learn the secret of victorious living has been the heart's desire of those who love the Lord, in every generation.

We feel we would give anything if only we could, in actual experience, live on the High Places of love and victory here on this earth and during this life—able always to react to evil, tribulation, sorrow, pain, and every wrong thing in such a way that they would be overcome and transformed into something to the praise and glory of God forever. As Christians we know, in theory at least, that in the life of a child of God there are no second causes, that even the most unjust and cruel things, as well as all seemingly pointless and undeserved sufferings, have been permitted by God as a glorious opportunity for us to react to them in such a way that our Lord and Savior is able to produce in us, little by little, His own lovely character.

The Song of Songs expresses the desire implanted in every human heart, to be reunited with God Himself, and to know perfect and unbroken union with Him. He has made us for Himself, and our hearts can never know rest and perfect satisfaction until they find it in Him.

It is God's will that some of His children should learn this deep union with Himself through the perfect flowering of natural human love in marriage. For others it is equally His will that the same perfect union should be learned through the experience of learning to lay down completely this natural and instinctive desire for marriage and parenthood, and accept the circumstances of life which deny them this experience. This instinct for love, so firmly implanted in the human heart, is the supreme way by which we learn to desire and love God Himself above all else.

But the High Places of victory and union with Christ cannot be reached by any mental reckoning of self to be dead to sin, or by seeking to devise some way or discipline by which the will can be crucified. The only way is by learning to accept, day by day, the actual conditions and tests permitted by God, by a continually repeated laying down of our own will and acceptance of His as it is presented to us in the form of the people with whom we have to live and work, and in the things which happen to us. Every acceptance of His will becomes an altar of sacrifice, and every such surrender and abandonment of ourselves to His will is a means of furthering us on the way to the High Places to which He desires to bring every child of His while they are still living on earth.

The lessons of accepting and triumphing over evil, of becoming acquainted with grief, and pain, and, ultimately, of finding them transformed into something incomparably precious; of learning through constant glad surrender to know the Lord of Love Himself in a new way and to experience unbroken union with Him—these are the lessons of the allegory in this book. The High Places and the hinds' feet do not refer to heavenly places after death, but are meant to be the glorious experience of God's children here and now—if they will follow the path He chooses for them.

Perhaps the Lord will use it to speak comfort to some of His loved ones who are finding themselves forced to keep company with Sorrow and Suffering, or who walk in darkness and have no light or feel themselves tossed with tempest and not comforted. It may help them to understand a new meaning in what is happening, for the experiences through which they are passing are all part of the wonderful process by which the Lord is making real in their lives the same experience which made David and Habakkuk cry out exultantly, "The Lord God maketh my feet like hinds' feet, and setteth me upon mine High Places" (Psa. 18:33 and Hab. 3:19).

# Hinds' Feet on High Places

*by Hannah Hurnard*

—— with a ——

# *Woman's Devotional*

*by Darien B. Cooper*

# Part One

## CHAPTER 1

# Invitation to the High Places

This is the story of how Much-Afraid escaped from her Fearing relatives and went with the Shepherd to the High Places where "perfect love casteth out fear."

For several years Much-Afraid had been in the service of the Chief Shepherd, whose great flocks were pastured down in the Valley of Humiliation. She lived with her friends and fellow workers Mercy and Peace in a tranquil little white cottage in the village of Much-Trembling. She loved her work and desired intensely to please the Chief Shepherd, but happy as she was in most ways, she was conscious of several things which hindered her in her work and caused her much secret distress and shame.

In the first place she was a cripple, with feet so crooked that they often caused her to limp and stumble as she went about her work. She had also the very unsightly blemish of a crooked mouth which greatly disfigured both expression and speech and was sadly conscious that these ugly blemishes must be a cause of astonishment and offense to many who knew that she was in the service of the great Shepherd.

Most earnestly she longed to be completely delivered from these shortcomings and to be made beautiful, gracious, and

2

# Loving Companionship

Planted deep within each of our hearts is an insatiable desire for a loving companionship that cannot be satisfied by any living thing except God Himself. David describes this feeling in Psalm 42:2.

*"My inner self thirsts for God, for the living God.*
*When shall I come and behold the face of God?"*
(AMP)

Are you searching for something you have not yet found? Do you have inner longings that are not met? Turn to the Shepherd, the Lord Jesus Christ, who alone can satisfy your thirst. Lift your heart up to Him.

Lord, I am trusting You to teach me how to give myself completely to You so my inner desires can be satisfied. Teach me to know Your love and to walk in that love as a way of life. I want to go with You to the High Places, where

*"perfect love casts out fear"*
(1 John 4:18 NKJ).

What a comfort to know You are

*"the Way and the Truth and the Life"*
(Jn. 14:6 AMP).

I thank You for the wonderful adventure before us.

strong as were so many of the Shepherd's other workers, and above all to be made like the Chief Shepherd Himself. But she feared that there could be no deliverance from these two crippling disfigurements and that they must continue to mar her service always.

There was, however, another and even greater trouble in her life. She was a member of the Family of Fearings, and her relatives were scattered all over the valley, so that she could never really escape from them. An orphan, she had been brought up in the home of her aunt, poor Mrs. Dismal Forebodings, with her two cousins Gloomy and Spiteful and their brother Craven Fear, a great bully who habitually tormented and persecuted her in a really dreadful way.

Like most of the other families who lived in the Valley of Humiliation, all the Fearings hated the Chief Shepherd and tried to boycott His servants, and naturally it was a great offense to them that one of their own family should have entered His service. Consequently they did all they could both by threats and persuasions to get her out of His employment, and one dreadful day they laid before her the family dictum that she must immediately marry her cousin Craven Fear and settle down respectably among her own people. If she refused to do this of her own free will, they threatened to use force and compel her.

Poor Much-Afraid was, of course, overwhelmed with horror at the mere idea, but her relatives always terrified her, and she had never learned to resist or ignore their threats, so she simply sat cowering before them, repeating again and again that nothing would induce her to marry Craven Fear, but she was quite unable to escape from their presence.

The unhappy interview therefore lasted a long time, and when finally they did leave her for awhile, it was already early evening. With a surge of relief, Much-Afraid remembered that the Chief Shepherd would then be leading His flocks to their accustomed watering place beside a lovely cascade and pool on the outskirts of the village. To this place she was in

# Never Forgotten

Have you ever felt abandoned, forsaken, or tormented by those closest to you, perhaps even by your own family members? Those closest to us can often bring a greater degree of torment or hurt than anyone else. However, we can be comforted by God's words to us:

*"Can a woman forget her nursing child, and have*
*no compassion on the son of her womb? Even these*
*may forget, but I will not forget you. Behold, I have*
*inscribed you on the palms of My hands; your walls*
*are continually before Me"*
(Is. 49:15-16 NAS).

Turn to Jesus as you would a trusted, precious friend. Realize that He is welcoming you into His presence with outstretched arms. Pour your heart out to Him; tell Him all about the pain. Ponder this thought: **Right now, just as you are, both the Father and the Son love you** as much as They love one another.

*"That they may all be one; even as Thou, Father, art*
*in Me, and I in Thee, that they also may be in Us..."*
(Jn. 17:21 NAS).

Lord, help me to grasp the depth of Your love. A love where I am never forgotten is hard for me to understand. Help me to grasp the depth of such unfathomable love. I have never known such love before, but I do thank You for it.

the habit of going very early every morning to meet Him and learn His wishes and commands for the day, and again in the evenings to give her report on the day's work. It was now time to meet Him there beside the pool, and she felt sure He would help her and not permit her relatives to kidnap her and force her to leave His service for the dreadful slavery of marriage with Craven Fear.

Still shaking with fear and without pausing to wash the tears from her face, Much-Afraid shut the door of the cottage and started off for the cascade and the pool.

The quiet evening light was filling the Valley of Humiliation with a golden glow as she left the village and started to cross the fields. Beyond the river, the mountains which bounded the eastern side of the Valley like towering ramparts were already tinged with pink, and their deep gorges were filled with lovely and mysterious shadows.

Through the quiet and peace of this tranquil evening, poor, terrified Much-Afraid came to the pool where the Shepherd was waiting for her and told Him of her dreadful plight.

"What shall I do?" she cried as she ended the recital. "How can I escape? They can't really force me to marry my cousin Craven, can they? Oh!" cried she, overwhelmed again at the very thought of such a prospect, "it is dreadful enough to be Much-Afraid, but to think of having to be Mrs. Craven Fear for the rest of my life and never able to escape from the torment of it is more than I can bear."

"Don't be afraid," said the Shepherd gently. "You are in My service, and if you will trust Me they will not be able to force you against your will into any family alliance. But you ought never to have let your Fearing relatives into your cottage, because they are enemies of the King who has taken you into His employment."

"I know, oh, I know," cried Much-Afraid, "but whenever I meet any of my relatives I seem to lose all my strength and simply cannot resist them, no matter how I strive. As long as I live in the Valley I cannot escape meeting them. They are

# Completely His

Join your Lord at the watering place beside the lovely cascade and pool in the village of your heart, alongside Much-Afraid. Enter into His presence with a sense of longing to be completely His. He gave His life so you could live in this daily companionship with Him.

*"God is faithful—reliable, trustworthy and [therefore] ever true to His promise, and He can be depended on; by Him you were called into companionship and participation with His Son, Jesus Christ our Lord"*
(1 Cor. 1:9 AMP).

Lord Jesus, show me whenever our companionship is broken because I doubted Your faithfulness to me by being fearful or angry at various times, in certain places, or with particular people. Teach me how to let Your love and faithfulness saturate every fiber of my being so our companionship can become the most important thing in my life. I choose to believe You are faithful and trustworthy, ever true to Your promises. I long to abide in Your presence alone. Thank You for Your faithful love to me.

everywhere and now that they are determined to get me into their power again I shall never dare venture outside my cottage alone for fear of being kidnapped."

As she spoke she lifted her eyes and looked across the Valley and the river to the lovely sunset-lighted peaks of the mountains, then cried out in desperate longing, "Oh, if only I could escape from this Valley of Humiliation altogether and go to the High Places, completely out of reach of all the Fearings and my other relatives!"

No sooner were these words uttered when to her complete astonishment the Shepherd answered, "I have waited a long time to hear you make that suggestion, Much-Afraid. It would indeed be best for you to leave the Valley for the High Places, and I will very willingly take you there Myself. The lower slopes of those mountains on the other side of the river are the borderland of My Father's Kingdom, the Realm of Love. No Fears of any kind are able to live there because 'perfect love casteth out fear and everything that torments.' "

Much-Afraid stared at Him in amazement. "Go to the High Places," she exclaimed, "and live there? Oh, if only I could! For months past the longing has never left me. I think of it day and night, but it is not possible. I could never get there. I am too lame." She looked down at her malformed feet as she spoke, and her eyes again filled with tears and despair and self-pity. "These mountains are so steep and dangerous. I have been told that only the hinds and the deer can move on them safely."

"It is quite true that the way up to the High Places is both difficult and dangerous," said the Shepherd. "It has to be, so that nothing which is an enemy of Love can make the ascent and invade the Kingdom. Nothing blemished or in any way imperfect is allowed there, and the inhabitants of the High Places do need 'hinds' feet.' I have them Myself," He added with a smile, "and like a young hart or a roebuck I can go leaping on the mountains and skipping on the hills with the greatest ease and pleasure.

# Yearning Heart

Do you want to serve the Lord more fully? Is your heart yearning to follow Him? Don't let fear of the unknown stop you. He has promised to help you:

*"For I am the Lord, your God, who takes*
*hold of your right hand and says to you,*
*Do not fear; I will help you"*
(Is. 41:13 NIV).

With desperate longing, release your inner being to Jesus and say, "I want to go to the High Places and live there with You too!" Listen to His promise to you:

*"Faithful is He Who is calling you [to Himself] and*
*utterly trustworthy, and He will also do it [that is*
*fulfill His call by hallowing and keeping you]"*
(1 Thess. 5:24 AMP).

What a comfort to know that as you rely upon Jesus, others cannot force you against your will to leave His presence. Your heart's desire can become a reality. Now sit quietly before Him and let your soul be saturated with His promise to you. Do not leave His presence until you are bathed with the belief that He means the following words to you: "I have waited a long time to hear you make this request. I will very willingly take you there Myself."

"But, Much-Afraid, I could make yours like hinds' feet also, and set you upon the High Places. You could serve Me then much more fully and be out of reach of all your enemies. I am delighted to hear that you have been longing to go there, for, as I said before, I have been waiting for you to make that suggestion. Then," He added, with another smile, "you would never have to meet Craven Fear again."

Much-Afraid stared at Him in bewilderment. "Make my feet like hinds' feet," she repeated. "How is that possible? And what would the inhabitants of the Kingdom of Love say to the presence of a wretched little cripple with an ugly face and a twisted mouth, if nothing blemished and imperfect may dwell there?"

"It is true," said the Shepherd, "that you would have to be changed before you could live on the High Places, but if you are willing to go with Me, I promise to help you develop hinds' feet. Up there on the mountains, as you get near the real High Places, the air is fresh and invigorating. It strengthens the whole body and there are streams with wonderful healing properties, so that those who bathe in them find all their blemishes and disfigurements washed away.

"But there is another thing I must tell you. Not only would I have to make your feet like hinds' feet, but you would have to receive another name, for it would be as impossible for a Much-Afraid to enter the Kingdom of Love as for any other member of the Fearing family. Are you willing to be changed completely, Much-Afraid, and to be made like the new name which you will receive if you become a citizen in the Kingdom of Love?"

She nodded her head and then said very earnestly, "Yes, I am."

Again He smiled, but added gravely, "There is still one thing more, the most important of all. No one is allowed to dwell in the Kingdom of Love, unless they have the flower of

# Promised Help

Going from the known to the unknown is often very frightening. The idea of being changed through difficulty and danger can make us tremble. However, God promises that He will help us and that His Word will make the necessary provisions in our hearts so we can walk the way He chooses for us.

*"The steps of a man are established by the Lord;*
*and He delights in his way"*
(Ps. 37:23 NAS).

*"I shall run the way of Thy commandments,*
*for Thou wilt enlarge my heart"*
(Ps. 119:32 NAS).

*"Behold God, my salvation! I will trust*
*and not be afraid, for the Lord God is*
*my strength and song; yes, He has*
*become my salvation"*
(Is. 12:2 AMP).

I do want to serve You, precious Lord. Still my trembling heart in Your loving hand. Quiet any anger when things don't go my way. Enlarge my heart to embrace Your choices, knowing Your love paves the way.

Love already blooming in their hearts. Has Love been planted in your heart, Much-Afraid?"

As the Shepherd said this He looked at her very steadily and she realized that His eyes were searching into the very depths of her heart and knew all that was there far better than she did herself. She did not answer for a long time, because she was not sure what to say, but she looked rather flinchingly into the eyes which were gazing at her so penetratingly and became aware that they had the power of reflecting what they looked upon.

She could thus really see her own heart as He saw it, so after a long pause she answered, "I think that what is growing there is a great longing to experience the joy of natural, human love and to learn to love supremely one person who will love me in return. But perhaps that desire, natural and right as it seems, is not the Love of which You are speaking?" She paused and then added honestly and almost tremblingly, "I see the longing to be loved and admired growing in my heart, Shepherd, but I don't think I see the kind of Love that You are talking about, at least, nothing like the love which I see in You."

"Then will you let Me plant the seed of true Love there now?" asked the Shepherd. "It will take you some time to develop hinds' feet and to climb to the High Places, and if I put the seed in your heart now it will be ready to bloom by the time you get there."

Much-Afraid shrank back, "I am afraid," she said. "I have been told that if you really love someone you give that loved one the power to hurt and pain you in a way nothing else can."

"That is true," agreed the Shepherd. "To love does mean to put yourself into the power of the loved one and to become very vulnerable to pain, and you are very Much-Afraid of pain, are you not?"

She nodded miserably and then said shamefacedly, "Yes, very much afraid of it."

# Vulnerable Honesty

As you turn to Jesus, remember His deep love for you. Let the cares of the day fade away. Sit calmly with Him, knowing that He's enjoying your undivided attention. Then, with vulnerable honesty, show Him anything deep within that causes you to shrink back from His purpose for you. Let Him search your heart to expose the kind of love that dominates your soul. We were designed to receive and return God's love, but it often gets replaced with self love or with a craving for others' love. Say with a yielded heart:

*"Search me [thoroughly], O God, and know my heart!*
*Try me, and know my thoughts! And see if there*
*is any wicked or hurtful way in me, and lead me*
*in the way everlasting"*
(Ps. 139:23-24 AMP).

Thank You, dear Lord Jesus, that I can relax as I wait for Your revelation. I know You will expose only what Your Spirit has prepared my soul to receive. I love You!

"But it is so happy to love," said the Shepherd quietly. "It is happy to love even if you are not loved in return. There is pain too, certainly, but Love does not think that very significant."

Much-Afraid thought suddenly that He had the most patient eyes she had ever seen. At the same time there was something in them that hurt her to the heart, though she could not have said why, but she still shrank back in fear and said (bringing the words out very quickly because somehow she was ashamed to say them), "I would never dare to love unless I were sure of being loved in return. If I let You plant the seed of Love in my heart will You give me the promise that I shall be loved in return? I couldn't bear it otherwise."

The smile He turned on her then was the gentlest and kindest she had ever seen, yet once again, and for the same indefinable reason as before, it cut her to the quick. "Yes," He said, without hesitation, "I promise you, Much-Afraid, that when the plant of Love is ready to bloom in your heart and when you are ready to change your name, then you will be loved in return."

A thrill of joy went through her from head to foot. It seemed too wonderful to be believed, but the Shepherd Himself was making the promise, and of one thing she was quite sure. He could not lie. "Please plant Love in my heart now," she said faintly. Poor little soul, she was still Much-Afraid even when promised the greatest thing in the world.

The Shepherd put His hand in His bosom, drew something forth, and laid it in the palm of His hand. The He held His hand out toward Much-Afraid. "Here is the seed of Love," He said.

She bent forward to look, then gave a startled little cry and drew back. There was indeed a seed lying in the palm of His hand, but it was shaped exactly like a long, sharply-pointed thorn. Much-Afraid had often noticed that the Shepherd's hands were scarred and wounded, but now she saw that the

14

# Surrendered Heart

With determined surrender, hand your heart into His hands. Ask for the same attitude, purpose, and humble mind that He has, as Paul instructed.

*"Let this same attitude and purpose and [humble] mind be in you which was in Christ Jesus…"*
(Phil. 2:5 AMP).

Request that

*"He would grant you, according to the riches of His glory, to be strengthened with power through His Spirit in the inner man; so that Christ may dwell in your hearts through faith; and that you, being rooted and grounded in love, may be able to comprehend with all the saints what is the breadth and length and height and depth, and to know the love of Christ which surpasses knowledge, that you may be filled up to all the fulness of God"*
(Eph. 3:16-19 NAS).

Ponder such a love. Rest in it… bask in it… glory in it! Thank Him that He always fulfills His Word, as He said:

*"For truly I say to you, until heaven and earth pass away, not the smallest letter or stroke shall pass away from the Law, until all is accomplished"*
(Mt. 5:18 NAS).

scar in the palm of the hand held out to her was the exact shape and size of the seed of Love lying beside it.

"The seed looks very sharp," she said shrinkingly. "Won't it hurt if You put it into my heart?"

He answered gently, "It is so sharp that it slips in very quickly. But Much-Afraid, I have already warned you that Love and pain go together, for a time at least. If you would know Love, you must know pain too."

Much-Afraid looked at the thorn and shrank from it. Then she looked at the Shepherd's face and repeated His words to herself. "When the seed of Love in your heart is ready to bloom, you will be loved in return," and a strange new courage entered into her. She suddenly stepped forward, bared her heart, and said, "Please plant the seed here in my heart."

His face lit up with a glad smile and He said with a note of joy in His voice, "Now you will be able to go with Me to the High Places and be a citizen of the Kingdom of My Father."

Then He pressed the thorn into her heart. It was true, just as He had said, it did cause a piercing pain, but it slipped in quickly and then, suddenly, a sweetness she had never felt or imagined before tingled through her. It was bittersweet, but the sweetness was the stronger. She thought of the Shepherd's words, "It is so happy to love," and her pale, sallow cheeks suddenly glowed pink and her eyes shone. For a moment Much-Afraid did not look afraid at all. The twisted mouth had relaxed into a happy curve, and the shining eyes and pink cheeks made her almost beautiful.

"Thank You, thank You," she cried, and knelt at the Shepherd's feet. "How good You are. How patient You are. There is no one in the whole world as good and kind as You. I will go with You to the mountains. I will trust You to make my feet like hinds' feet, and to set me, even me, upon the High Places."

"I am more glad even than you," said the Shepherd, "and now you really act as though you are going to change your

# True Privilege

There are many things people can give their lives to. We tend to get caught up in our families, in our careers, and even in things. But the Lord says this:

*"Let not a wise man boast of his wisdom,*
*and let not the mighty man boast of his might,*
*let not a rich man boast of his riches; but let*
*him who boasts boast of this, that he understands*
*and knows Me, that I am the Lord who exercises*
*lovingkindness, justice, and righteousness on earth;*
*for I delight in these things..."*
(Jer. 9:23-24 NAS).

I choose knowing You, Lord Jesus. Thank You that You allow me to know You and that You even desire for me to know You. It is such a privilege to be in Your presence and to learn to open my heart to You!

Continue in praise of your wonderful Lord. Praise releases your spirit to flow with His Spirit in love. Let your words flow freely.

name already. But there is one thing more I must tell you. I shall take you to the foot of the mountains Myself, so that there will be no danger from your enemies. After that, two special companions I have chosen will guide and help you on all the steep and difficult places while your feet are still lame and while you can only limp and go slowly.

"You will not see Me all the time, Much-Afraid, for as I told you, I shall be leaping on the mountains and skipping on the hills, and you will not at first be able to accompany Me or keep up with Me. That will come later. However, you must remember that as soon as you reach the slopes of the mountains there is a wonderful system of communication from end to end of the Kingdom of Love, and I shall be able to hear you whenever you speak to Me. Whenever you call for help I promise to come to you at once.

"At the foot of the mountains My two servants whom I have chosen to be your guides will be waiting for you. Remember, I have chosen them Myself, with great care, as the two who are most able to help you and assist you in developing hinds' feet. You will accept them with joy and allow them to be your helpers, will you not?"

"Oh, yes," she answered at once, smiling at Him happily. "Of course I am quite certain that You know best and that whatever You choose is right." Then she added joyfully, "I feel as though I shall never be afraid again."

He looked very kindly at the little shepherdess who had just received the seed of Love into her heart and was preparing to go with Him to the High Places, but also with full understanding. He knew her through and through, in all the intricate labyrinth of her lonely heart, better far than she knew herself. No one understood better than He, that growing into the likeness of a new name is a long process, but He did not say this. He looked with a certain tender pity and compassion at the glowing cheeks and shining eyes which had so suddenly transformed the appearance of plain little Much-Afraid.

# Abundant Provision

Of all creation, we are the most privileged. Listen to the priceless opportunity we have:

*"Let us then approach the throne of grace*
*with confidence, so that we may receive mercy*
*and find grace to help us in our time of need"*
(Heb. 4:16 NIV).

With wholehearted sincerity, joyfully embrace your future with your Lord. He promises us:

*"Because he has set his love upon Me, therefore*
*will I deliver him; I will set him on high, because*
*he knows and understands My name....He shall*
*call upon Me, and I will answer him; I will be*
*with him in trouble, I will deliver him and*
*honor him. With long life will I satisfy him,*
*and show him My salvation"*
(Ps. 91:14-16 AMP).

Assure Him that you are certain that He knows best and that whatever He chooses is right. Rejoice over knowing His provision.

Dear Jesus, strengthen my heart so I can obey and gladly follow Your voice. Thank You that You will do all I have asked, and even more.

Then He said, "Now you may go home and make your preparations for leaving. You are not to take anything with you, only leave everything in order. Do not tell anyone about it, for a journey to the High Places needs to be a secret matter. I cannot now give you the exact time when we are to start for the mountains, but it will be soon, and you must be ready to follow Me whenever I come to the cottage and call. I will give you a secret sign. I shall sing one of the Shepherd's songs as I pass the cottage, and it will contain a special message for you. When you hear it, come at once and follow Me to the trysting place."

Then, as the sun had already gone down in a blaze of red and gold, and the eastern mountains were now veiled in misty mauve and grey, and the shadows were lengthening, He turned and led His flock away toward the sheepfolds.

Much-Afraid turned her face homeward, her heart full of happiness and excitement, and still feeling as though she would never be frightened again. As she started back across the fields she sang to herself one of the songs from an old book of songs which the Shepherds often used. Never before had it seemed to her so sweet, so applicable.

> *"The Song of Songs," the loveliest song,*
> *The song of Love the King,*
> *No joy on earth compares with his,*
> *But seems a broken thing.*
> *His Name as ointment is poured forth,*
> *And all his lovers sing.*
>
> *Draw me—I will run after thee,*
> *Thou art my heart's one choice,*
> *Oh, bring me to thy royal house,*
> *To dwell there and rejoice.*
> *There in thy presence, O my King,*
> *To feast and hear thy voice.*
>
> *Look not upon me with contempt,*
> *Though soiled and marred I be,*

# Close Friendship

Thank You, Jesus, for this time alone to just focus on You. Thank You that You are closer than my breath...nearer than my eyelids. Thank You that You understand all about me and still want my companionship! How wonderful to have a Friend like You!

Bask in the quietness with Him. Relax in His presence. Know that He is thrilled at your wanting to know Him. Jesus prayed to the Father:

*"And I have made Thy name known to them,*
*and will make it known; that the love*
*wherewith Thou didst love Me may be*
*in them, and I in them"*
(Jn. 17:26 NAS).

*"And we have known and believed the love*
*that God hath to us. God is love; and he that*
*dwelleth in love dwelleth in God, and God in him"*
(1 John 4:16 KJV).

Let your mind embrace the fact that the Father and the Son love you just as you are at this moment, the same way They love each other. Realize that They will never stop loving you in this way.

*The King found me—an outcast thing—*
*And set his love on me.*
*I shall be perfected by Love,*
*Made fair as day to see.*

(Cant. 1:1-6)

She walked singing across the first field and was halfway over the next when suddenly she saw Craven Fear himself coming toward her. Poor Much-Afraid: for a little while she had completely forgotten the existence of her dreadful relatives, and now here was the most dreaded and detested of them all slouching toward her. Her heart filled with a terrible panic. She looked right and left, but there was no hiding place anywhere, and besides it was all too obvious that he was actually coming to meet her, for as soon as he saw her he quickened his pace and in a moment or two was right beside her.

With a horror that sickened her very heart she heard him say, "Well, here you are at last, little Cousin Much-Afraid. So we are to be married, eh, what do you think of that?" and he pinched her, presumably in a playful manner, but viciously enough to make her gasp and bite her lips to keep back a cry of pain.

She shrank away from him and shook with terror and loathing. Unfortunately this was the worst thing she could have done, for it was always her obvious fear which encouraged him to continue tormenting her. If only she could have ignored him, he soon would have tired of teasing and of her company and would have wandered off to look for other prey. In all her life, however, Much-Afraid had never been able to ignore Fear. Now it was absolutely beyond her power to conceal the dread which she felt.

Her white face and terrified eyes immediately had the effect of stimulating Craven's desire to bait her. Here she was, alone and completely in his power. He caught hold of her, and poor Much-Afraid uttered one frenzied cry of terror and pain. At that moment Craven Fear loosed his grasp and cringed away.

# Clear Perspective

Times of rejoicing, insight, or understanding are often followed by a time of application. These times are meant by our Lord to

*"set [our] feet upon a rock making [our] footsteps firm"*
(Ps. 40:2b NAS).

Often these application times involve an attack of the enemy. Satan hates Jesus and all those who follow Him. His goal is to draw us away from Jesus' presence and cause us to lose the inheritance Jesus purchased for us. After all, he lost his inheritance and privilege of being in Jesus' presence, so he does not like us having what he cannot have.

*"The thief comes only in order that he may steal
and may kill and may destroy..."*
(Jn. 10:10 AMP).

If we're not prepared, we can be knocked off balance in the same way a clap of thunder or a sudden bolt of lightning on a relatively clear day would! The good news is, Jesus says:

*"...I came that they may have and enjoy life, and
have it in abundance —to the full, till it overflows"*
(Jn. 10:10 AMP).

Thank You, Lord Jesus, for Your marvelous provision! As I walk with You, my perspective becomes clearer and it is easier to face my enemies. I love You!

The Shepherd had approached them unperceived and was standing beside them. One look at His stern face and flashing eyes and the stout Shepherd's cudgel grasped in His strong, uplifted hand was more than enough for the bully. Craven Fear slunk away like a whipped cur, actually running from the village instead of toward it, not knowing where he was going, urged by one instinct alone, to find a place of safety.

Much-Afraid burst into tears. Of course she ought to have known that Craven was a coward and that if only she had lifted her voice and called for the Shepherd, he would have fled at once. Now her dress was torn and disordered, and her arms bruised by the bully's grip, yet that was the least part of her distress. She was overwhelmed with shame that she had so quickly acted like her old name and nature, which she had hoped was beginning to be changed already.

It seemed so impossible to ignore the Fearings, still less to resist them. She did not dare look at the Shepherd, but had she done so she would have seen with what compassion He was regarding her. She did not realize that the Prince of Love is "of very tender compassions to them that are afraid." She supposed that, like everybody else, He was despising her for her silly fears, so she muttered a shamed "thank you."

Then, still without looking at Him, she limped painfully toward the village, weeping bitterly as she went and saying over and over again to herself, "What is the use of even thinking of going to the High Places? I could never reach them, for the least little thing is enough to turn me back."

However, when at last she reached the security of the cottage she began to feel better, and by the time she had drunk a cup of tea and taken her evening meal she had recovered so far that she was able to remind herself of all that had happened there beside the cascade and the pool. Suddenly she remembered, with a thrill of wonder and delight, that the seed of Love had been planted in her heart. As she thought of it, the same almost intolerable sweetness stole over her, the bittersweet, indefinable but wholly delightful ecstasy of a new happiness.

# Complete Acceptance

Come into Jesus' outstretched arms knowing that He welcomes you into His presence. Quietly sit with Him for a while. Acknowledge the deep sense of love He has for you. Receive His love for you by faith. If you struggle with guilt as Much-Afraid did, remember God's provision. For when Jesus

*"had by offering Himself accomplished our cleansing of sins and riddance of guilt, He sat down at the right hand of the divine Majesty on high"*
(Heb. 1:3b AMP).

He laid down His life so the entangling works of the enemy in your life might be unraveled. That's how much He loves you.

*"The reason the Son of God was made manifest (visible) was to undo (destroy, loosen and dissolve) the works the devil [has done]"*
(1 John 3:8b AMP).

And Jesus said:

*"It is finished!"*
(See John 19:30.)

Thank You, Jesus, for dying so I might not have to wear the garment of guilt. I choose to take it off like a dirty shirt and I put it aside. Let me understand that You love me, that You accept me, because I am in You!

"It is happy to love," said little Much-Afraid to herself and then she repeated: "It is happy to love." After putting the cottage in order for the night, because she was utterly tired out with all the conflicting emotions of that strange day, she went to bed. Lying there before falling asleep, she sang over and over again to herself another of the lovely songs from the old song book.

*O thou whom my soul loveth,*
*Tell me where thou dost feed,*
*And where thy flocks at noonday*
*To rest and browse dost lead.*
*For why should I*
*By others be,*
*And not by thee?*

*O fairest among women,*
*Dost thou indeed not know?*
*Then lead my little flocklet*
*The way that my flocks go;*
*And be to me,*
*As I to thee,*
*Sweet company.*

(Cant. 1:7,8)

Then she fell into a heavy, dreamless sleep.

# Gratitude Expressed

With your heart overflowing with great appreciation, thank Jesus for being your God. Thank Him
for being your Savior, your Lord, and your Friend.
Express your gratitude to Him as the Bridegroom of the
Church. Ponder for a time upon each name and what it
means to you. List the special things He's done for you
recently that you appreciate. Take your time. Let Him remind you of the ways He works in your life.

Being in Your presence, Lord Jesus, and learning to open my heart completely to You is such
a wonderful adventure. How lovely You are! Like
Paul, I say to You with fresh commitment:

> *"...I count all things to be loss in view of*
> *the surpassing value of knowing*
> *Christ Jesus my Lord..."*
> (Phil. 3:8 NAS).

I make it my goal in life to

> *"know Him, and the power of His resurrection*
> *and the fellowship of His sufferings, being*
> *conformed to His death; in order that I may*
> *attain to the resurrection from the dead"*
> (Phil. 3:10-11 NAS).

What an honor, Lord. Thank You!

# CHAPTER 2

# Fearing Invasion

Much-Afraid woke early the next morning and all her fears were gone. Her first thought was, "Probably sometime today I am to start for the High Places with the Shepherd." This so excited her that she could hardly eat her breakfast, and as she began making arrangements for her departure, she could not help singing.

It seemed to her that ever since the seed of Love had been planted in her heart, songs of joy were welling up in her innermost being. And the songs which best expressed this new happiness and thankfulness were from the old book which the shepherds so loved to use as they worked among the flocks and led them to the pastures. As she carried out the simple arrangements the Shepherd had told her to make, she sang another of these songs.

*Now when the King at table sits,*
*My spikenard smelleth sweet,*
*And myrrh and camphire from my store*
*I pour upon his feet.*
*My thankful love must be displayed,*
*He loved and wooed a beggar maid.*

*Ye daughters of Jerusalem,*
*I'm black to look upon*
*As goatskin tents; but also as*

# Abiding Love

Enter the presence of your Lord knowing that His arms are reaching out to welcome you. Commit yourself to His loving care. With Much-Afraid, sing your love to your Lord. If you feel awkward, break through that barrier by releasing your soul to Jesus. You can begin by simply reading aloud, word for word, the song of Much-Afraid that begins on the opposite page. As you become freer in your expression, add your own words. Then wait before Him with an open, seeking heart and listen to what He wants to say to you.

*"I have loved you [just] as the Father has loved Me; abide in My love—continue in His love with Me"*
(Jn. 15:9 AMP).

Precious Lord Jesus, it is still a little difficult for me to realize that I am in Your presence conversing with You as with an old friend. I'm beginning to realize that this is what You want and what my inner being craves. Lord Jesus, I give myself to You once again, saying, "Let me always abide in Your love."

*The tent of Solomon.*
*Without, I bear the marks of sin,*
*But Love's adorning is within.*

*Despise me not that I am black,*
*The sun hath burned my face,*
*My mother's children hated me,*
*And drove me from my place.*
*In their vineyards I toiled and wept.*
*But mine own vineyard have not kept.*

*I am not fair save to the King,*
*Though fair my royal dress,*
*His kingly grace is lavished on*
*My need and worthlessness.*
*My blemishes he will not see*
*But loves the beauty that shall be.*

(Cant. 1:12-15,5,6)

From time to time as she went about her work her heart fluttered, half with excitement, half with dread of the unknown, but whenever she remembered the thorn in her heart, she tingled from head to foot with the same mysterious sweetness. Love was for her, too, even for her, crippled little Much-Afraid. When she reached the High Places she was to lose her humiliating disfigurements and be made beautiful, and when the plant in her heart was ready to bloom she was to be loved in return. Even as she thought of this, doubt mingled with the sweetness. Surely it could not possibly be true; just a beautiful dream, but not reality.

"Oh, I am afraid it won't ever happen," she would say to herself, and then, when she thought of the Shepherd, her heart quickened again and she would run to the door or window to see if He were coming to call her.

The morning wore on and still He had not come, but just after midday something else came: an invasion by her terrible relatives. All of a sudden, before she realized what was happening,

30

# Magnificent Provision

Calm your heart as you come into your Lord's presence. Know that He loves you and welcomes you. Thank Him for His complete acceptance of you just as you are. Sin may have left a mark on you, but praise God that His love toward you does not depend on what you do or don't do, but on the fact that you are "in Christ" because you received His payment for your sins.

*"There is therefore now no condemnation*
*for those who are in Christ Jesus"*
(Rom. 8:1 NAS).

Thank You, Lord, that Your love is completely released toward me and will continue to be for all eternity. Help me to comprehend the breadth and depth of Your all-encompassing love.

Meditate on His love a little while until you feel that you can begin to grasp the wonder of His magnificent provision. Ask Him to continue with His revelation until you see and receive all He has for you.

they were upon her. There was tramping of feet and a clamor of voices and then she was surrounded by a whole army of aunts and uncles and cousins. Craven, however, was not with them. The family, hearing of his reception the evening before, and realizing that she shrank from him with peculiar dread and terror, had decided that it would not be wise to take him with them.

They were determined to overrule Much-Afraid's objections to the marriage, and if possible get her out of the cottage and into one of their own dwelling places. Their plan was to make a bold attack while she would be alone in the cottage and the Shepherd far away with His flocks, so they hoped she would be at their mercy. She could not be forcibly abducted in broad daylight; there were too many of the Shepherd's servants in the village who would instantly come to her assistance.

However, they knew Much-Afraid's timidity and weakness and they believed that, if there were enough of them present, they could cow her into consenting to go with them to the Mansion of old Lord Fearing. Then they would have her in their power.

The old Lord himself was actually with them, assuring her in a fatherly tone of voice that they had come with the kindest and friendliest intentions. He understood that she had some objections to the proposed marriage, and he wanted to have the opportunity of quietly talking them over with her, to see if he could set them at rest. It seemed to him that it was a suitable and attractive match in every way and that there must be some extraordinary misconception in her mind which a little understanding talk together would set right. If not, he assured her kindly, he would not permit her to be married against her will.

When he had finished, a babel of other Fearing voices broke in, reasoning with her and making all sorts of suggestions. The fact was, they told her, that she had cut herself off from her relatives for so long, it was now quite apparent that she had all kinds of strange notions about their feelings and intentions toward her. It was really only right that she should

# Protective Love

The Lord Jesus Christ loves you with all His being. He proved that love by laying down His life for you. However, the enemy hates you with his entire being. Listen to God's warning:

*"Be of sober spirit, be on the alert. Your adversary,*
*the devil, prowls about like a roaring lion,*
*seeking someone to devour"*
(1 Pet. 5:8 NAS).

God also points out to us the enemy's strategy. He says,

*"...They count it a pleasure to...[entice] unstable souls...*
*forsaking the right way....These are springs*
*without water, and mists driven by a storm, for*
*whom the black darkness has been reserved. ...*
*[They promise you] freedom while they themselves*
*are slaves of corruption; for by what a man is*
*overcome, by this he is enslaved"*
(2 Pet. 2:13-15; 17,19 NAS).

Thank You, precious Lord, that You are aware of the enemy's methods and I can turn to You for help. Help me to take satan's strategies seriously, but to rest in Your protective love. How blessed I am to be "in You."

now spend a little time with them and thus give them the opportunity of proving that she had misjudged and misunderstood them.

Craven might not be just as handsome and pleasing in appearance as a prince in a fairy tale, and it was true that he had, unfortunately, rather a rough manner, but that was because he had known nothing of the softening and refining influences of marriage. Certainly the responsibilities and joys of married life would quickly alter this, and would indeed effect a transformation in him. It was to be her delightful privilege to assist as principal mover in bringing about this reformation which they all so eagerly wished to see.

The whole gang talked on and on, while poor Much-Afraid sat cowering in their midst, almost too dazed to know what they were saying and suggesting. Just as they had hoped, they were gradually bringing her to a state of bewilderment and incoherent fear. It looked as though they would soon be able to persuade her that it was her duty to attempt the impossible task of trying to convert Craven Fear into something less objectionable than he really was. Suddenly there came an interruption from without.

The Fearings had carefully closed the door when they entered the cottage and even contrived to bolt it, so that Much-Afraid could not escape. Now came the distant sound of a man's voice raised in song, singing one of the songs from the old book which Much-Afraid knew and loved so well. Then the singer Himself came in view, slowly passing along the lane. It was the Chief Shepherd, already leading His flock to the watering place. The words floated in through the open window, accompanied by the soft bleating of the sheep and the scuffling of many little dusty feet as they pattered after Him.

It seemed as though all other sounds were hushed to stillness on that quiet summer afternoon as the Shepherd sang while passing the cottage. Inside, the clamor of voices had ceased instantly and was succeeded by a silence which could be felt. This is what He sang:

# Evil Resisted

God created us in His image as image bearers. He knows what fulfills us because He designed us with great care. Therefore, He gives instructions to protect us from being harmed.

*"Oh, the joys of those who do not follow evil men's advice, who do not hang around with sinners, scoffing at the things of God"*
(Ps. 1:1 TLB).

God also warns us to never underestimate the subtlety and power of the enemy. The enemy presents his destructive plans for us wrapped in a logic that appeals to our thinking and caters to our weaknesses. God's Word describes this method perfectly:

*"His speech was smoother than butter, but his heart was war; his words were softer than oil, yet they were drawn swords"*
(Ps. 55:21 NAS).

Lord Jesus, give me wisdom to separate the vile from the precious. Allow me to immediately see the evil and resist it in Your wonderful name.

*The Voice of my Beloved!*
*Through all my heart it thrills,*
*He leaps upon the mountains,*
*And skips upon the hills.*

*For like a roe or young hart,*
*So swift and strong is he,*
*He looketh through my window,*
*And beckoneth unto me.*

*"Rise up, my love, fair one,*
*And come away with me,*
*Gone are the snows of winter,*
*The rains no more we see.*

*"The flowers are appearing,*
*The little birds all sing,*
*The turtle dove is calling,*
*Through all the land 'tis spring.*

*"The shoots are on the grapevines,*
*The figs are on the tree,*
*Arise, my love, my fair one,*
*And come away with me.*

*"Why is my dove still hiding?*
*When all things else rejoice,*
*Oh, let me see thee, fair one,*
*Oh, let me hear thy voice."*

(Cant. 2:8-14)

As she sat listening in the cottage, Much-Afraid knew with a pang of agonizing pain that the Shepherd was calling her to go with Him to the mountains. This was the secret signal He had promised, and He had said that she must be ready to leave instantly, the moment she heard it. Now here she was, locked inside her own cottage, beleaguered by her terrible Fears and unable to respond in any way to His call or even to give any sign of her need.

# Loving Approval

When God starts dealing with a particular weakness in our lives, we often progress through stages before our victory is complete. What a comfort to know that

*"no temptation has overtaken you but such as is common to man; and God is faithful, who will not allow you to be tempted beyond what you are able, but with the temptation will provide the way of escape also, that you may be able to endure it"*
(1 Cor. 10:13 NAS).

God will help us work through these areas. If you feel that these weaknesses make you less acceptable to God, do this: Think of a person you would put at the top of your list of "spiritually mature" people. Once you have thought upon God's complete love, approval, and acceptance of this person, transfer that same acceptance and approval to yourself. Both of you are equally acceptable to the Father, not for what either of you has or has not done, but because you are "in Christ."

*"Accept one another, then, just as Christ accepted you, in order to bring praise to God"*
(Rom. 15:7 NIV).

Lord Jesus, thank You for Your love and acceptance of me even with my weaknesses. Draw me ever closer to You, Lord.

There was one moment indeed, when the song first started and everyone was startled into silence, when she might have called to Him to come and help her. She did not realize that the Fearings were holding their breath lest she did call, and had she done so, they would have fled helter-skelter through the door. However, she was too stunned with fear to seize the opportunity, and then it was too late.

The next moment she felt Coward's heavy hand laid tightly over her mouth, then other hands gripped her firmly and held her in the chair. So the Shepherd slowly passed the cottage, "showing Himself at the window," and singing the signal song, but receiving no response of any kind.

When He had passed and the words of the song and the bleating of the sheep had died away in the distance, it was found that Much-Afraid had fainted. Her cousin Coward's gagging hands had half-choked her. Her relatives would dearly have liked to seize this opportunity and carry her off while she was unconscious, but as this was the hour when everybody was returning from work it was too dangerous. The Fearings decided therefore that they would remain in the cottage until darkness fell, then gag Much-Afraid and carry her off unperceived.

When this plan had been decided upon, they laid her upon the bed to recover as best she might, while some of the aunts and cousins went out into the kitchen to see what provisions for refreshing themselves might be plundered. The men sat smoking in the sitting room, and Gloomy was left to guard the half-conscious victim in the bedroom.

Gradually Much-Afraid regained her senses, and as she realized her position she nearly fainted again with horror. She dared not cry out for help, for all her neighbors would be away at their work; but were they? No, it was later than she had thought, for suddenly she heard the voice of Mrs. Valiant, her

# Greater Grace

The results of sin paralyze our very life. Our life flows to us through the Spirit in much the same way an unborn baby receives life from its mother through the umbilical cord. When there's a kink or a knot in the cord, life is restricted. It is the same with sin. When we fall into sin, we block our life flow of relationship to our Lord.

> *"But your iniquities have separated between you and your God, and your sins have hid His face from you..."*
> (Is. 59:2 KJV).

Nevertheless, no matter how deep a pit we might fall into, His mercy is deeper. No matter how far our weakness extends, His grace is greater.

> *"But You, O Lord, are a God merciful and gracious, slow to anger and abounding in mercy and loving-kindness and truth"*
> (Ps. 86:15 AMP).

Close out all thoughts or circumstances around you as you focus on Him and quietly wait.

Thank You, Jesus, that You are bigger than my weakness and that You live within me. I want to turn entirely away from evil and completely toward You. Help me to hate sin and love You.

neighbor in the cottage next door. At the sound, Much-Afraid braced herself for one last desperate bid for escape.

Gloomy was quite unprepared for such a move, and before she realized what was happening, Much-Afraid sprang from the bed and shouted through the window as loudly as her fear permitted, "Valiant! Valiant! Come and help me. Come quickly. Help!"

At the sound of her first cry, Mrs. Valiant looked across the garden and caught a glimpse of Much-Afraid's white, terrified face at the window and of her hand beckoning entreatingly. The next moment the face was jerked away from view and a curtain suddenly drawn across the window. That was enough for Mrs. Valiant, whose name described her exactly. She hurried straight across to her neighbor's cottage and tried the door, but finding it locked, she looked in through a window and saw the room full of Much-Afraid's relatives.

Mrs. Valiant was not the sort of person to be the least intimidated by what she called, "a pack of idle Fears." Thrusting her face right in through the window, she cried in a threatening voice, "Out of this house you go, this minute, every one of you. If you have not left in three seconds, I shall call the Chief Shepherd. This cottage belongs to Him, and won't you catch it if He finds you here."

The effect of her words was magical. The door was unbolted and thrown open and the Fearings poured out pell-mell, tumbling over one another in their haste to get away. Mrs. Valiant smiled grimly as she watched their ignominious flight. When the last one had scuttled away she went into the cottage to Much-Afraid, who seemed quite overcome with fear and distress. Little by little she learned the story of those hours of torment and the plan to kidnap the poor victim after darkness fell.

Mrs. Valiant hardly knew herself what it was to feel fear, and had just routed the whole gang of Fearings singlehanded. She felt much inclined to adopt a bracing attitude and to chide the silly girl for not standing up to her relatives at once, boldly repulsing them before they got her into their clutches. But as

# Eternal Refuge

Come to the Father as a little child seeking to know Him and be taught by Him. Pour out your heart to Him as a trusting child pours out her heart to a loving, caring father. Know that He hears, cares, and loves you. After a few moments, while safely resting in His arms, recall the greatest battle you are facing. Then be buoyed up by His promise and provision for you:

> *"Behold! I have given you authority and power to trample upon serpents and scorpions, and (physical and mental strength and ability) over all the power that the enemy [possesses], and nothing shall in any way harm you"*
> (Lk. 10:19 AMP).

Be cheered and encouraged by His heart for His children:

> *"There is none like God, O Jeshurun [Israel], Who rides through the heavens to your help, and in His majestic glory through the sky. The eternal God is your refuge and dwelling place, and underneath are the everlasting arms; He drove the enemy before you and thrust them out, saying, Destroy!....Happy are you, O Israel, and blessing is yours! Who is like you, a people saved by the Lord, the shield of your help, the sword that exalts you! Your enemies shall come fawning and cringing, and submit feigned obedience to you, and you shall march on their high places"*
> (Deut. 33:26-27; 29 AMP).

Thank You, Lord, for Your provision. Teach me to use the power You have provided and to exercise the ability You have entrusted to me.

she looked at the white face and terrified eyes and saw the quaking body of poor Much-Afraid, she checked herself. "What is the use of saying it? She can't act upon it, poor thing; she is one of them herself and has got Fearing in the blood, and when the enemy is within you it's a poor prospect. I think no one but the Shepherd Himself can really help her," she reflected.

So instead of an admonition, she patted the trembling girl and said with all the kindness of her motherly heart, "Now, my dear, while you are getting over your fright, I'll just pop into the kitchen and make a good cup of tea for both of us and you'll feel better at once. My! If they haven't been in here and put the kettle on for us," she added, as she opened the kitchen door and found the cloth already on the table and the preparations for the plundered meal which the unwanted visitors had so hastily abandoned.

"What a pack of harpies," she muttered angrily to herself, then smiled complacently as she remembered how they had fled before her.

By the time they had drunk their tea and Mrs. Valiant had energetically cleared away the last traces of the unwelcome invaders, Much-Afraid had nearly recovered her composure. Darkness had long since fallen, and now it was much too late for her to go to the pool to keep tryst with the Shepherd and explain why she had not responded to His call. She would have to wait for the morning light.

So at Mrs. Valiant's suggestion, as she was feeling utterly exhausted, she went straight to bed. Her neighbor saw her safely tucked in, and kissed her warmly and reassuringly. Indeed, she offered to sleep in the cottage herself that night, but Much-Afraid, knowing that she had a family waiting for her at home, refused the kind offer. However, before leaving, Mrs. Valiant placed a bell beside the bed and assured her that if anything alarmed her in the night she had only to ring the bell and the whole Valiant family would be over instantly to assist her. Then she went away and Much-Afraid was left alone in the cottage.

# Divine Focus

When the struggle for victory is waging heavy warfare in our souls, it's often easy to doubt that we can get through it or that we are valuable enough to be worth saving. Perhaps you feel like you're dressed in rags—torn, ragged, unkempt rags. Visualize Jesus spreading wide the voluminous robe He is wearing and completely covering you with it. Hear Him say, "My Father does not see your 'yet to be refined areas.' He sees you as a finished product because you are 'in Me'." Our stability and security does not rest upon us or what we do, but on who God is. He eagerly waits upon us to recognize His character and draw upon His strength.

*"But You, O Lord, are a God merciful and gracious, slow to anger and abounding in mercy and loving-kindness and truth. O turn to me, and have mercy and be gracious to me; grant strength—might and inflexibility [to temptation]— to Your servant, and save the son of Your handmaiden"*
(Ps. 86:15-16 AMP).

Lord Jesus, it is often so difficult to get my eyes off of myself and to focus on You. Enable me to seek Your face. Unto You, O Lord, do I bring my whole life.

# CHAPTER 3

# Flight in the Night

For hours poor Much-Afraid lay sleepless on her bed, too bruised in mind and body to rest in one position, but tossing and turning wearily from side to side until long after midnight. Somewhere at the back of her mind was a dreadful uneasiness, as though there was something she ought to remember, but was unable to do so. When at last she fell asleep this thought still haunted her.

She woke suddenly an hour or two later, her mind intensely alert, conscious of an agonizing pain such as she had never known before. The thorn in her heart was throbbing and aching in a manner she could scarcely bear. It was as though the pain was hammering out something which at first she was still too confused to be able to understand. Then, all of a sudden, in a terrible flash, it became clear to her, and she found herself whispering over and over again, "The Shepherd came and called me as He promised, but I didn't go to Him or give any answer. Supposing He thought that I had changed my mind and didn't want to go with Him. Supposing He has gone and left me behind! Gone without me! Yes, left me behind!"

The shock of this thought was awful. This was the thing she had forgotten. He would not be able to understand why she had not gone out to Him as He had told her.

He had urged her to be ready to go with Him the instant that He called, that there must be no delay, that He Himself had to go

44

# Sustaining Power

Has the thought ever crossed your mind, "This mistake is too big; it's all over for me"? Did the consequences of that wrong decision cause you to end up in the proverbial mud puddle? The psalmist, David, also expressed such feelings, but he recognized that once we have given ourselves to the Lord, He takes us at our word. He is committed to carry us and draw us. He will clean the mud off us and help us take another step forward.

*"I waited patiently for the Lord; He turned to me and heard my cry. He lifted me out of the slimy pit, out of the mud and mire; He set my feet on a rock and gave me a firm place to stand"*
(Ps. 40:1-2 NIV).

Jesus, melt my heart so I can see when I'm in a mud puddle and enable me to anxiously turn to You so I may be cleansed. Make me teachable, that I may hear You and others when they see and tell me about my dripping mud. Thank You, precious Lord, for Your drawing and sustaining power.

to the mountains on urgent business. She had not been able to go even to the trysting place as usual that evening.

Of course He would think that she was afraid. Perhaps He was gone already and alone. Much-Afraid turned icy cold and her teeth chattered, but it was the pain in her heart which was the most awful part of her distress. It seemed to suffocate her as she lay there in bed. She sat up, shivering with cold and with the horror of the thought. She could not bear it if He had gone and left her behind.

On the table beside her lay the old song book. Glancing down at it in the light of the lamp, she saw it was open at the page whereon was written a song about another shepherdess. She, just like herself, had failed to respond to the call of love and then found, too late, that Love had gone away.

It had always seemed to her such a sad song that she could hardly read it, but now as she read the words again in the dark loneliness of the night, it seemed as though it was the cry of her own forlorn and terrified heart.

> *By night on my bed I sought him,*
> *He whom my soul loveth so.*
> *I sought—but I could not find him,*
> *And now I will rise and go—*
>
> *Out in the streets of the city,*
> *And out on the broad highway;*
> *For he whom my soul so loveth,*
> *Hath left me and gone away.*

The page in the little song book ended there, and she did not turn the leaf. Suddenly she could bear the uncertainty no longer. She must see for herself at once if He really had gone away and left her behind. She slipped out of bed, dressed herself as quickly as her shaking fingers would permit, and then unlocked the cottage door. She, too, would go out into the street and the broad highway and would see if she could find Him, would see if He had gone and left her behind, or—oh, if only it were possible—if He had waited to give her another chance.

# Joy Restored

What a sinking, sickening feeling it is to realize that we have unintentionally, or what felt like unavoidably, done the opposite to our hearts' desire—especially if those we dearly love suffer for it. At such times we can say:

> *"Be gracious to me, O God, according to Thy lovingkindness; according to the greatness of Thy compassion blot out my transgressions. Wash me thoroughly from my iniquity, and cleanse me from my sin. ...Against Thee, Thee only, I have sinned.... Create in me a clean heart, O God, and renew a steadfast spirit within me. ...Restore to me the joy of Thy salvation, and sustain me with a willing spirit"*
> (Ps. 51:1-2; 4,10,12 NAS).

Lord Jesus, whenever I begin to dwell on how wrong I am, help me to

> *"remember the days of old, [to] meditate on all Your doings; [to] ponder on the work of Your hands"*
> (Ps. 143:5 AMP).

Take time to review each marvelous thing He has done for you. Bask in each one until your being is filled with His provision and love for you. Thank Him for being a God who cares.

Opening the door, she went out into the darkness. A hundred Craven Fears lurking in the lonely street could not have deterred her at that moment, for the pain in her heart swallowed up fear and everything else and drove her forth. So in the dark hours, just before the dawn, Much-Afraid started off to look for the Shepherd.

She could not go quickly because of her lameness, but limped along the village streets toward the open fields and the sheepfolds. As she went she whispered to herself, "O Shepherd, when You said that Love and pain go together, how truly You spoke."

Had she but known or even dimly sensed what it would be like, would she, could she, possibly have consented to let Him put the thorn in her heart? It was too late now: it was there. Love was there and pain, too, and she must find the Shepherd. At last, limping and breathless, she came to the sheepfolds, still and silent in the dim starlight. One or two undershepherds were there, keeping watch over the flocks through the night, and when they heard footsteps approaching they rose up from the ground and went to meet the intruder.

"Who are you?" they challenged her in the darkness, then stared in amazement as their lanterns flashed on the white face and frightened eyes of Much-Afraid.

"Is the Chief Shepherd here?" she gasped as she leaned against the wall of the sheepfold, panting and trying to recover her breath.

"No," said the watchman, staring at her curiously. "He left the flocks in our charge this night and gave His orders. He said that He had to make a journey to the mountains, as He often does, and did not say when He would be back."

Much-Afraid could not speak. She moaned and pressed her hands to her heart, feeling as though it would break. What could she do now? He was gone. He had thought that she did not want to go and had not waited for her. Then, aching with despair, as she leaned trembling against the wall of the fold, she remembered the Shepherd's face and the loving-kindness

# Without Fault

If our hearts cry out, "Father, isn't there some other way than the one having pain woven through Your love?" we would hear the Father answer, "If there was, don't you think I'd have chosen it for My Son, whom I love?"

*"Although He was a Son, He learned obedience*
*from the things which He suffered"*
(Heb. 5:8 NAS).

If the Father used suffering in our Lord's life, why shouldn't He do the same in ours, His chosen children?

*"Long ago, even before He made the world, God chose*
*us to be His very own, through what Christ would*
*do for us; He decided then to make us holy in His eyes,*
*without a single fault—we who stand before*
*Him covered with His love"*
(Eph. 1:4 TLB).

Strength and confidence rise up in my heart as I think upon Your loving kindness, Lord Jesus. Thank You that any pain I presently experience is not worth being compared to the glory that will be conferred on me as I continue walking in Your presence.

of the look with which He had invited her to accompany Him to the mountains.

It came to her mind that He who understood her so well, who knew all about her fears and had compassion on her, would not leave until He was quite sure that she really meant to refuse to go with Him. She lifted her eyes, looked across the Valley toward the eastern mountains and the High Places. A faint streak of light was appearing in the east, and she knew that soon the sun would rise. Suddenly she remembered the last verse of the sad song which she had read, the last verse on the page which she had not waited to turn over. It came whispering into her mind just as a little bird began to sing in one of the bushes beside her.

> *And then—in the dawn I saw him,*
> *He whom my heart loveth so.*
> *I found him, held him and told him*
> *I never could let him go.*

(Cant. 3:1-5)

Much-Afraid ceased trembling and said to herself, "I will go to the trysting-place, and see if He is waiting for me there." With scarcely a word to the watchmen she turned and hurried southward, over the field where Craven Fear had met her toward the sheep pool. Almost forgetting that she was lame, she sped toward the distant trees which fringed the pool.

Just as the sky turned red above the mountains, the joyous, babbling sound of cascading water reached her ears, and as she hurried forward Much-Afraid suddenly found a cascade of song pouring forth from her own heart. He was there, standing by the pool, looking toward her with the light of the sunrise shining on His face. As Much-Afraid stumbled toward Him, He stepped quickly to her side and she fell at His feet sobbing, "O my Lord, take me with You as You said. Don't leave me behind."

"I knew you would come," He said gently, "but Much-Afraid, why were you not at the trysting-place last evening?

# Tender Love

Sometimes we have difficulty coming to our Father because of an imperfect relationship with our earthly father or with others. We are not sure of His heart toward us. However, we need **never** be hesitant or fearful to come honestly and vulnerably to our Lord, revealing every minute detail of our beings. Listen to His words to us:

*"He will feed His flock like a shepherd, He will gather the lambs in His arm, He will carry them in His bosom, and will gently lead those that have their young"*
(Is. 40:11 AMP).

*"For the eyes of the Lord run to and fro throughout the whole earth, to show Himself strong in behalf of those whose heart is blameless toward Him..."*
(2 Chron. 16:9 AMP).

"Blameless" means the absence of even a charge or accusation against us because of Jesus' shed blood covering us.

Thank You, Jesus, for Your tender care. I desire to abandon myself into Your care without scruples, without fear, without any agitating thoughts. Thank You for Your great faithfulness. I love You, Lord.

Did you not hear Me when I passed your cottage and called? I wanted to tell you to be ready to start with Me this morning at sunrise." As He spoke the sun rose fully over the peaks of the mountains and bathed them both in a lovely golden light.

"I am here," said Much-Afraid, still kneeling at His feet, "and I will go with You anywhere."

Then the Shepherd took her by the hand and they started for the mountains.

# Divine Delight

We can count on God to give us the desires of our hearts as we walk in His presence because He Himself placed those desires there.

*"Delight yourself also in the Lord, and He will give you the desires and secret petitions of your heart"*
(Ps. 37:4 AMP).

He will probably bring about our desires in a way so different from what we expected that we may think He is not fulfilling His word. But as we keep our eyes on Him and our hearts "squeezably" soft in His hand, He will pull back the curtain one day and then all the arrangements on the stage of life will make perfect sense.

*"In the same way, we can see and understand only a little about God now, as if we were peering at His reflection in a poor mirror; but someday we are going to see Him in His completeness, face to face. Now all that I know is hazy and blurred, but then I will see everything clearly, just as clearly as God sees into my heart right now"*
(1 Cor. 13:12 TLB).

Thank You, Jesus, that Your ways are perfect, even though I can't see them. I embrace them for myself today.

# CHAPTER 4

# Start for the High Places

It was early morning of a beautiful day. The valley lay as though still asleep. The only sounds were the joyful laughter of the running streams and the gay little songs of the birds. The dew sparkled on the grass and the wild flowers glowed like little jewels. Especially lovely were the wild anemones, purple, pink and scarlet, which dotted the pastures everywhere, thrusting their beautiful little faces up through the straggling thorns. Sometimes the Shepherd and Much-Afraid walked over patches of thousands of tiny little pink or mauve blossoms, each minutely small and yet all together forming a brilliant carpet, far richer than any seen in a king's palace.

Once the Shepherd stooped and touched the flowers gently with His fingers, then said to Much-Afraid with a smile, "Humble yourself, and you will find that Love is spreading a carpet of flowers beneath your feet."

Much-Afraid looked at Him earnestly. "I have often wondered about the wild flowers," she said. "It does seem strange that such unnumbered multitudes should bloom in the wild places of the earth where perhaps nobody ever sees them and the goats and the cattle can walk over them and crush them to death. They have so much beauty and sweetness to give and no one on whom to lavish it, nor who will even appreciate it."

The look the Shepherd turned on her was very beautiful. "Nothing My Father and I have made is ever wasted," He said

# Yielded Heart

Enter Jesus' presence today with a light heart. Skip along with Him hand-in-hand through the flower-laden valley of your heart. Bask in the untold privilege of facing and embracing life in His wonderful presence. Whisper words of love and gratitude to Him for choosing you as His beloved.

*"...I am my beloved's, and his desire is toward me!"*
(Song 7:10 AMP)

As birds chatter and sing, praising their Creator, so you too offer to your Lord praise from your lips. Just as leaves rustle in the wind as an act of yieldedness to their Creator, you too humble yourself under His hand.

*"...be clothed with humility: for God resisteth the proud,*
*and giveth grace to the humble"*
(1 Pet. 5:5 KJV).

Lord Jesus, I completely yield myself to Your will. I want to flow with Your Spirit as freely and easily as the leaves yield to the wind!

quietly, "and the little wild flowers have a wonderful lesson to teach. They offer themselves so sweetly and confidently and willingly, even if it seems that there is no one to appreciate them. Just as though they sang a joyous little song to themselves, that it is so happy to love, even though one is not loved in return.

"I must tell you a great truth, Much-Afraid, which only the few understand. All the fairest beauties in the human soul, its greatest victories, and its most splendid achievements are always those which no one else knows anything about, or can only dimly guess at. Every inner response of the human heart to Love and every conquest over self-love is a new flower on the tree of Love.

"Many a quiet, ordinary, and hidden life, unknown to the world, is a veritable garden in which Love's flowers and fruits have come to such perfection that it is a place of delight where the King of Love Himself walks and rejoices with His friends. Some of My servants have indeed won great visible victories and are rightly loved and reverenced by other men, but always their greatest victories are like the wild flowers, those which no one knows about. Learn this lesson now, down here in the valley, Much-Afraid, and when you get to the steep places of the mountains it will comfort you."

Then He added, "Come, the birds are all singing so joyously, let us join them too, and the flowers shall suggest the theme of our song." So, as they walked down the Valley toward the river, they sang together another of the old songs in the Shepherd's book, singing the parts in turn.

*I am the Rose of Sharon,*
*A wild anemone.*
*As lily 'mong the thorn trees*
*So is my love to me.*

*An apple tree 'mong wild trees,*
*My Love is in my sight,*

# Eternal Royalty

Just as the wild flowers offer themselves so sweet-ly, confidently, and willingly to their Creator, so should we. They reflect His glory—and we not only have the opportunity of reflecting His glory, but also the added privilege of being a chosen image bearer of the most High God.

> *"But you are a chosen race, a royal priesthood,*
> *a holy nation, a people for God's own possession,*
> *that you may proclaim the excellencies of Him who*
> *has called you out of darkness into His marvelous light"*
> (1 Pet. 2:9 NAS).

All earthly royalty will fade as the bloom of a flower, but His royalty begins now and lasts for eternity. People, things, or circumstances cannot remove Him from His King-ship. However, our human heart, damaged by sin, must be continually reminded that He has bestowed that royalty on us!

Lord Jesus, let my life be hidden completely in Your majesty. It is still hard for me to grasp that You have me as a special person belonging to You, as royalty! Let my heart bloom with fresh new flow-ers that reflect Your glorious image.

*I sit down in his shadow,*
*His fruit is my delight.*

*He brought me to his palace,*
*And to the banquet hall,*
*To share with me his greatness,*
*I, who am least of all.*

*Oh, give me help and comfort,*
*For I am sick with shame,*
*Unfit to be his consort,*
*Unfit to bear his Name.*

*I charge you, O ye daughters,*
*Ye roes among the trees,*
*Stir not my sleeping loved one,*
*To love me e'er he please.*

(Cant. 2:1-4,7)

Just as they finished singing this song they came to a place where a rushing stream poured itself across the path they were following and went cascading down the other side. It was running so swiftly and singing so loudly that it seemed to fill the valley around them with its laughing voice.

As the Shepherd lifted Much-Afraid across the slippery, wet stones she said to Him, "I do wish I knew what it is that all running water sings.

"Sometimes in the silence of the night I lie in bed and listen to the voice of the little stream which runs past our cottage garden. It sounds so happy and so eager, and as though it were repeating to itself over and over again some very lovely, secret message. I think all running water seems to be singing the same song, either loud and clear or soft and low. I do wish I knew what the waters were saying. It is quite different from the voice of the sea and of salt waters, but I never can understand it. It is an unknown tongue. Tell me, Shepherd, do you know what all the waters sing as they hurry on their way?"

# Divine Life

The Christian life is a paradox to our natural way of thinking: We die to live. Jesus made this clear in Luke 9:23-24:

> *"If anyone wishes to come after Me, let him deny himself, and take up his cross daily, and follow Me. For whoever wishes to save his life shall lose it, but whoever loses his life for My sake, he is the one who will save it"*
> (NAS).

Our dying to have life is also explained in Galatians 2:20:

> *"I have been crucified with Christ; and it is no longer I who live, but Christ lives in me..."*
> (NAS).

Lord Jesus, I know I have so much to learn about losing my life and releasing Yours in me. It is awe-inspiring to realize that the Most High God, who created the splendorous heavens as well as the minute details in plants and animals, *lives within me.* Please teach me and lead me in living Your life.

The Shepherd smiled again, and they stood silently for a few moments by the little torrent, which seemed to shout even more loudly and exultantly as though it knew they had paused to listen. Suddenly, as Much-Afraid stood beside the Shepherd it seemed as though her ears and her understanding were open, and bit by bit, the water-language became clear. It is, of course, impossible to write it in water-language, but this is the best I can do to translate it. Of course, it is a very poor effort, for though a water song perhaps may be set to music, words are quite a different matter. But it went something like this:

### The Water Song

*Come, oh come! let us away—*
*Lower, lower every day,*
*Oh, what joy it is to race*
*Down to find the lowest place.*
*This the dearest law we know—*
*"It is happy to go low."*
*Sweetest urge and sweetest will,*
*"Let us go down lower still."*

*Hear the summons night and day*
*Calling us to come away.*
*From the heights we leap and flow*
*To the valleys down below.*
*Always answering to the call,*
*To the lowest place of all.*
*Sweetest urge and sweetest pain,*
*To go low and rise again.*

"That is very puzzling," said Much-Afraid, after she had listened for a little and found that this was the refrain, repeated over and over again, though with a thousand variations of little trills and murmurs and bubbles and splashing sighs. " 'Let us go down lower still,' the water seems to be singing so gladly, because it is hurrying to go down to the

60

# Omniscient Care

The knowledge of who our God is forms a solid foundation for our lives. Isn't it comforting to know that our loving Father is omniscient, that He knows everything–including what is best for us?

*"Lord, You know all things"*
(see John 21:17).

He is also omnipresent; He is always everywhere caring for us.

*"The eyes of the Lord are everywhere"*
(Prov. 15:3a NIV).

And just think, as large and as great as God is, He desires to open our ears and eyes to know Him, to walk with Him, and to receive and embrace His truth. The omniscient and omnipresent God will show us as much truth as we can embrace. As we obey the truth that we do know, He will give us more.

*"…No eye has seen, no ear has heard, no mind has conceived what God has prepared for those who love Him"*
(1 Cor. 2:9 NIV).

As I dwell upon Your character, my Lord, it becomes so much easier to receive and return You love and to let it splash on whomever and whatever You bring into my path. I give myself to You freely and hilariously, as the water gives itself to the course that You lay before it. Help me to hold You in affectionate reverence, promptly obeying You and gratefully recognizing the benefits You in Your greatness have bestowed upon me.

lowest place, and yet You are calling me to the Highest Places. What does it mean?"

"The High Places," answered the Shepherd, "are the starting places for the journey down to the lowest place in the world. When you have hinds' feet and can go 'leaping on the mountains and skipping on the hills,' you will be able, as I am, to run down from the heights in gladdest self-giving and then go up to the mountains again. You will be able to mount to the High Places swifter than eagles, for it is only up on the High Places of Love that anyone can receive the power to pour themselves down in an utter abandonment of self-giving."

This saying seemed very mysterious and strange, but now that her ears had been opened to understand the water song, she heard it repeated over and over again by all the little streams which crossed their pathway or ran beside it. It seemed, too, that the wild flowers were also singing the same sort of song, only in yet another language, a color language, which, like the water tongue, could only be understood by the heart and not by the mind. They seemed to have a little chorus all their own which thousands upon thousands of them were singing in different color notes.

> *This is the law by which we live—*
> *It is so sweet to give and give.*

After that it seemed to Much-Afraid that all the little birds were chirping and trilling and lilting a tiny theme song also, with unnumbered variations, but still with one chorus breaking in all the time.

> *This is the joy of all winged life above—*
> *Happy it is to be able to love.*

"I never knew before," said Much-Afraid suddenly, "that the Valley is such a beautiful place and so full of song."

The Shepherd laughed and answered, "Only Love can really understand the music and the beauty and the joy which was planted in the heart of all created things. Have you forgotten

# Total Love

The Lord says:

*"For My thoughts are not your thoughts, neither are*
*your ways My ways… For as the heavens are higher*
*than the earth, so are My ways higher than your ways"*
(Is. 55:8-9 NAS).

Do you desire to mount to the High Places more swiftly than eagles? Do you want to be clothed with strength, dignity, and His peace so you can pour yourself out in utter abandonment of self-giving to others? Then you must learn to follow the most important commandment:

*"…The Lord our God is the one and only God.*
*And you must love Him with all your heart and*
*soul and mind and strength"*
(Mk. 12:29-30 TLB).

Only when you are completely absorbed with who your God is, and are controlled by Him, are you fulfilled and ready to be released to obey His second most important commandment:

*"You must love others as much as yourself"*
(see Mark 12:31 TLB).

Thank You, Lord Jesus, for the insight I am beginning to have about love. Continue opening my heart to understand You and Your ways.

that two days ago I planted the seed of Love in your heart? Already it has begun to make you hear and see things which you did not notice before.

"As Love grows in you, Much-Afraid, you will come to understand many things which you never dreamed of before. You will develop the gift of understanding many 'unknown tongues' and you will learn to speak Love's own language too, but first you must learn to spell out the alphabet of Love and to develop hinds' feet. Both these things you will learn on the journey to the High Places, and now here we are at the river, and over on the other side the foothills of the mountains begin. There we shall find your two guides waiting for you."

It was strange and wonderful indeed, thought Much-Afraid, that they had reached the river so quickly and were already approaching the mountains. Upheld by the Shepherd's hand and supported by His strength, she had really forgotten her lameness and had been unconscious of either tiredness or weakness. Oh, if only He would take her the whole way to the mountain places, instead of giving her over to the care of other guides.

When she thought of this, she said to Him imploringly, "Will You not take me all the way? When I am with You I am strong and I am sure no one else but You can get me up to the High Places."

He looked at her most kindly, but answered quietly, "Much-Afraid, I could do what you wish. I could carry you all the way up to the High Places Myself, instead of leaving you to climb there. But if I did, you would never be able to develop hinds' feet, and become My companion and go where I go. If you will climb to the heights this once with the companions I have chosen for you, even though it may seem a very long and in some places a very difficult journey, I promise you that you will develop hinds' feet.

"Afterwards you will be able to go with Me, 'leaping on the mountains,' and be able to make the ascent and the descent in

# Victorious Strength

Strong physical muscles are developed by use and exercise. The same process holds true for having healthy muscles in the inner soul also. However, the only way to exercise and practice those muscles is to face problems through God's strength and walk through them.

*"He teaches my hands to war, so that*
*my arms bend a bow of bronze"*
(Ps. 18:34 AMP).

As we walk, we learn about ourselves—we learn when we stop trusting Him and start trusting ourselves.

Lord, help me to close out thoughts of my activities and worries and to turn my mind toward You. I want to trust You and rely upon You. I exercise my spiritual muscles in this area. Thank You for making me victorious over this weak area of distrust.

*"For you shall go out... with joy, and be led forth...*
*with peace; the mountains and the hills shall*
*break forth before you into singing, and all the*
*trees of the field shall clap their hands"*
(Is. 55:12 AMP).

the twinkling of an eye. Moreover, if I carry you up to the High Places now, with only a tiny seed of Love in your heart, you will not be able to live in the Kingdom of Love. You will have to stay outside on places not so high, still within reach of your enemies.

"Some of them, you know, can visit the lower parts of the mountain. I have no doubt that you will meet them as you make the ascent. That is why I have most carefully chosen for you two of the very best and strongest guides. I assure you, however, that never for a moment shall I be beyond your reach or call for help, even when you cannot see Me. It is just as though I shall be present with you all the time, even though invisible. And you have My faithful promise that this journey which you are now to make will be the means of developing your hinds' feet."

"You will give me a new name when I get to the top?" quavered poor Much-Afraid, who all of a sudden seemed to have become deaf to the music around her and to be full of fears and forebodings again.

"Yes, certainly. When the flower of Love is ready to bloom in your heart, you will be loved in return and will receive a new name," replied the Shepherd.

Much-Afraid paused on the bridge and looked back over the way they had come. The Valley looked very green and peaceful, while the mountains to whose foot they had come towered above them like gigantic and threatening ramparts. Far away in the distance she could see the trees growing around the village of Much-Trembling, and with a sudden pang she pictured the Shepherd's helpers going about their happy work, the flocks wandering over the pastures and the peaceful little white cottage in which she had lived.

As these scenes rose before her, tears began to prick in her eyes and the thorn pricked in her heart, but almost at once she turned to the Shepherd and said thankfully, "I will trust You and do whatever You want."

# Freedom's Choice

Choice is a key word to life. Jesus gave mankind a choice because He wants His Bride, the Church, to choose Him, not be forced to come to Him or become a robot who cannot receive and return His love. To be our future Bridegroom, however, carried a heavy price: death on the cross. He chose to pay that price. When we choose to walk with Jesus, the price we pay is small in comparison to the benefits we receive—especially when we consider that those benefits were bought with His blood! Our best day without Him is worse than the worst day we had while walking with Him!

*"So, beloved, since you are expecting these things,*
*be eager to be found by Him [at His coming] without*
*spot or blemish, and at peace—in serene confidence, free*
*from fears and agitating passions and moral conflicts"*
(2 Pet. 3:14 AMP).

I choose to give all of myself to You, Jesus. Be the center of my life—be my joy, my strength, and my power. Do in my heart what I have so long been a failure in trying to do myself. Be my God.

Then, as she looked up in His face, He smiled most sweetly and said something He had never said before, "You have one real beauty, Much-Afraid, you have such trustful eyes. Trust is one of the most beautiful things in the world. When I look at the trust in your eyes I find you more beautiful to look upon than many a lovely queen."

In a very short time they were over the bridge, and had come to the foot of the mountains, where the path began the ascent of the lower slopes. Here great boulders were scattered all around, and suddenly Much-Afraid saw the figures of two veiled women seated on one of the rocks at the side of the path. As the Shepherd and she came up to that place, the two rose and bowed silently to Him.

"Here are the two guides which I promised," said the Shepherd quietly. "From now on until you are over the steep and difficult places, they will be your companions and helpers."

Much-Afraid looked at them fearfully. Certainly they were tall and appeared to be very strong, but why were they veiled? For what reason did they hide their faces? The longer and closer she looked at them, the more she began to dread them. They were so silent, so strong, and so mysterious. Why did they not speak? Why give her no friendly word of greeting?

"Who are they?" she whispered to the Shepherd. "Will You tell me their names, and why don't they speak to me? Are they dumb?"

"No, they are not dumb," said the Shepherd very quietly, "but they speak a new language, Much-Afraid, a dialect of the mountains which you have not yet learned. But as you travel with them, little by little, you will learn to understand their words.

"They are good teachers; indeed, I have few better. As for their names, I will tell you them in your own language, and later you will learn what they are called in their own tongue. This," said He, motioning toward the first of the silent figures, "is named Sorrow. And the other is her twin sister, Suffering."

# Daring Trust

Growth comes when we choose godliness instead of relief from people, things, and circumstances in the face of the unpleasant. Be comforted by His words to us:

*"Do not let your hearts be troubled (distressed, agitated)....I will not leave you as orphans— comfortless, desolate, bereaved, forlorn, helpless— I will come [back] to you"*
(Jn. 14:1,18 AMP).

Propelled by His love, we can dare to trust Him for the things we cannot see, for the results that are yet hidden to us.

*"Since we consider and look not to the things that are seen but to the things that are unseen; for the things that are visible are temporal (brief and fleeting), but the things that are invisible are deathless and everlasting"*
(2 Cor. 4:18 AMP).

Lord Jesus, enable me to reach from the visible into the invisible to live as You have designed me to live. I trust You.

Poor Much-Afraid! Her cheeks blanched and she began to tremble from head to foot. She felt so like fainting that she clung to the Shepherd for support.

"I can't go with them," she gasped. "I can't! I can't! O my Lord Shepherd, why do You do this to me? How can I travel in their company? It is more than I can bear. You tell me that the mountain way itself is so steep and difficult that I cannot climb it alone. Then why, oh why, must You make Sorrow and Suffering my companions? Couldn't You have given Joy and Peace to go with me, to strengthen me and encourage me and help me on the difficult way? I never thought You would do this to me!" And she burst into tears.

A strange look passed over the Shepherd's face as He listened to this outburst, then looking at the veiled figures as He spoke, He answered very gently, "Joy and Peace. Are those the companions you would choose for yourself? You remember your promise, to accept the helpers that I would give, because you believed that I would choose the very best possible guides for you. Will you still trust Me, Much-Afraid? Will you go with them, or do you wish to turn back to the Valley, and to all your Fearing relatives, to Craven Fear himself?"

Much-Afraid shuddered. The choice seemed terrible. Fear she knew only too well, but Sorrow and Suffering had always seemed to her the two most terrifying things which she could encounter. How could she go with them and abandon herself to their power and control? It was impossible. Then she looked at the Shepherd and suddenly knew she could not doubt Him, could not possibly turn back from following Him; that if she were unfit and unable to love anyone else in the world, yet in her trembling, miserable little heart, she did love Him. Even if He asked the impossible, she could not refuse.

She looked at Him piteously, then said, "Do I wish to turn back? O Shepherd, to whom should I go? In all the world I have no one but You. Help me to follow You, even though it

# Fearless Surrender

We do not have a choice over where we are born, who our parents are, what we look like, or what talents and gifts we possess. But we do have a choice over the most important issue in our lives: how we live life. When suffering touches us, it is natural to resist. Yet suffering is a friend, not a foe, when we are yielded to and controlled by the Lord Jesus Christ. When we are under His care, He allows nothing to enter our lives that is not first filtered through His tender, loving hand. He allows nothing that He cannot use for our good. His compassionate heart has perfectly proportioned these things to transform our weaknesses into strengths. First, though, we must surrender to Him. We do not need to fear suffering when He is with us.

*"Fear not...for I am with you; do not look around you in terror and be dismayed, for I am your God. I will strengthen and harden you [to difficulties]; yes, I will help you; yes, I will hold you up and retain you with My victorious right hand of rightness and justice"*
(Is. 41:10 AMP).

Lord, I choose to live life by walking with You. I trust You with everything in my life.

seems impossible. Help me to trust You as much as I long to love You."

As He heard these words the Shepherd suddenly lifted His head and laughed—a laugh full of exultation and triumph and delight. It echoed round the rocky walls of the little canyon in which they stood until for a moment or two it seemed as though the whole mountain range was laughing with Him. The echoes bounded higher and higher, leaping from rock to rock, and from crag to crag, up to the highest summits, until it seemed as though the last faint echoes of it were running into heaven itself.

When the last note had faded into silence, His voice said very softly, "Thou art all fair, my love; there is no spot in thee" (Cant. 4:7). Then He added, "Fear not, Much-Afraid, only believe. I promise that you shall not be put to shame. Go with Sorrow and Suffering, and if you cannot welcome them now, when you come to the difficult places where you cannot manage alone, put your hands in theirs confidently and they will take you exactly where I want you to go."

Much-Afraid stood quite still, looking up into His face, which now had such a happy, exultant look, the look of one who above all things else delights in saving and delivering. In her heart the words of a hymn, written by another of the Shepherd's followers, began to run through her mind and she started to sing softly and sweetly:

> *Let Sorrow do its work, send grief or pain;*
> *Sweet are thy messengers, sweet their refrain.*
> *If they but work in me, more love, O Christ, to thee,*
> *More love to thee, more love to thee.*

"Others have gone this way before me," she thought, "and they could even sing about it afterwards. Will He who is so strong and gentle be less faithful and gracious to me, weak and cowardly though I am, when it is so obvious that the thing He delights in most of all is to deliver His followers from all

# Captivating Love

Precious Lord Jesus, the very thought of You draws my heart to want to know You with my entire being. Let me cling to nothing of this world and to be satisfied with nothing less than You–Your love, Your ways, Your very life! Captivate my heart, O Lord; let me drink deeply from You.

*"Whom have I in Heaven but You? And I have no delight or desire on earth beside You. My flesh and my heart may fail, but God is the rock and firm strength of my heart, and my portion for ever"*
(Ps. 73:25-26 AMP).

*"For Your mercy and loving-kindness are great and high as the heavens! Your truth and faithfulness reach to the skies!"*
(Ps. 108:4 AMP)

Let your heart rest in His tender, gloriously sweet care. Worship at His feet.

I choose to draw near to You, my God. Help me to trust You as much as I long to love You. Thank You that You do even more than I ask. I thank You that I am Your workmanship.

*"For we are God's [own] handiwork (His workmanship), recreated in Christ Jesus…"*
(Eph. 2:10 AMP).

their fears and to take them to the High Places?" With this came the thought that the sooner she went with these new guides, the sooner she would reach those glorious High Places.

She stepped forward, looking at the two veiled figures, and said with a courage which she had never felt before, "I will go with you. Please lead the way," for even then she could not bring herself to put out her hands to grasp theirs.

The Shepherd laughed again and then said clearly, "My Peace I leave with you. My Joy be fulfilled in you. Remember that I pledge Myself to bring you to the High Places at the top of these mountains and that you shall not be put to shame and now 'till the day break and the shadows flee away, I will be like a roe or a young hart on the mountains' " (Cant. 2:17).

Then before Much-Afraid could realize what was happening, He had leaped on to a great rock at the side of the path and from there to another and to yet another, swifter almost than her eyes could follow His movements. He was leaping up the mountains, springing from height to height, going on before them until in a moment or two He was lost to sight.

When they could see Him no longer, Much-Afraid and her two new companions began to ascend the foothills. It would have been a curious sight, had there been anyone to watch, as Much-Afraid started on her journey, limping toward the High Places, shrinking as far as possible from the two veiled figures beside her, pretending not to see their proffered hands. But there was no one there to see, for if there is one thing more certain than another, it is that the development of hinds' feet is a secret process, demanding that there should be no onlookers.

# Obedient Steps

Much-Afraid began her journey in a hard place—something we all must face at one time or another. The process toward victory, though, starts with being willing to begin. Often we would rather wait for courage to well up inside us before stepping out to do a difficult assignment. However, if we step out in obedience to His voice, He will meet us at that place of obedience.

*"And God is able to make all grace abound to you, that always having all sufficiency in everything, you may have an abundance for every good deed"*
(2 Cor. 9:8 NAS).

As we choose to follow Him, we will find ourselves delighting in the process because He is continually drawing us to Himself through it!

Lord, I appreciate the work that You are doing in me. Bring the fruit of Your work in perfecting my character to full harvest. I love You.

# CHAPTER 5

# **Encounter With Pride**

From the very beginning the way up the mountains proved to be steeper than anything Much-Afraid had supposed herself capable of tackling, and it was not very long before she was forced to seek the help of her companions. Each time she shrinkingly took hold of the hand of either Sorrow or Suffering a pang went through her, but once their hands were grasped she found they had amazing strength, and seemed able to pull and even lift her upwards and over places which she would have considered utterly impossible to reach. Indeed, without their aid they would have been impossible, even for a strong and sure-footed person.

It was not very long, too, before she began to realize how much she needed their help in another way, for it was not only the steepness of the climb and her own lameness and weakness which made the journey difficult. To her surprise and distress she found there were enemies to meet on the way who would certainly have succeeded in making her turn back had she been alone.

To explain this we must now go back to the Valley of Humiliation and see what was happening there. Great was the wrath and consternation of the whole Fearing clan when it was discovered that Much-Afraid had made her escape from the Valley and had actually gone off to the mountains in the

# Inner Satisfaction

Turn to Jesus. Allow Him to quiet your mind and still your emotions. When you are relaxed in Him, consider the person or situation that you are having trouble embracing. Perhaps it would help you to know that God wants you to look through the people, things, and circumstances that you face as if they were transparent glass—to see His hand at work in the situation. He uses your life circumstances to bring you into His arms, where He can teach you to allow Him to satisfy your inner longings.

Teach me, Lord Jesus, to see Your workings in the situations I face. Help me to give my deep desires to You. Lord, thank You that

*"Your mercy and loving-kindness, O Lord,*
*extend to the skies, and Your*
*faithfulness to the clouds"*
(Ps. 36:5 AMP).

I know You will not let me down.

company of the Shepherd they so much hated. So long as she had been just ugly, crippled, and miserable little Much-Afraid, her relatives had cared nothing about her. Now they found it quite intolerable that of them all she alone should be singled out in this way and be taken to live on the High Places. Perhaps she would be given service in the palace of the great King Himself.

Who was Much-Afraid that this should happen to her while the rest of the family drudged away in the Valley of Humiliation? It was not that they wanted to go to the mountains themselves, far be it, but it was intolerable that Much-Afraid should do so.

So it happened that instead of being a little nobody in the eyes of her relatives, Much-Afraid had suddenly become the central figure in their interest and thought. Not only was her own immediate circle of Fearing relatives concerned about the matter but all of her more distant connections as well. Indeed, the whole population of the Valley, apart from the King's own servants, were angered by her departure, and determined that by some means she must be brought back and the hated Shepherd be robbed of His success in filching her from them.

A great consultation went on between all the more influential relatives, and ways and means discussed by which she could be captured most effectively and be brought back to the Valley as a permanent slave. Finally, it was agreed that someone must be sent after her as quickly as possible in order to force her to return. But they could not conceal from themselves that force might prove impossible, as apparently she had put herself under the protection of the Great Shepherd. Some means, then, would have to be found to beguile her into leaving Him of her own free will. How could this be accomplished?

In the end it was unanimously decided to send a distant connection of the family named Pride. The choice fell on him for several reasons. First, he was not only very strong and powerful but was also a handsome young man, and when he

# Heavenly Perspective

The enemy hates Jesus, he hates you, and he hates me. He knows that Jesus defeated him on the cross. He knows his sentence of doom has been sealed. But he will cause as much destruction as he can in the meantime.

> *"If the world hates you, you know that it*
> *has hated Me before it hated you"*
> (Jn. 15:18 NAS).

We need to keep our perspective on God if we do not want to be overwhelmed by the obstacles the enemy puts in our way. Here is the Lord's provision for our victory:

> *"[And He] has now entered into heaven and is*
> *at the right hand of God, with [all] angels and*
> *authorities and powers made subservient to Him"*
> (1 Pet. 3:22 AMP).

Lord Jesus, please break me of the unhealthy habit of going to others for help instead of to You. When the enemy is about to overcome me, remind me of the wonderful provision You have made for my victory over him!

> *"Jesus replied, I am the Bread of Life. He who*
> *comes to Me will never be hungry and he who*
> *believes on and cleaves to and trusts in and relies*
> *on Me will never thirst any more—at any time"*
> (Jn. 6:35 AMP).

chose, could be extremely attractive. It was emphasized that if other means proved unsuccessful he was to feel no scruples against exerting all his powers of fascination in order to coax Much-Afraid away from the Shepherd.

Besides, it was a well-known fact that the young man was by nature far too proud to admit defeat or lack of success in any undertaking, and that there would be no giving up on his part until he accomplished his purpose. As everybody knew, to confess defeat and return without Much-Afraid would be the last thing possible to Pride, so when he consented to undertake the task it was felt that the matter was as good as settled.

Much-Afraid and her two companions therefore had only been a few days upon their journey and had made but slow though steady progress, when one morning, on turning a corner of the rocky pathway, Pride was seen striding toward them. She was certainly surprised and discomfited at this unexpected apparition, but not unduly alarmed. This cousin had always so disdained and ignored her very existence that at first it never occurred to her that he would even speak to her, but expected to see him pass by in the same haughty manner as usual.

Pride himself, who had been skulking and spying for several hours before he showed himself, was on his part delighted to find that though Much-Afraid seemed to be traveling in the care of two strong companions, yet the Shepherd Himself apparently was not with her. He approached her therefore quite confidently but with a most unusual affability of manner, and to Much-Afraid's great surprise stopped when they met, and greeted her.

"Well, Cousin Much-Afraid, here you are at last. I have had such ado to catch up with you."

"How do you do, Cousin Pride?" said that poor little simpleton. Much-Afraid, of course, ought to have known better than to greet, much less to stop and talk with one of her own relatives from the Valley. But it is rather pleasant, after being snubbed and ignored for years, suddenly to be greeted as an

# Wisdom Learned

God planted within each of us a legitimate need for unconditional love and acceptance which only He can completely fill. Unfortunately, we try to satisfy that need in illegitimate ways—by turning to others, to things, or to circumstances. Now, we are not forced to turn to these things; we choose to sin with our own free will. Granted, the enemy uses the most inviting "bait" customized to our weaknesses to lure us from our Lord. The enemy knows the way we have habitually walked and what to dangle before us. God, however, has no tolerance toward sin; therefore, He will not compromise with it. He knows the pain and destruction it leaves in its path. We seem to need to learn that by experience. So how can we turn from sin?

*"Do not be wise in your own eyes; fear the*
*Lord and turn away from evil"*
(Prov. 3:7 NAS).

Dear Lord, I choose to not continue in sin. Show me when I begin to fall into the same old weakness. Help me to hate sin as You hate it.

equal. Besides this, her curiosity was awakened. Of course, had it been that awful and detestable Craven, nothing would have induced her to stop and speak with him.

"Much-Afraid," said Pride seriously, actually taking her hand in a kindly and friendly manner (it so happened that at that place the path was not quite so steep and she had freed her hands from those of both Sorrow and Suffering), "I have made this journey on purpose to try to help you. I do beg you to allow me to do so and to listen very attentively and seriously.

"My dear cousin, you must give up this extraordinary journey and come back with me to the Valley. You don't realize the true position in which you have put yourself, nor the dreadful future before you. The One who has persuaded you to start this improper journey" (Pride could not bring himself even to mention the Shepherd by name) "is well known to have seduced other helpless victims in this same way.

"Do you know what will happen to you, Much-Afraid, if you persist in going forward? All those fair promises He has made about bringing you into His Kingdom and making you live happily ever afterward will prove false. When He gets you up to the wild, desolate parts of the mountains, He will abandon you altogether, and you will be put to lasting shame."

Poor Much-Afraid tried to pull her hand away, for now she began to understand the meaning of his presence there and his bitter hatred of the Shepherd, but as she struggled to free her hand, he only grasped it tighter. She had to learn that once Pride is listened to, struggle as one may, it is the hardest thing in the world to throw him off. She hated the things that he said, but with her hand grasped in his they had the power to sound horribly plausible and true.

Did she not often find herself in her heart of hearts thrusting back the same idea and possibility which Pride was suggesting to her? Even if the Shepherd did not abandon her (and that she could not believe), might it not be that He who did allow Sorrow and Suffering to be her companions, would also allow her (for her soul's good, of course) to be put to shame before all her relatives and connections? Was she not almost certainly

# Growing Discernment

In order to mature, we must all learn to discern between the truth and a lie. We must learn to separate the vile from the precious in each and every situation.

*"…if you separate the precious from the vile…*
*you shall be as My mouthpiece…"*
(Jer. 15:19 AMP).

Only the Spirit of God can give us this discernment. However, too often we go through the maturing process the hard way–learning by making a mistake and finding out the painfulness of the consequences. When we become self-confident, rebellious, or ignorant, our guard is down and the enemy can move in. When he gains that ground in our lives, only the power of God can break his hold on it. That is the reason we are warned:

*"And do not give the devil an opportunity"*
(Eph. 4:27 NAS).

We can help ourselves stay out of satan's clutches by following this advice:

*"Do not be so deceived and misled! Evil companionships,*
*(communion, associations) corrupt and deprave*
*good manners and morals and character"*
(1 Cor. 15:33 AMP).

Lord Jesus, give me the ability to recognize and avoid the enemy's manipulations, schemes, and traps. I look to You for release, healing, and protection.

exposing herself to ridicule? Who could know what the Shepherd might allow her to go through (for her ultimate good, perhaps, but quite unbearable to contemplate).

It is a terrible thing to let Pride take one by the hand, Much-Afraid suddenly discovered; his suggestions are so frightfully strong, and through the contact of touch he can press them home with almost irresistible force.

"Come back, Much-Afraid," he urged vehemently. "Give it up before it is too late. In your heart of hearts you know that what I am saying is true and that you will be put to shame before everybody. Give it up while there is still time. Is a merely fictitious promise of living on the High Places worth the cost you are asked to pay for it? What is it that you seek there in that mythological Kingdom above?"

Entirely against her will, and simply because he seemed to have her at his mercy, Much-Afraid let the words be dragged out of her. "I am seeking the Kingdom of Love," she said faintly.

"I thought as much," sneered Pride. "Seeking your heart's desire, eh? And now, Much-Afraid, have a little pride, ask yourself honestly, are you not so ugly and deformed that nobody even in the Valley really loves you? That is the brutal truth. Then how much less will you be welcome in the Kingdom of Love, where they say nothing but unblemished beauty and perfection is admitted? Can you really expect to find what you are seeking; no, I tell you again that you feel this yourself and you know it. Then be honest at least and give it up. Turn back with me before it is too late."

Poor Much-Afraid! The urge to turn back seemed almost irresistible, but at that moment when she stood held in the clutch of Pride, feeling as though every word he spoke was the hideous truth, she had an inner vision of the face of the Shepherd. She remembered the look with which He had promised her, "I pledge Myself to bring you there, and that you shall not be put to shame." Then it was as though she heard Him again,

# Sure Hope

The truth is, the Christian life is difficult and very hard at times. Can you identify with these words from the psalmist:

*"Lord, how they are increased who trouble me! Many are they who rise up against me. Many are saying of me, There is no help for him in God..."*
(Ps. 3:1-2 AMP).

The price we pay in difficulty, however, is nothing in comparison to the rewards He gives us now and for eternity. So if you feel abandoned or ashamed, realize that they are only feelings, not reality. This is reality:

*"...Behold, I am laying in Zion a chosen, (honored,) precious chief Cornerstone; and he who believes in Him...shall never be disappointed or put to shame"*
(1 Pet. 2:6 AMP).

Lord Jesus, thank You that I am beginning to separate the precious from the vile and to see truth. Even though I have many imperfections to be worked out in my life yet, I still put my hope in You because not only do You love me, You also *like me!* Thank You, Jesus!

repeating softly, as though looking at some radiant vision in the distance:

> *Behold, thou art fair, my love; thou hast dove's eyes.*
> *Thou art all fair, my love; there is no spot in thee.*

Before Pride could realize what was happening, Much-Afraid uttered a desperate cry for help and was calling up the mountain. "Come to me, Shepherd! Come quickly! Make no tarrying, O my Lord."

There was a sound of loose rattling stones and of a prodigious leap, and the next moment the Shepherd was on the path beside them, His face terrible to look at, His Shepherd's staff raised high above His head. Only one blow fell, and then Pride dropped the hand he had been grasping so tightly and made off down the path and round the corner, slipping and stumbling on the stones as he went, and was out of sight in a moment.

"Much-Afraid," said the Shepherd, in a tone of gentle but firm rebuke, "why did you let Pride come up to you and take your hand? If you had been holding the hands of your two helpers this could never have happened."

For the first time, Much-Afraid of her own free will held out both hands to her two companions, and they grasped her strongly, but never before had their hold upon her been so full of pain, so bitter with sorrow.

She learned in this way the first important lesson on her journey upward, that if one stops to parley with Pride and listens to his poisonous suggestions and, above all, if he is allowed to lay his grasp upon any part of one, Sorrow becomes unspeakably more unbearable afterwards and anguish of heart has bitterness added to it. Moreover, for a while she limped more painfully than ever she had since leaving the Valley. Pride had trodden on her feet at the moment she called for help and left them more lame and sore than ever.

# Faithful Mercy

Sin will take us further than we want to go. It will keep us longer than we want to stay and it will cost us more than we want to pay. God, in His mercy, will work through those people He places in authority over us to protect us, bless us, and sensitize our consciences. Consider the beginning of Romans 13:

> *"...The authorities that exist have been established by God. Consequently, he who rebels against the authority is rebelling against what God has instituted..."*
> (vv. 1-2 NIV).

We often leave this God-given protection when we feel we know what is best. Then we need to turn in repentance back to God. When we do, He is faithful to forgive.

> *"If we confess our sins, He is faithful and righteous to forgive us our sins and to cleanse us from all unrighteousness"*
> (1 John 1:9 NAS).

O lovely Lord Jesus, what a haven of blessing to retreat from the problems and pressures of the day and sink into Your warm, caring, loving arms. Let my inner being be drawn to Your heart. I rejoice that Your mercies are greater than my faults. Thank You for receiving me.

# CHAPTER 6

# Detour Through the Desert

After meeting Pride, Much-Afraid and her companions went on their way, but she was obliged to hobble painfully and could go but slowly. However, she accepted the assistance of her two guides with far greater willingness than before, and gradually the effects of the encounter wore off and she was able to make better progress.

Then one day the path turned a corner, and to her amazement and consternation she saw a great plain spread out beneath them. As far as the eye could see there seemed to be nothing but desert, an endless expanse of sand dunes, with not a tree in sight. The only objects breaking the monotony of the desert were strange, towering pyramids, rising above the sand dunes, hoary with age and grimly desolate. To the horror of Much-Afraid her two guides prepared to take the steep path downward.

She stopped dead and said to them, "We mustn't go down there. The Shepherd has called me to the High Places. We must find some path which goes up, but certainly not down there." But they made signs to her that she was to follow them down the steep pathway to the desert below.

Much-Afraid looked to left and right, but though it seemed incredible, there was no way possible by which they could continue

# Desires Fulfilled

People, things, and circumstances will always change. Our God, however, never changes.

*"Jesus Christ, the Messiah, [is always] the same, yesterday, today, [yes,] and forever—to the ages"*
(Heb. 13:8 AMP).

Also, since people are not perfect, they will disappoint us sooner or later. On the other hand, Jesus always fulfills the desires of our hearts, the desires that He has placed in us. It's just that He almost always does it differently than we expected. We think He's tossing aside our desires like unwanted gifts. When you feel this way, remember Jesus' words to Peter:

*"You do not understand now what I am doing, but you will understand later on"*
(Jn. 13:7 AMP).

Lord Jesus, help me to sink the roots of my soul deeply into the fact that You are loving, good, reliable, nurturing, accepting, just, and impartial—that You love me and have my best interests in mind. Thank You that You are faithfully orchestrating each minute detail in my life for my good, even when things don't happen as I want them.

Now release the details of today's expectations to Him, and allow Him to accomplish His will in your life.

to climb upward. The hill they were on ended abruptly at this precipice, and the rocky cliffs towered above them in every direction straight as walls with no possible foothold.

"I can't go down there," panted Much-Afraid, sick with shock and fear. "He can never mean that—never! He called me up to the High Places, and this is an absolute contradiction of all that He promised."

She then lifted up her voice and called desperately, "Shepherd, come to me. Oh, I need You. Come and help me."

In a moment He was there, standing beside her.

"Shepherd," she said despairingly, "I can't understand this. The guides You gave me say that we must go down there into that desert, turning right away from the High Places altogether. You don't mean that, do You? You can't contradict Yourself. Tell them we are not to go there, and show us another way. Make a way for us, Shepherd, as You promised."

He looked at her and answered very gently, "That is the path, Much-Afraid, and you are to go down there."

"Oh, no," she cried. "You can't mean it. You said if I would trust You, You would bring me to the High Places, and that path leads right away from them. It contradicts all that You promised."

"No," said the Shepherd, "it is not contradiction, only postponement for the best to become possible."

Much-Afraid felt as though He had stabbed her to the heart. "You mean," she said incredulously, "You really mean that I am to follow that path down and down into that wilderness and then over that desert, away from the mountains indefinitely? Why" (and there was a sob of anguish in her voice) "it may be months, even years, before that path leads back to the mountains again. O Shepherd, do You mean it is indefinite postponement?"

He bowed His head silently, and Much-Afraid sank on her knees at His feet, almost overwhelmed. He was leading her away from her heart's desire altogether and gave no promise

# Holy Detour

When there appears to be a contradiction between what God has promised and what we see happening, remember that we see from a limited perspective. We see, as it were, only one narrow slice out of the whole pie of life. God, though, sees it all—His knowledge is perfect. This seemingly contradictory situation is similar to the one in which Jesus predicted His suffering and death. His disciples' reaction was the same as Much-Afraid's when she faced what appeared to be a detour away from the High Places and through the desert. Then Jesus challenged His disciples with these words:

*"If anyone wishes to come after Me, let him deny himself, and take up his cross, and follow Me. For whoever wishes to save his life shall lose it; but whoever loses his life for My sake shall find it"*
(Mt. 16:24-25 NAS).

Losing one's life is painful. It's death! Upon hearing a missionary's report of God's work, a woman commented, "I'd give my life to be used like that!" The missionary replied, "That's what it would cost!"

Lord, remind me that there's more than only what I see. Help me to want what You want for me. Let me "die" as gracefully as possible!

at all as to when He would bring her back. As she looked out over what seemed an endless desert, the only path she could see led farther and farther away from the High Places, and it was all desert.

Then He answered very quietly, "Much-Afraid, do you love Me enough to accept the postponement and the apparent contradiction of the promise, and to go down there with Me into the desert?"

She was still crouching at His feet, sobbing as if her heart would break, but now she looked up through her tears, caught His hand in hers, and said, trembling, "I do love You, You know that I love You. Oh, forgive me because I can't help my tears. I will go down with You into the wilderness, right away from the promise, if You really wish it. Even if You cannot tell me why it has to be, I will go with You, for You know I do love You, and You have the right to choose for me anything that You please."

It was very early morning, and high above them, hanging in the sky over the silent expanse of desert, was a young crescent moon and the morning star shining like a brilliant jewel close beside it. There Much-Afraid built her first altar on the mountains, a little pile of broken rocks, and then, with the Shepherd standing close beside her, she laid down on the altar her trembling, rebelling will. A little spurt of flame came from somewhere, and in an instant nothing but a heap of ashes was lying on the altar. That is to say, she thought at first there were only ashes, but the Shepherd told her to look closer, and there among the ashes she saw a little stone of some kind, a dark-colored, common-looking pebble.

"Pick it up and take it with you," said the Shepherd gently, "as a memorial of this altar which you built, and all that it stands for."

Much-Afraid took the stone out of the ashes, scarcely looking at it and feeling that to her life's end she would never need a reminder of that altar, for how could she ever forget it or the anguish of that first surrender, but she dropped the pebble into

# Transparent Confession

Gently turn to Jesus and lay your head upon His bosom. Tell Him all the contents of your heart the same way an innocent child would spill all the details of her day to a loving, caring mother. It is important to our maturing to not suppress, conceal, or deny what is happening inside us, but to be transparent and completely vulnerable to our Lord. We need to lay down our trembling, rebellious wills on the altar to Him. Our greatest gift to Him is to relinquish our will to Him.

> *"My sacrifice [the sacrifice acceptable] to God is a broken spirit; a broken and a contrite heart [broken down with sorrow for sin and humbly and thoroughly penitent] such, O God, You will not despise"*
> (Ps. 51:17 AMP).

Let's build an altar as a memorial to God's mighty deeds and offer our wills there. Then it would serve as encouragement during a time of discouragement, to remind us of our yieldedness to Him.

Lord Jesus, I lay my will down on the altar. I say with Much-Afraid that I will go with You, for You know I do love You, and You have the right to choose for me anything that You please.

a little purse or bag which the Shepherd gave her and put it away carefully.

Then they began the descent into the desert, and at the first step Much-Afraid felt a thrill of the sweetest joy and comfort surge through her, for she found that the Shepherd Himself was going down with them. She would not have Sorrow and Suffering as her only companions, but He was there too. As she started down the path He began a song which Much-Afraid had not heard before, and it sounded so sweet and comforting that her pain began to melt away. It was as though the song suggested to her a part at least of the reason for this strange postponement of all her hopes. This is the song He sang:

### The Closed Garden

*A garden closed art thou, my love,*
*Where none thy fruits can taste,*
*A spring shut up, a fountain sealed,*
*An orchard run to waste.*

*Awake, north wind! and come, thou south!*
*Blow on my garden fair,*
*That all the spices may flow out*
*As perfume on the air.*

(Cant. 4:12-16)

They reached the desert surprisingly quickly, because, although the path was very steep indeed, Much-Afraid was leaning on the Shepherd, and did not feel her weakness at all. By the evening of that same day they were down on the pale sand dunes and walking toward some huts built in the shadow of one of the great pyramids, where they were to rest that night. At sunset, when the sky burned fiery red over the western rim of the desert, the Shepherd led Much-Afraid away from the huts, to the foot of the pyramid.

"Much-Afraid," He said, "all of My servants on their way to the High Places have had to make this detour through the desert. It is called 'The furnace of Egypt, and an horror of great

# Nurturing Love

Come to your Lord in sweetness and quiet attention. His cords of love draw you to Him, nurturing you as a day of sunshine does the flowers. Rest there in His presence with your heart lifted up to Him. Let your complete hope be in God. His nurturing love will prepare and strengthen you for the purification that comes from pain. Why must pain be mixed with purification? What is the reason for His working in such a way? Hosea 2:19-20 tells us:

> *"And I will betroth you to Me for ever; yes, I will betroth you to Me in righteousness and justice, and in steadfast love, and in mercies. I will even betroth you to Me in stability and in faithfulness, and you shall know—recognize, be acquainted with, appreciate, give heed to and cherish—the Lord"*
> (AMP).

Yes, my Lord, I want to *know You*, not merely about You. I love You more today than I did yesterday, but I long to love and cherish You more tomorrow than I do today. Help me to grow through the pain to reach the purification.

darkness' (Gen. 15:12,17). Here they have learned many things which otherwise they would have known nothing about.

"Abraham was the first of My servants to come this way, and this pyramid was hoary with age when he first looked upon it. Then came Joseph, with tears and anguish of heart, and looked upon it too and learned the lesson of the furnace of fire. Since that time an endless succession of My people have come this way. They came to learn the secret of royalty, and now you are here, Much-Afraid. You, too, are in the line of succession. It is a great privilege, and if you will, you also may learn the lesson of the furnace and of the great darkness just as surely as did those before you. Those who come down to the furnace go on their way afterwards as royal men and women, princes and princesses of the Royal Line."

Much-Afraid looked up at the towering pyramid, now shadowy and black against the sunset sky, and desolate as it looked in the waste of desert, yet it seemed to her to be one of the most majestic objects she had ever seen.

Then all of a sudden the desert was full of people, an endless procession of them. There was Abraham himself and Sarah his wife, those first lonely exiles in a strange land; there was Joseph, the betrayed and wounded brother who had been sold into slavery, who when he wept for his father's tent, saw only the alien pyramid. Then one after another she saw a great host which no man could number stretching across the desert in an endless line. The last one in the line held out a hand which she took, and there she was in the great chain herself. Words came to her ears also, and she heard them quite plainly.

"Fear not, Much-Afraid, to go down into Egypt; for I will there make of thee a great nation; I will go down with thee into Egypt; and I will also surely bring thee up again" (Gen. 46:3).

After this they went back to the huts to rest that night. In the morning the Shepherd called Much-Afraid again and led her away, but this time He opened a little door in the wall of the pyramid and took her inside. There was a passage which

# Glorious Transition

Life with Jesus is much like living in a Victorian house where the rooms all come into a central hall that leads down the middle of the house. Sometimes we are in His "glory" room. Those are the times to embrace, rejoice over, and savor with glee! Then He says, "It's time to enter the dark hall to go to another room." In the darkness we have only the handrail (God's Word and the Spirit's empowering) to sustain us. This route is necessary to make it to the next "glory" room. We can trust Him as we walk down this dark hall because He is good. Not only is He good, but He also does good!

*"The goodness of God endureth continually"*
(Ps. 52:1b KJV).

*"Thou art good, and doest good"*
(Ps. 119:68a KJV).

Trust Him. His is building you into a house!

*"You also, as living stones, are being built up*
*as a spiritual house for a holy priesthood,*
*to offer up spiritual sacrifices acceptable*
*to God through Jesus Christ"*
(1 Pet. 2:5 NAS).

Lord Jesus, help me to embrace and cherish the times in Your hall as much as I do in Your "glory" room. Let me always remember that each is precious to You and should be also to me. I love You!

led to the center, and from there a spiral staircase went up to the floors above.

But the Shepherd opened another door leading out of the central chamber on the ground floor and they entered a very large room which looked like a granary. There were great piles of grain everywhere except in the middle. There on the open space men were threshing the different kinds of grain in many different ways and then grinding them to powder, some coarse and some finer. At one side were women sitting on the ground with hollow smooth stones before them, grinding the very best of the wheat into the finest possible powder.

Watching them for awhile, Much-Afraid saw how the grains were first beaten and bruised until they crumbled to pieces, but still the grinding and beating process continued, until at last the powder was fine enough to be used for baking the best wheat bread.

"See," said the Shepherd gently, "how various are the methods used for grinding the different varieties of grain, according to their special use and purpose." Then He quoted, "Dill is not threshed with a threshing instrument, neither is a cart wheel turned about upon the cummin; but dill is beaten out with a staff, and the cummin with a rod. Bread corn is bruised, but no one crushes it forever; neither is it broken with the wheel of a cart nor bruised with horsemen driving over it" (Isa. 28:27,28).

As Much-Afraid watched the women pounding the bread corn with their heavy stones she noticed how long the process took before the fine white powder was finished and ready for use. Then she heard the Shepherd saying, "I bring My people into Egypt that they, too, may be threshed and ground into the finest powder and may become bread corn for the use of others. But remember, though bread corn is bruised, no one threshes it forever; only until the bruised and broken grain is ready for its highest use. This also cometh forth from the Lord of Hosts, which is wonderful in counsel and excellent in working" (v. 29).

# Submitted Steps

One way to suffer is to have what you do not want and want what you do not have. Thus the hardest choice in life is to embrace our Lord's lordship and give Him the right to make our choices. It is to lay down the control of our own lives and refuse to be "as God" in them. Let these words encourage you to make that choice:

" 'For I know the plans that I have for you,' declares
the Lord, 'plans for welfare and not for calamity
to give you a future and a hope' "
(Jer. 29:11 NAS).

So don't despise suffering. Grapes give the greatest yield, but are the easiest to go wild if not pruned.

"Before I was afflicted I went astray, but now
Your word do I keep [hearing, receiving,
loving and obeying it]"
(Ps. 119:67 AMP).

Thank You, Jesus, that times of suffering are for my benefit and Your glory. What a comfort to know such times are privileges ordained by You to take me one step farther with You. I yield, knowing You will see me through.

After this the Shepherd took her back to the central chamber and they ascended the spiral staircase, twisting up and up into the darkness above. There, on the next floor, they came to another and smaller room, in the center of which stood a great wheel, flat, like a table. Beside it stood a potter who wrought a work on the wheel. As he spun the wheel he fashioned his clay into many beautiful shapes and objects. The material was cut and kneaded and shaped as he saw fit, but always the clay lay still upon the wheel, submitting to his every touch, perfectly, unresisting.

As they watched, the Shepherd said, "In Egypt, too, I fashion My fairest and finest vessels and bring forth instruments for My work, according as I see fit" (Jer. 18). Then He smiled and added, "Cannot I do with you, Much-Afraid, as this potter? Behold, as the clay is in the hand of the potter so are you in My hand" (Jer. 18:6).

Last of all He took her up the stairway to the highest floor. There they found a room with a furnace in which gold was being smelted and refined of all its dross. Also in the furnace were rough pieces of stone and rock containing crystals. These were put in the great heat of the oven and left for a time. On being taken out, behold, they were glorious jewels, flashing as though they had received the fire into their very hearts. As Much-Afraid stood beside the Shepherd, looking shrinkingly into the fire, He said the loveliest thing of all.

"O thou afflicted, tossed with tempest, and not comforted, behold, I will lay thy stones with fair colors, and lay thy foundations with sapphires. And I will make thy windows of agates, and thy gates of carbuncles, and all thy borders of pleasant stones" (Isa. 54:11). Then He added, "My rarest and choicest jewels and My finest gold are those who have been refined in the furnace of Egypt," and He sang one verse of a little song:

> *I'll turn my hands upon thy heart,*
> *And purge away thy dross,*
> *I will refine thee in my fire*
> *Remake thee at my cross.*

# Passing Pressures

Our compassionate, loving Father puts limits on our suffering. We can be assured that it will not last forever. The psalmist wrote:

*"Sing to the Lord, you saints of His; praise His holy name. For His anger lasts only a moment, but His favor lasts a lifetime; weeping may remain for a night, but rejoicing comes in the morning"*
(Ps. 30:4-5 NIV).

We can relax in the Potter's tender hands, letting the truth of His Word bring to us a complete, restful, and submissive attitude even in the midst of being "squeezed."

*"Yet, O Lord, You are our Father; we are the clay, and You our potter, and we all are the work of Your hand"*
(Is. 64:8 AMP).

Thank You, Lord Jesus, that as I keep my eyes on You, You will never give me more than I can stand. I can embrace that suffering in my life knowing that You, as the Potter, set its limits and regulate its size and duration. Thank You for arranging so carefully and affectionately the details of my life.

They stayed at the huts in the desert for several days, and Much-Afraid learned many things which she had never heard before.

One thing, however, made a special impression upon her. In all that great desert, there was not a single green thing growing, neither tree nor flower nor plant save here and there a patch of straggly grey cacti.

On the last morning she was walking near the tents and huts of the desert dwellers, when in a lonely corner behind a wall she came upon a little golden-yellow flower, growing all alone. An old pipe was connected with a water tank. In the pipe was one tiny hole through which came an occasional drop of water. Where the drops fell one by one, there grew the little golden flower, though where the seed had come from, Much-Afraid could not imagine, for there were no birds anywhere and no other growing things.

She stopped over the lonely, lovely little golden face, lifted up so hopefully and so bravely to the feeble drip, and cried out softly, "What is your name, little flower, for I never saw one like you before."

The tiny plant answered at once in a tone as golden as itself, "Behold me! My name is Acceptance-with-Joy."

Much-Afraid thought of the things which she had seen in the pyramid: the threshing-floor and the whirring wheel and the fiery furnace. Somehow the answer of the little golden flower which grew all alone in the waste of the desert stole into her heart and echoed there faintly but sweetly, filling her with comfort. She said to herself, "He has brought me here when I did not want to come for His own purpose. I, too, will look up into His face and say, 'Behold me! I am Thy little handmaiden Acceptance-with-Joy.' " Then she stooped down and picked up a pebble which was lying in the sand beside the flower and put it in the purse with the first altar stone.

# Thankful Persistence

One of life's strategic keys is learning to embrace what our Lord brings into our lives with thanksgiving. When we do so, we recognize His sovereign control and completely yield ourselves to Him. He will never waste our sorrows. On the contrary, He turns them into precious jewels! As for our suffering, He uses it to birth beautiful new things into our lives. So if we keep these things in mind, it makes the pain more bearable and it seems less senseless.

*"Thank [God] in everything—no matter what*
*the circumstances may be, be thankful and give*
*thanks; for this is the will of God for you [who are]*
*in Christ Jesus [the Revealer and Mediator of that will]"*
(1 Thess. 5:18 AMP).

O Lord Jesus, Lover of my soul, You and only You understand the inner craving of my being. Thank You for loving me, never leaving me, and caring about every detail of my life. Help me to begin each day with a thankful spirit, until I can do so as a way of life. Let me never be found resisting what You are birthing or bringing forth in me. I love You and want to love You even more.

# CHAPTER 7

# On the Shores
# of Loneliness

After they walked together through the burning desert sands, then one day, quite unexpectedly, a path crossed the main track which they were following. "This," said the Shepherd quietly, "is the path which you are now to follow." So they turned westward with the High Places right behind their backs and came in a little while to the end of the desert. They found themselves on the shore of a great sea.

"It is now time for Me to leave you, Much-Afraid," He said, "and return to the mountains. Remember, even though you seem to be farther away than ever from the High Places and from Me, there is really no distance at all separating us. I can cross the desert sands as swiftly as I can leap from the High Places to the valleys, and whenever you call for Me, I shall come. This is the word I now leave with you. Believe it and practice it with joy. My sheep hear My voice and they follow Me.

"Whenever you are willing to obey Me, Much-Afraid, and to follow the path of My choice, you will always be able to hear and recognize My voice, and when you hear it you must always obey. Remember also that it is always safe to obey My voice, even if it seems to call you to paths which look impossible or even crazy." On saying this He blessed her and went from them, leaping and bounding over the desert toward the High Places, which were now actually right behind her.

# Eternal Companion

Walking with Jesus means we have companionship with Him. Much-Afraid traveled through the desert with relative ease because of His companionship. As we walk with Him, we need to be sensitive to His voice. Isaiah 30:20-21 shows how sensitive we are to be to Him and to His voice:

*"And though the Lord give you the bread of adversity and the water of affliction, yet your Teacher will not hide Himself any more, but your eyes shall constantly behold your Teacher. And your ears shall hear a word behind you, saying, This is the way, walk in it, when you turn to the right hand and when you turn to the left"*
(AMP).

We need to hear His voice to follow Him. If we hold anything to ourselves, refusing to give it to Jesus, or if we do not obey a request He makes of us, then that has blocked His voice to us. We need to give those things to Him and get back into His companionship.

Lord Jesus, give me eyes and ears for You only. Let me completely hide myself in You and thrive only on our companionship.

Much-Afraid and her two companions walked along the shores of the great sea for many days, and at first it seemed to her that up till then she had never known real loneliness.

The green valley where all her friends and she had lived was far away behind her. Even the mountains were out of sight, and there seemed to be nothing in the whole wide world but the endless sandy desert on one side and the endless sea moaning drearily on the other. Nothing grew there, neither tree nor shrub nor even grass, but the shores were scattered with broken driftwood and with great tangled masses of brown and shriveled seaweed. Nothing lived in the whole region save the sea gulls wheeling and crying overhead and the crabs scuttling across the sand into their burrows. At intervals, too, an icy wind came shrilling across the billows, stabbing sharp as a knife.

In those days Much-Afraid never let go the hands of her two companions, and it was amazing how swiftly they helped her along. Stranger still, perhaps, was the way in which Much-Afraid walked, swifter and more upright than ever before, and with scarcely a limp, for something had happened in the wilderness which had left a mark upon her for the rest of her life. It was an inner and secret mark, and no one would have noticed any difference outwardly, but all the same, a deep inner change had taken place which indicated a new stage in her life.

She had been down into Egypt and had looked upon the grinding-stones, the wheel, and the furnace, and knew that they symbolized an experience which she herself must pass through. Somehow, incredible as it was, she, Much-Afraid, had been enabled to accept the knowledge and to acquiesce in it, and she knew within herself that with that acceptance a gulf had opened between herself and her past life, even between her past self; a gulf which could never again be closed.

She could look back across it to the green valley between the mountains and see herself there with the Shepherd's workers, feeding her little flock, cringing before her relatives and going to

# Love's Mark

Loneliness can lead to a place of abandonment to Jesus. Complete abandonment to Him, regardless of the cost, releases us to a new stage of growth in our pilgrimage of being made into His likeness as an image bearer.

> *"And I will give them one heart—a new heart—and I will put a new spirit within them; and I will take the stony [unnaturally hardened] heart out of their flesh, and will give them a heart of flesh [sensitive and responsive to the touch of their God]"*
> (Ezek. 11:19 AMP).

We are becoming like Him. Even though we may not feel spiritual or look spiritual, He has stamped us with His mark:

> *"In Him you also who have heard the Word of Truth, the glad tidings (Gospel) of your salvation, and have believed in and have adhered to and have relied on Him, were stamped with the seal of the long-promised Holy Spirit"*
> (Eph. 1:13 AMP).

Lord Jesus, You alone completely understand my weakness and my loneliness. Draw me close to Your heart. I release and abandon myself to You!

the pool morning and evening to keep tryst with the Shepherd. But it was looking at somebody else together, and she said to herself, "I was that woman, but am not that woman now."

She did not understand how it happened, but what the Shepherd had said had come to pass in herself, for those who go down into the furnace of Egypt and find there the flower of Acceptance come up changed and with the stamp of royalty upon them. It is true that Much-Afraid did not feel at all royal, and certainly did not as yet look it. Nevertheless, she had been stamped with the mark, and would never be the same again.

Therefore, though she went with Sorrow and Suffering day after day along the shores of the great sea of Loneliness, she did not go cringingly or complainingly. Indeed, gradually an impossible thing seemed to be happening. A new kind of joy was springing up in her heart, and she began to find herself noticing beauties in the landscape of which until then she had been quite unconscious.

Her heart often thrilled with an inner ecstasy when she caught sight of the sun shining on the wings of the wheeling seagulls, making them gleam as dazzlingly white as the snow on the peaks of the far-off High Places. Even their wild, mournful cries and the moanings of the water stirred in her a sorrow which was strangely beautiful. She had the feeling that somehow, in the very far-off places, perhaps even in far-off ages, there would be a meaning found to all sorrow and an answer too fair and wonderful to be as yet understood.

Often, too, she found herself laughing aloud as she watched the antics of the funny little scuttling crabs. When the sun shone brightly, as it did at times, even the grey, dreary sea was transformed into a thing of surpassing beauty, with the light gleaming on the curving green breakers and the foaming spray and the horizon blue as a midnight sky. When the sun thus shone on the wild wastes of waters it seemed as though all their sorrows had been swallowed up in joy, and then she would whisper to herself, "When He hath tried me, I shall

# Patient Expectation

Impatience with God's ways results in our cringing away from life and complaining about what is happening in it. In order to grow the flower of Acceptance-with-Joy in our hearts, we must choose to embrace life with thanksgiving. With this thankful heart we can see His beauty in all of creation. For example, think about the pulsating, rolling waves on the seashore. Ponder His mighty handiwork:

> "...I made the sand a boundary for the sea, an
> everlasting barrier it cannot cross. The waves
> may roll, but they cannot prevail; they may roar,
> but they cannot cross it"
> (Jer. 5:22 NIV).

Tiny grains of sand, so light they can be carried by the wind, hold the world's oceans in their boundaries because God sets the waters upon a barrier.

I lift my heart to You, my Lord, crying out "My God and my Lord, I adore You! I lay my life before You." Let me not cringe away, but accept with joy whatever You have for me.

come forth as gold. Weeping may endure for a night, but joy cometh in the morning."

One day they came to a place on the shore where there were high cliffs and great rocks scattered all about. In this place they were to rest for a time, and while there Much-Afraid wandered off by herself. After climbing the cliff she found herself looking down into a lonely little cove completely enclosed on three sides by the cliffs and with nothing in it but driftwood and stranded seaweed. The chief impression it made upon her was its emptiness. It seemed to lie there like an empty heart, watching and longing for the far-off tide which had receded to such a distance that it could never again return.

When, however, drawn by an urge to revisit the lonely cove, Much-Afraid went back to the same spot some hours later, all was changed. The waves were now rushing forward with the strength of a high tide urging them onward. Looking over the edge of the cliff, she saw that the cove which had been so empty was now filled to the brim. Great waves, roaring and laughing together, were pouring themselves through the narrow inlet and were leaping against the sides, irresistibly taking possession of every empty niche and crevice.

On seeing this transformation, she knelt down on the edge of the cliff and built her third altar. "O my Lord," she cried, "I thank Thee for leading me here. Behold me, here I am, empty as was this little cove, but waiting Thy time to be filled to the brim with the flood-tide of Love." Then she picked up a little piece of quartz and crystal which was lying on the rocky cliff and dropped it beside the other memorial stones in the little bag which she carried with her.

It was only a short time after the building of that new altar that her enemies were all upon her again. Far away in the Valley of Humiliation, her relatives had been awaiting the return of Pride with his victim, but as time passed and he did not return and Much-Afraid did not reappear it became obvious

# Secret Treasure

Into the secret place of the Most High do I run today, my Lord. There my heart melts when I think about Your Father's heart that You have toward me. You sent Your Son to the cross so I might have an intimate relationship with You. My identity is settled when I remember that I am Your child and that I am *complete in Christ* because of His work, not my performance. I bow down to You, my Lord, to worship You and say that I appreciate Your all-consuming love.

*"This is love: not that we loved God, but that*
*He loved us and sent His Son as an*
*atoning sacrifice for our sins"*
(1 John 4:10 NIV).

As I wait before You, I receive Your love. I receive the love of You, my Father. Your love is another treasure that I place into my remembrance. Just as a piece of quartz or crystal shimmers in the reflection of the sun, so does the many facets of Your love shine in my heart. Let me never forget that Your love has placed me "in You."

that he must have been unsuccessful in his undertaking and was too proud to admit it. They decided that reinforcements must be sent as soon as possible, before Much-Afraid could reach the really High Places and be altogether beyond their reach.

Spies were sent out, who met Pride and brought back word that Much-Afraid was nowhere on the mountains but was far away on the shores of the Sea of Loneliness. She was going in quite a different direction from the mountains altogether. This was unexpectedly delightful and encouraging news, and quickly suggested to them the best reinforcements to be sent to the help of Pride. There was complete unanimity in deciding that Resentment, Bitterness, and Self-Pity should hurry off at once to assist in bringing back Much-Afraid to her eagerly-awaiting relatives.

Off they went to the shores of Loneliness, and Much-Afraid now had to endure a time of really dreadful assaults. It is true that her enemies soon discovered that this was not the same Much-Afraid with whom they had to deal. They could never get within close reach, because she kept so near to Sorrow and Suffering and accepted their assistance so much more willingly than before. However, they kept appearing before her, shouting out their horrid suggestions and mocking her until it really seemed that wherever she went one or another popped up (there were so many hiding-places for them among the rocks) and hurled their darts at her.

"I told you so," Pride would shout viciously. "Where are you now, you little fool? Up on the High Places? Not much! Do you know that everyone in the Valley of Humiliation knows about this and is laughing at you? Seeking your heart's desire, eh, and left abandoned by Him ( just as I warned you) on the shores of Loneliness. Why didn't you listen to me, you little fool?"

Then Resentment would raise his head over another rock. He was extremely ugly to look at, but his was a horribly fascinating ugliness. Sometimes Much-Afraid could hardly turn

# Grace Embraced

Have you ever thought: "I wouldn't mind if my tests were like my best friend's (or my sister's, or my neighbor's). Why are mine so hard?" We need to learn to separate the precious from the vile in life, especially while undergoing tests, trials, and afflictions. We should remember that

> *"the Lord God is a sun and shield; the Lord bestows [present] grace and favor and [future] glory—honor, splendor and heavenly bliss! No good thing will He withhold from those who walk uprightly"*
> (Ps. 84:11 AMP).

Let's embrace what our Lord brings into our lives, keeping in mind the end product, which is the purpose of the process.

> *"He will sit as a refiner and a purifier of silver; He will purify the sons of Levi, and purge them as gold and silver..."*
> (Mal. 3:3 NKJ).

I choose to embrace, Lord, with a grateful spirit, knowing that what You bring will be for my good. Your grace is completely sufficient for whatever I find myself in. Thank You for the opportunity to learn and grow.

her eyes away when he stared at her boldly and shouted, "You know, Much-Afraid, you act like a blind idiot. Who is this Shepherd you follow? What sort of a person is He to demand everything you have and take everything you offer and give nothing in return but suffering and sorrow and ridicule and shame? Why do you let Him treat you like this? Stand up for yourself and demand that He fulfill His promise and take you at once to the High Places. If not, tell Him that you feel absolved from all necessity to follow Him any longer."

Bitterness would then break in with his sneering voice, "The more you yield to Him, the more He will demand from you. He is cruel to you, and takes advantage of your devotion. All He has demanded from you so far is nothing to what He will demand if you persist in following Him. He lets His followers, yes, even women and children, go to concentration camps and torture chambers and hideous deaths of all kinds. Could you bear that, you little whiner? Then you'd better pull out and leave Him before He demands the uttermost sacrifice of all. Sooner or later, He'll put you on a cross of some sort and abandon you to it."

Self-Pity would chime in next, and in some dreadful way he was almost worse than any of the others. He talked so softly and in such a pitying tone that Much-Afraid would feel weak all over.

"Poor little Much-Afraid," he would whisper. "It is too bad, you know. You really are so devoted, and you have refused Him nothing, absolutely nothing; yet this is the cruel way in which He treats you. Can you really believe when He acts toward you like this that He loves you and has your real good at heart? How can that be possible?

"You have every right to feel sorry for yourself. Even if you are perfectly willing to suffer for His sake, at least other people ought to know about it and pity you instead of misunderstanding and ridiculing as they do. It really seems as though the One you follow takes delight in making you suffer and leaving you

# Comforting Arms

To what are many of our fears attached? Only the Spirit of God can reveal their exact connection, but often they are tied to a fear that our rights will not be recognized or our needs fulfilled. However, we dare not fix our eyes, our attention, on those fears.

*"O our God, will You not exercise judgment upon them? For we have no might to stand against this great company that is coming against us. We do not know what to do, but our eyes are upon You"*
(2 Chron. 20:12 AMP).

When fears hurl themselves at you, that is the time to inwardly run under Jesus' wing the same way chicks are gathered under the mother hen's wings.

*"And He has said to me, 'My grace is sufficient for you, for power is perfected in weakness.' Most gladly, therefore, I will rather boast about my weaknesses, that the power of Christ may dwell in me"*
(2 Cor. 12:9 NAS).

Lord, You are the Perfecter of my faith. How safe I feel wrapped in Your arms, because I know You are also the Finisher of my life, bringing me to maturity. Thank You for the careful attention You give to all the details of my life.

to be misunderstood, for every time you yield to Him He thinks up some new way of wounding and bruising you."

That last remark of Self-Pity's was a mistake, because the word "bruising" suddenly reminded Much-Afraid of what the Shepherd had said when they stood together on the threshing-floor in the pyramid. "Bread corn is bruised," He had said, "but no one threshes it forever, only till it is ready to be made bread for others. This also cometh forth from the Lord of Hosts who is wonderful in counsel and excellent in working" (Isa. 28:28,29).

When she thought of this, to Self-Pity's dismayed astonishment, Much-Afraid actually picked up a piece of rock and hurled it at him, and as he said afterwards to the other three in an aggrieved tone of voice, "If I hadn't ducked and bolted like a hare it could have laid me out altogether, the little vixen!"

But it is exhausting to be assaulted day after day with suggestions like these, and while Sorrow and Suffering were holding her hands, naturally Much-Afraid could not cover her ears, so her enemies were really able to give her a dreadful time. At last, things came to a crisis.

One day when her companions actually seemed to be sleeping for a little while, Much-Afraid unwarily wandered off alone. Not this time to her favorite spot looking down into the little cove, but in a new direction, and she came to a place where the cliffs jutted out into the sea, forming a very narrow peninsula, which ended in a sheer precipice.

When she reached the end of this promontory she stood looking out over the endless expanse of sea, and suddenly found to her horror all four of her enemies approaching and closing in on her. That already she was becoming a different person was then quite apparent, for instead of nearly fainting with fright at their approach, although she did look very pale and frightened, she actually seized a stone in each hand and, putting her back against a great rock, prepared to resist them to the

# Safe Refuge

When you feel bombarded by the assaults of the enemy, remember this: The enemy eventually "hangs" himself with his lies and evil deeds, which he cannot stop performing. He will overplay his hand. Run into the secret place of the Most High, or your "safe" place with Jesus, and say:

> *"My eyes are ever toward the Lord, for He*
> *will pluck my feet out of the net"*
> (Ps. 25:15 AMP).

If your relatives or friends come visiting you, pouring forth Pride, Resentment, Bitterness, or Self-Pity, don't be dragged down or succumb to wallowing in those feelings with them. Instead, dwell upon Jesus, who He is and how privileged you are to walk with Him. Then your strength and dignity will return to you in His time.

Lord, I keep my eyes on You. Lord, I say of You,

> *"He is my refuge and my fortress, my God, on Him*
> *I lean and rely, and in Him I (confidently) trust!"*
> (Ps. 91:2 AMP)

limit of her strength. Fortunately the place was too narrow for all four to approach together, but Pride put himself in front of the others and stepped toward her holding a strong cudgel.

"You can put down those stones, Much-Afraid," said he savagely. "There are four of us here, and we mean to do as we please with you now that you are in our power. You shall not only listen to us but shall go with us."

Much-Afraid lifted her face toward the seemingly empty sky, and with all her strength called out, "Come to my deliverance and make no tarrying, O my Lord."

To the horror of the four ruffians, there was the Shepherd Himself, leaping toward them along the narrow promontory more terrible than a great mountain stag with thrusting horns. Resentment, Bitterness, and Self-Pity managed to hurl themselves flat on the ground and edge away as He bounded toward the place where Pride was just seizing hold of Much-Afraid. Catching him by the shoulders, the Shepherd spun him around, lifted him in the air, where he uttered a loud, despairing shriek, and then dropped him over the edge of the cliff into the sea.

"O Shepherd," gasped Much-Afraid, shaking with relief and hope, "thank You. Do You think Pride is really dead at last?"

"No," said the Shepherd, "it is most unlikely." He glanced over the cliff as He spoke, and caught sight of Pride swimming like a fish toward the shore, and added, "There he goes, but he has had a fall today which he will not forget, and I fancy he will limp for some time to come. As for the other three, they have made off into some hiding place, and are not likely to trouble you again in the same way now that they realize that I am within call."

"Shepherd," asked Much-Afraid earnestly, "tell me why I nearly got into Pride's clutches again, and why Resentment, Bitterness, and Self-Pity have been able to pester me for so long in this dreadful way. I did not call You before, because they never dared to come close to me or to make a real attack, but

# Constant Care

The process of breaking out of a destructive life pattern is much like the process of discovering a hole you did not know was in front of you. You fall in. After a while you realize that you are in a hole and climb out. The next time you catch yourself on the way down. Finally, you recognize the hole as you near it and can go around it or jump over it. All these steps are "victory" steps, even though jumping over it is more pleasant than hitting the bottom and climbing out. That's why it is a process. So if you feel overwhelmed, just call out to Jesus. He is right there to help you. It has been said that one drop of Jesus' blood can paralyze all the demons in hell. What a joy to be able to call upon the Lord and know that He scatters our enemies!

*"But [even] the very hairs of your head are all numbered. Do not be struck with fear or seized with alarm; you are of greater worth than many [flocks] of sparrows"*
(Lk. 12:7 AMP).

My Lord, my Lover, my spirit turns to You. What a mighty God You are! Thank You for all the grace I have tasted. You are my portion. I adore You.

they have been lurking around all the time and making their horrible suggestions, and I couldn't get away from them. Why was it?"

"I think," said the Shepherd gently, "that lately the way seemed a little easier and the sun shone, and you came to a place where you could rest. You forgot for a while that you were My little handmaiden Acceptance-with-Joy and were beginning to tell yourself it really was time that I led you back to the mountains and up to the High Places. When you wear the weed of impatience in your heart instead of the flower Acceptance-with-Joy, you will always find your enemies get an advantage over you."

Much-Afraid blushed. She knew how right He was in His diagnosis. It had been easier to accept the hard path and to be patient when the sea was grey and dull than now when the sun shone and everything else around looked bright and happy and satisfied. She put her hand in the Shepherd's and said sorrowfully, "You are quite right. I have been thinking that You are allowing me to follow this path too long and that You were forgetting Your promise." Then she added, looking steadfastly into His face, "But I do tell You now with all my heart that You are my Shepherd whose voice I love to hear and obey, and that it is my joy to follow You. You choose, my Lord, and I will obey."

The Shepherd stooped down and picked up a stone which was lying beside her feet and said smilingly, "Put this in your bag with the other stones as a memorial of this day when for the first time you saw Pride toppled over before you, and of your promise that you will wait patiently until I give you your heart's desire."

# Holy Occupation

Have you ever wondered if you would ever see certain "fleshly" or "soulish" tendencies in you again? Romans 6:11-12 speaks to this issue:

*"In the same way, count yourselves dead to sin but alive to God in Christ Jesus. Therefore do not let sin reign in your mortal body so that you obey its evil desires"*
(NIV).

God designed us to be completely absorbed and occupied with Him in much the same way a fish is submerged, sustained, and surrounded by water. If the fish is laid on the bank, it begins to die because it's removed from the water which gives it life. When we live in the flesh, we are like the fish stranded on the sand. Can you recall a time when you "slipped" into the flesh path? Confess it and release it all into His hands.

Lord Jesus, when I crawl out of the water of Your presence onto the bank of life, thinking that You are not doing things right or that You need my help, do whatever is necessary to place me back into the water of life with You. You are my Shepherd, and it is my joy to follow You.

# CHAPTER 8

# On the Old Sea Wall

A few days had passed after the victory over Pride, and Much-Afraid and her companions were continuing their journey along the shore of the great sea. One morning the path unexpectedly turned inland again and they found themselves facing back over the desert in the direction of the mountains, although, of course, they were too far away to be visible. With a thrill of indescribable joy Much-Afraid saw that at last the path did actually run straight toward the east and that it would lead them back to the High Places.

She dropped the hands of her two guides in order to clap her own, and gave a little skip of joy. No matter how great the distance between them and the mountains, now at last they were to go in the right direction. All three started back across the desert, but Much-Afraid could not wait for her guides, and actually ran on ahead as though she had never been lame at all.

Suddenly the path took another turn at right angles and went straight before her as far as she could see, not toward the mountains at all, but southward again to where far ahead the desert seemed to end in some sort of hill country. Much-Afraid stood quite still, dumb with dismay and shock. Then she began to tremble all over. It could not be possible, no, it couldn't, that yet again the Shepherd was saying "No," and turning her right away from the High Places.

# Patient Pace

How easy it is to take our eyes off of Jesus and run ahead when we think we see His plan for us and become presumptuous. In our presumption we set ourselves up for a fall. Peter ran to Jesus when he saw Him walking on the water, but lost his balance when his eyes slipped off Jesus. Yet, when Peter began to sink,

*"…he cried, saying, Lord, save me. And immediately Jesus stretched forth His hand, and caught him…"*
(Mt. 14:30-31 KJV).

Peter lifted himself up and fell, just like the physical law of gravity says—if we jump from a high building, we will fall. However, even beyond physical laws are spiritual laws. One spiritual law says that the way up is to go down!

*"Humble yourselves, therefore, under the mighty hand of God, that He may exalt you at the proper time"*
(1 Pet. 5:6 NAS).

Lord Jesus, I want to walk in Your timing, not run ahead in my presumption or lag behind in irresponsibility. I choose today to humble myself, that I may not fall.

"Hope deferred maketh the heart sick," said the wise man of long ago, and how truly he spoke! Now she had been skipping and running so excitedly along the path toward the mountains that she had left Sorrow and Suffering quite behind, and while they were catching up with her she was standing quite alone at the place where the path turned away from the mountains.

Up from behind a sand dune close beside her rose the form of her enemy Bitterness. He did not come any nearer, having learned a little more prudence, and was not going to make her call for the Shepherd if he could avoid it, but simply stood and looked at her and laughed and laughed again, the bitterest sound that Much-Afraid had heard in all her life.

Then he said, as venomously as a viper, "Why don't you laugh too, you little fool? You knew this would happen." There he stood, uttering those awful bursts of laughter until it seemed that the whole desert was filled with the echoes of his mockery. Sorrow and her sister came up to Much-Afraid and stood by her side quite silently, and for a little while everything was swallowed up in pain and "an horror of great darkness." A sudden swirling wind shrieked over the desert and raised a storm of dust and sand which blinded them.

In the silence which succeeded the storm Much-Afraid heard her voice, low and trembling, but quite distinct, saying, "My Lord, what dost Thou want to say to me? Speak—for Thy servant heareth."

Next moment the Shepherd was standing beside her. "Be of good cheer," He said, "it is I, be not afraid. Build Me another altar and lay down your whole will as a burnt offering."

Obediently Much-Afraid raised a little heap of sand and loose stones, which was all that she could find in the desert, and again laid down her will and said with tears (for Sorrow had stepped forward and knelt beside her), "I delight to do Thy will, O my God."

From somewhere, though they could not see the source, there came a spurt of flame which consumed the offering and

# *Immeasurable Worth*

As we struggle to be free from old patterns of bondage, there are often short times of disorientation before our minds, wills, and emotions learn to yield to the Spirit rather than to impulses or to old habits. What a comfort to know that His acceptance of us does not depend on our performance! Always remember that our great worth and value comes from the price Jesus paid for our lives.

> *"But [you were purchased] with the precious blood of Christ, the Messiah, like that of a [sacrificial] lamb without blemish or spot"*
> (1 Pet. 1:19 AMP).

The worth of an object is measured by the price paid. What does that statement tell us about our worth?

Lord Jesus, when I slip back into a performance mode, please remind me of the basis for my worth and value. In honor of You, I lay my whole will down before You as completely as I can. I release the contents of my heart to You as a living sacrifice. Burn away all of self and let nothing but Your purity remain.

left a little heap of ashes on the altar. Then came the Shepherd's voice. "This further delay is not unto death, but for the glory of God; that the Son of God may be glorified."

Another gust of wind sprang up and whirled the ashes away in every direction, and the only thing remaining on the altar was a rough, ordinary-looking stone which Much-Afraid picked up and put into the bag with the others. Then she rose to her feet, turned her face away from the mountains, and they all started southward. The Shepherd went with them for a little way so that Resentment and Self-Pity, who were hiding close at hand awaiting an opportunity to attack, lay flat behind the sand dunes and were not seen at that time at all.

Presently they reached a place where the sea, which they had left behind when they turned inland, came sweeping into the desert, forming a great estuary. A strong tide was surging into it, filling it completely with swiftly-flowing waters. However, a stone causeway with many arches had been built across the estuary, and an earthen ramp led up to it. The Shepherd led Much-Afraid to the foot of the ramp and told her to follow this path across the sea. Once more He repeated with great emphasis the words which He had spoken beside the altar, then departed.

Much-Afraid, followed by her two companions, scrambled up the ramp and found themselves on top of the old sea wall. From the height on which they now stood they could look back over the desert. On one side was the sea, and on the other, so blurred with distance that they could not be sure if they really saw it, was a haze which might be part of the mountains, or was it only wishful thinking?

Then, looking ahead they saw that the causeway would indeed bring them across the estuary into a different kind of country altogether, a well-wooded land of hills and valleys with cottages and farmsteads among orchards and fields. The sun was shining brilliantly, and up there on the wall they could feel the full force of the great wind which was urging

# Reverent Desire

Reverently come into the Lord's presence. Tenderly crawl up in His lap, hug Him, and pour your heart out to Him. Quietly wait upon Him.

*"You have said, Seek you My face—inquire for and require My presence [as your vital need]. My heart says to You, Your face [Your presence], Lord, will I seek, inquire for and require....Teach me Your way, O Lord, and lead me in a plain and even path because of my enemies—those who lie in wait for me"*
(Ps. 27:8,11 AMP).

Lord Jesus, let my heart be as an open hand before You. Show me anything today to which I am clinging that is not of You. Thank You that Your arm always reaches out to meet me at my point of need to establish me in Your ways, like an estuary that extends inland to meet the mouth of a river.

*"It was not by their sword that they won the land, nor did their arm bring them victory; it was Your right hand, Your arm, and the light of Your face, for You loved them"*
(Ps. 44:3 NIV).

and lashing the rushing waves to flow swifter and swifter. It reminded Much-Afraid of a pack of hounds, urged on by the huntsmen, following one another, leaping and surging and roaring beneath the causeway and then flowing forward far inland, brimming the shores of the estuary.

Somehow the roar of the wind and the surge of the waters seemed to get into her blood and course through her being like a glorious wine of life. The wind whipped her cheeks and tore at her hair and clothes and nearly toppled her over, but she stood there, shouting at the top of her voice, though the wind seized the sound of it and carried it off, drowned in a deafening roar of its own. What Much-Afraid was shouting up there on the old sea wall was this:

"And now shall mine head be lifted up above mine enemies round about; therefore I will sing praises unto the Lord; yea I will offer the sacrifice of joy and will praise the Name of the Lord" (Psa. 27:6).

As she sang she thought to herself, "It must be really dreadful to be the Shepherd's enemies. Always, always to find themselves frustrated. Always, always to have their prey snatched away. How simply maddening it must be to see even the silliest little weaklings set up out of reach on the High Places and made to triumph over all their enemies. It must be unbearable."

While still on the causeway she picked up another stone as the Shepherd had taught her, this time as a memorial of His victory in making her triumph over her enemies, and dropped it into the little bag of treasured memories. So they made their way across the causeway and down the ramp on the other side and immediately found themselves in a wood.

The change in scene after their long journey through the desert was wonderful. A long-deferred spring was just loosening everything from the grip of winter, and all the trees were bursting into fairest green and the buds were swelling. In between the trees were glades of bluebells and wild anemones,

# Precious Sacrifice

When we speak the truth and praise our Lord, our faith is increased and our enemies are put on the run.

*"And now shall mine head be lifted up above mine enemies round about me: therefore will I offer in His tabernacle sacrifices of joy; I will sing, yea, I will sing praises unto the Lord"*
(Ps. 27:6 KJV).

Continue to speak His Word aloud and meditate upon it until the sacrifice of praise fills your soul with strength and dignity. Your enemies will then flee from you in terror.

*"The heavens declare the glory of God, and the firmament shows and proclaims His handiwork"*
(Ps. 19:1 AMP).

*"The Lord lives! Blessed be my rock, and let the God of my salvation be exalted"*
(Ps. 18:46 AMP).

Lord Jesus, let Your Spirit and Your Word invigorate my being in much the same way as the sound of the roar of the wind and the surge of the waters get into a person's blood. Course through my being like a glorious wine of life!

and violets and primroses grew in clumps along the mossy banks. Birds sang and called to one another and rustled about, busily absorbed in nest-building.

Much-Afraid told herself that never before had she realized what the awakening from the death of winter was like. Perhaps it had needed the desert wastes to open her eyes to all this beauty, but she walked through the wood, almost forgetting for a little that Sorrow and her sister also walked with her.

Everywhere she looked it seemed that the unfurling green on the trees and the nesting birds and the leaping squirrels and blossoming flowers were all saying the same thing, greeting one another in their own special language with a sort of ecstasy and calling cheerfully, "You see, the winter has gone at last. The delay was not unto death but for the glory of God. Never was there a fairer spring than this."

At the same time Much-Afraid herself was conscious of a wonderful stirring in her own heart, as though something were springing up and breaking into new life there too. The feeling was so sweet, yet so mixed with pain that she hardly knew which predominated. She thought of the seed of Love which the Shepherd had planted in her heart, and half-afraid and half-eager, she looked to see if it had really taken root and was springing up. She saw a mass of leaves, and at the end of the stem a little swelling which might almost prove to be a bud.

As Much-Afraid looked at it another stab went through her heart, for she remembered the words of the Shepherd that when the plant of Love was ready to bloom she would be loved in return and would receive a new name up there on the High Places. But here she was, still far away from them, indeed farther than ever before, and with apparently no possibility of going there for a long time to come. How could the Shepherd's promise prove true? When she thought of that her tears fell again.

You may think that Much-Afraid was altogether too much given to shedding tears, but remember that she had Sorrow

# Holy Liberty

The most wonderful part of pain is the contrast of release and liberty we feel when it stops. Afterwards, we are left with a greater appreciation and sensitivity of soul to Him because we have embraced His will.

*"For [our earthly fathers] disciplined us for only a short period of time and chastised us as seemed proper and good to them, but He disciplines us for our certain good, that we may become sharers in His own holiness"*
(Heb. 12:10 AMP).

However, when we allow sin to tie us in a knot that takes the form of selfishness or self-protection, it takes a long time for the truth that our Lord is indeed faithful and dependable to penetrate our souls.

*"The Lord is my rock and my fortress and my deliverer, my God, my rock, in whom I take refuge; my shield and the horn of my salvation, my stronghold"*
(Ps. 18:2 NAS).

Lord, I look to You as my Protector. What a privilege it is to serve You, who not only has the power, but who also delights to use it to bring forth Your holiness from our imperfection.

for a companion and teacher. There is this to be added, that her tears were all in secret, for no one but her enemies knew about this strange journey on which she had set out. The heart knoweth its own sorrow and there are times when, like David, it is comforting to think that our tears are put in a bottle and not one of them forgotten by the One who leads us in paths of sorrow.

But she did not weep for long, for almost at once she caught sight of something else, a gleam of gold. Looking closer, what should she see but an exact replica of the little golden flower which she had found growing near the pyramids in the desert. Somehow it had been transplanted and was actually growing in her own heart. Much-Afraid gave a cry of delight, and the tiny golden thing nodded and said in its little golden voice, "Behold me, here I am, growing in your heart, 'Acceptance-with-Joy.' "

Much-Afraid smiled and answered, "Why, yes, of course, I was forgetting," and she knelt down there in the wood, put a pile of stones together and laid sticks on them. As you have noticed, altars are built of whatever materials lie close at hand at the time. Then she hesitated. What should she lay on the altar this time? She looked at the tiny swelling on the plant of Love which might be a bud and again might not, then she leaned forward, placed her heart on the altar and said, "Behold me, here I am; Thy little handmaiden Acceptance-with-Joy and all that is in my heart is Thine."

This time, though there came a flame of fire and burned up the sticks, the bud was still on the stem of the plant. Perhaps, thought Much-Afraid, because it was too small to offer. But nevertheless something lovely had happened. It was as though a spark from the flame had entered her heart and was still glowing there, warm and radiant. On the altar among the ashes was yet another stone for her to pick up and put with the rest, so now there were six stones of remembrance lying in

# Cleansing Passion

Lord Jesus, teach me to appreciate and not despise my struggles. Give me Your perspective. Let me remember the awesome privilege You have given me to be completely molded into Your image—that You chose to conform *me* to Your image. No one has ever cared for me like You do, Jesus. Lord, I freely lay myself upon Your altar of love. I release myself to Your warm flames of love. Burn out of me everything that is not of You so only what is fueled by Your Spirit remains. I want to be tried as silver is tried, refined, and purified.

> "...He will sift out everything without solid foundations, so that only unshakable things will be left. Since we have a kingdom nothing can destroy, let us please God by serving Him with thankful hearts, and with holy fear and awe. For our God is a consuming fire" (Heb. 12:27-29 TLB).

All that is in my heart I give to You, Lord Jesus.

the bag she carried. Going on their way, in a very short time they came to the edge of the wood and she uttered a cry of joy, for who should be standing there, waiting to meet them, but the Shepherd Himself. She ran toward Him as though she had wings on her feet.

"Oh, welcome, welcome, a thousand times welcome!" cried Much-Afraid, tingling with joy from head to foot. "I am afraid there is nothing much in the garden of my heart as yet, Shepherd, but all that there is, is Yours to do with as You please."

"I have come to bring you a message," said the Shepherd. "You are to be ready, Much-Afraid, for something new. This is the message, 'Now shalt thou see what I will do' " (Ex. 6:1).

The color leaped into her cheeks, and a shock of joy went through her, for she remembered the plant in her heart and the promise that when it was ready to bloom she would be up on the High Places and ready to enter the Kingdom of Love.

"O Shepherd," she exclaimed, almost breathless with the thought. "Do You mean that I am really to go to the High Places at last? Really—at last?"

She thought He nodded, but He did not answer at once, but stood looking at her with an expression she did not quite understand.

"Do you mean it?" she repeated, catching His hand and looking up at Him with almost incredulous joy. "Do you mean You soon will be taking me to the High Places?"

This time He answered, "Yes," and added with a strange smile, "now shalt thou see what I will do."

# Sweet Serenity

What causes us to tingle with joy as Much-Afraid did when she ran into the Shepherd's arms? Knowing that God chose us because He knew He could succeed in bringing about His likeness through us should give us a joyful, thankful spirit.

Lord, thank You that You took the initiative to reach out to me and to choose me.

*"You did not choose Me, but I chose you, and appointed you, that you should go and bear fruit..."*
(Jn. 15:16 NAS).

Lord Jesus, with quiet confidence I rest securely in Your choosing me to be made like You. You know me better than I know myself, and You still chose me! I will honor You by resting in Your choice and love for me today. Before You I will simply remain peaceful and calm. In the warm, divine beams of Your love, I rest.

Quietly meditate on His Word.

*"As for God, His way is perfect! The Word of the Lord is tested and tried; He is a shield to all those who take refuge and put their trust in Him"*
(Ps. 18:30 AMP).

# CHAPTER 9

# Great Precipice Injury

After that, for a little while Much-Afraid had a song in her heart as she walked among the fields and orchards and the low hills of the country to which they had come. It hardly seemed to matter now that Sorrow and Suffering were still with her because of the hope leaping up in her heart that soon they would cease to be her companions altogether, for when she came to the mountains again and they had helped her up to the High Places she would need them no longer. Neither did it matter that the path they followed still led southward, twisting among the hills and leading through quiet valleys, because she had the Shepherd's own promise that soon it would lead her back to the eastern mountains and to the place of her heart's desire.

After a time the path began sloping upward toward the summits of the hills.

One day they suddenly reached the top of the highest of the hills and just as the sun rose found themselves on a great plateau. They looked eastward toward the golden sunrise, and Much-Afraid burst into a cry of joy and thankfulness. There, at no great distance, on the farther side of the plateau, were the mountains, quite distinct and rising like a great wall, crowned with ramparts and towers and pinnacles, all of which were glowing rose-red and gold in the sunrise. Never, thought she, had she seen anything so beautiful.

As the sun rose higher and the glow faded from the sky, she saw that the highest peaks were covered with snow, so white

# Hope Eternal

Turn to your Lord today as you would if you felt a song in your heart flowing from fresh hope. As you sit before Him, ponder this thought: Your great and holy God loved you before He called heaven and earth into existence. Just as God Himself is eternal, without beginning or end, so is His love for you. God has always loved you and He always will love you.

*"... I have loved you with an everlasting love;*
*therefore I have drawn you with lovingkindness"*
(Jer. 31:3 NAS).

With quiet confidence rejoice over the privilege of walking with and serving a God who loves you so much that He will always be available to you, no matter what situation you are in.

*"The name of the Lord is a strong tower;*
*the righteous run to it and are safe"*
(Prov. 18:10 NIV).

Wait before Him. Allow the magnitude of such love begin to saturate you. Sit before Him, welcoming and receiving His love.

Thank You, Lord, for the refuge You provide. How comforting to know You always give me a place where I am safe and held strongly in Your care—regardless of the situation.

and glittering that her eyes were dazzled with their glory. She was looking at the High Places themselves. Best of all, the path they were following here turned eastward and led directly toward the mountains.

Much-Afraid fell on her knees on the hilltop, bowed her head and worshipped. It seemed to her at that moment that all the pain and the postponement, all the sorrows and trials of the long journey she had made, were as nothing compared to the glory which shone before her. It seemed to her, too, that even her companions were smiling with her. When she had worshiped and rejoiced she rose to her feet and all three started to cross the plateau. It was amazing how quickly they went, for the path was flat and comparatively smooth, and before they could have believed it possible they found themselves approaching the mountains and were among the slopes and boulders at their very feet.

As they approached, Much-Afraid could not help being struck by the steepness of these slopes, and the nearer they drew, the more like impassable walls the mountains appeared to become. But she told herself that when she was right up to them they would find a valley or gorge, or a pass up which they could proceed, and that she certainly would not mind how steep the way was if only it led upward. In the late afternoon they did come to the top of the lower slopes and to the very foot of the mountains. The path they were following led them right up to the foot of an impassable precipice and there stopped dead.

Much-Afraid stood still and stared. The more she looked, the more stunned she felt. Then she began to tremble and shake all over, for the whole mountain range before her, as far as she could see to left and right, rose up in unbroken walls of rock so high that it made her giddy when she put her head back and tried to look up to the top. The cliffs completely blocked the way before her, yet the path ran right up to them, then stopped. There was no sign of a track in any other direction, and there was no way at all by which the overhanging, terrifying wall of cliff could be ascended. They would have to turn back.

# Refreshing Transformation

When we can lose ourselves in who our God is and what a great God we are privileged to know and have live within us, our steps become lighter and they have a fresh new spring to them.

> *"But we all, with unveiled face beholding as in a*
> *mirror the glory of the Lord, are being transformed*
> *into the same image from glory to glory, just*
> *as from the Lord, the Spirit"*
> (2 Cor. 3:18 NAS).

As we continue walking and come across blocked or impassable roads, we need to remember that He always leads in right paths for "His name's sake."

> *"…He guides me in the paths of*
> *righteousness for His name's sake"*
> (Ps. 23:3 NAS).

He would lose His good name if He didn't. Our problem is we start gazing at our circumstances instead of upon the Lord, and we lose our balance.

Lord Jesus, when I begin to grow dizzy and faint because of what I see before me, draw my perspective back to You. Thank You, dear Shepherd, that You lead me in right paths.

Just as this overwhelming realization came to her, Suffering caught her hand and pointed to the rocky walls. A hart, followed by a hind, had appeared from among the jumbled rocks around them and were now actually beginning to ascend the precipice.

As the three stood watching, Much-Afraid turned dizzy and faint, for she saw that the hart, which was leading the way, was following what appeared to be a narrow and intensely steep track which went zigzagging across the face of the cliff. In some parts it was only a narrow ledge, in others there appeared to be rough steps, but in certain places she saw that the track apparently broke right off.

Then the hart would leap across the gap and go springing upward, always closely followed by the hind, who set her feet exactly where his had been, and leaped after him, as lightly, as sure-footed, and apparently unafraid as it was possible for any creature to be. So the two of them leaped and sprang with perfect grace and assurance up the face of the precipice and disappeared from sight over the top.

Much-Afraid covered her face with her hands and sank down on a rock with a horror and dread in her heart such as she had never felt before. Then she felt her two companions take her hands in theirs and heard them say, "Do not be afraid, Much-Afraid, this is not a dead end after all, and we shall not have to turn back. There is a way up the face of the precipice. The hart and the hind have shown it to us quite plainly. We shall be able to follow it too and make the ascent."

"Oh, no! No!" Much-Afraid almost shrieked. "That path is utterly impossible. The deer may be able to manage it, but no human being could. I could never get up there. I would fall headlong and be broken in pieces on those awful rocks." She burst into hysterical sobbing. "It's an impossibility, an absolute impossibility. I cannot get to the High Places that way, and so can never get there at all." Her two guides tried to say something more, but she put her hands over her ears and broke into another clamor of terrified sobs. There was the Shepherd's Much-Afraid, sitting at

# Strong Fortress

When facing a difficulty, we have a choice. Do we run into "Panic Palace" and hide or perhaps invite in friends for a "pity party," or do we run into the arms of our God who is a strong fortress?

*"God is my strong fortress; He guides the blameless in His way and sets him free"*
(2 Sam. 22:33 AMP).

All of us, at one time or another, have said, "I can't do it; I can't." The next time we face a difficulty, let's instead exhale out to Him our concerns and impossible problems–knowing that He gladly receives each and every one. His answer to us is, "I never said you could, but I always said I would!" Zechariah 4:6 says:

*"...Not by might nor by power, but by My Spirit...says the Lord of hosts"*
(AMP).

Lord Jesus, as I face obstacles that seem impossible to me, keep me from dissolving into a pool of fear or exploding in a fit of rage. Allow me to be invigorated and led by Your Spirit. I choose to trust You today in all the paths before me.

the foot of the precipice, wringing her hands and shaking with terror, sobbing over and over again, "I can't do it; I can't. I shall never get to the High Places." Nothing less like royalty could be imagined, but far worse was to follow.

As she crouched on the ground, completely exhausted, they heard a crunching sound and a rattling of loose stones, then a voice close beside her.

"Ha, ha! My dear little cousin, we meet again at last! How do you find yourself now, Much-Afraid, in this delightfully pleasant situation?"

She opened her eyes in fresh terror and found herself looking right into the hideous face of Craven Fear himself.

"I thought somehow," he went on with a look of the most horrible gloating. "Yes, I really thought that we could come together again at last. Did you really believe, you poor little fool, that you could escape from me altogether? No, no, Much-Afraid, you are one of the Fearings, and you can't evade the truth, and what is more, you trembling little idiot, you belong to me. I have come to take you back safely and make sure that you don't wander off again."

"I won't go with you," gasped Much-Afraid, too shocked by this awful apparition to have her wits about her. "I absolutely refuse to go with you."

"Well, you can take your choice," sneered Craven. "Take a look at the precipice before you, my dear cousin. Won't you feel lovely up there! Just look where I'm pointing, Much-Afraid. See there, halfway up, where that dizzy little ledge breaks right off and you have to jump across the chasm on to that bit of rock. Just picture yourself jumping that, Much-Afraid, and finding yourself hanging over space, clutching a bit of slippery rock which you can't hold on to another minute. Just imagine those ugly, knife-like rocks at the foot of the precipice, waiting to receive and mangle you to pieces as your strength gives out, and you plunge down on them.

# Healing Touch

Are there days when you feel there are bruises, welts, and raw wounds throbbing from the soles of your feet to the top of your head? Do you sometimes feel that there is nothing sound in you? That is what the enemy has in mind for all of us. He wants to make us victims. A victim is someone who has been taken advantage of and who becomes injured. Our Shepherd, however, has other plans for us.

> "You prepare a table before me in the presence
> of my enemies; You anoint my head with oil;
> my [brimming] cup runs over"
> (Ps. 23:5 AMP).

He came to bring victory and healing.

> "And Jesus went about all the cities and villages,
> teaching in their synagogues, and preaching
> the gospel of the kingdom, and healing every
> sickness and every disease among the people"
> (Mt. 9:35 KJV).

Lord Jesus, I praise You that I belong to You. I choose to have You soften my wounds with Your oil. Anoint me with Your oil for healing. I do not want to be a victim any longer.

Tell Him about the wounds you may have. Be specific. Rejoice for the healing He gives.

"Doesn't it give you a lovely feeling, Much-Afraid? Just take time to picture it. That's only one of many such broken places on the track, and the higher you go, you dear little fool, the farther you will have to fall. Well, take your choice. Either you must go up there, where you know that you can't, but will end in a mangled heap at the bottom, or you must come back and live with me and be my little slave ever afterward." And the rocks and cliffs seemed to echo again with his gloating laughter.

"Much-Afraid," said the two guides, stooping over her and shaking her by the shoulder gently but firmly. "Much-Afraid, you know where your help lies. Call for help."

She clung to them and sobbed again. "I am afraid to call," she gasped. "I am so afraid that if I call Him, He will tell me that I must go that way, that dreadful, dreadful way, and I can't. It's impossible. I can't face it. Oh, what shall I do? Whatever shall I do?"

Sorrow bent over her and said very gently but urgently, "You must call for Him, Much-Afraid. Call at once."

"If I call Him," shuddered Much-Afraid through chattering teeth, "He will tell me to build an altar, and I can't. This time I can't."

Craven Fear laughed triumphantly and took a step toward her, but her two companions put themselves between him and his victim. Then Suffering looked at Sorrow, who nodded back. In answer to the nod Suffering took a small but very sharp knife which hung at her girdle, and bending over the crouching figure, pricked her. Much-Afraid cried out in anguish, and then, in utter despair at finding herself helpless in the presence of all three, did that which she ought to have done the moment the path brought them to the foot of the precipice. Though now she felt too ashamed to do it, she did so because she was forced by her extremity. She cried out, "O Lord, I am oppressed; undertake for me. My fears have taken hold upon me, and I am ashamed to look up."

# Heavenly Thoughts

It is not God's plan for us to be tormented with evil. However, our sentence to such victimization is lengthened when we give in to vain imaginations. When such pictures start playing in the theater of our minds, we should not struggle or wrestle with them, but immediately lead them directly to Jesus.

*"Casting down imaginations, and every high thing
that exalteth itself against the knowledge
of God, and bringing into captivity every
thought to the obedience of Christ"*
(2 Cor. 10:5 KJV).

A classic symptom of sinking into the victimization syndrome is to not believe that God has our best interests in mind. If we give in to this wrong thinking, we become victims of the enemy. Consider your life. What have you embraced, or are about to embrace, that is drawing you out of His presence? Decide to refuse it.

O Lord, my fears are about to take hold of me; undertake for me! I give You my mind and my emotions. Thank You for Your help and provision.

"Why, Much-Afraid." It was the Shepherd's voice close beside her. "What is the matter? Be of good cheer, it is I, be not afraid."

He sounded so cheery and full of strength, and, moreover, without a hint of reproach, that Much-Afraid felt as though a strong and exhilarating cordial had been poured into her heart and that a stream of courage and strength was flowing into her from His presence.

She sat up and looked at Him and saw that He was smiling, almost laughing at her. The shame in her eyes met no answering reproach in His, and suddenly she found words echoing in her heart which other trembling souls had spoken. "My Lord is of very tender compassion to them that are afraid." As she looked, thankfulness welled up in her heart and the icy hand of fear which had clutched her broke and melted away and joy burst into bloom. A little song ran through her mind like a trickling stream.

> *My Beloved is the chiefest*
> *Of ten thousand anywhere.*
> *He is altogether lovely*
> *He is altogether fair,*
> *My Beloved is so gentle*
> *And is strong beyond compare.*

"Much-Afraid," said the Shepherd again, "tell Me, what is the matter. Why were you so fearful?"

"It is the way You have chosen for me to go," she whispered. "It looks so dreadful, Shepherd, so impossible. I turn giddy and faint whenever I look at it. The roes and hinds can go there, but they are not limping, crippled, or cowardly like me."

"But, Much-Afraid, what did I promise you in the Valley of Humiliation?" asked the Shepherd with a smile.

Much-Afraid looked startled, and the blood rushed into her cheeks and ebbed again, leaving them as white as before. "You said," she began and broke off and then began again. "O Shepherd,

# Compassionate Lovingkindness

With reverent expectation come into Jesus' presence today. As you are quieted before Him, hear Him say to you, "Is anything wrong?" He doesn't ask because He doesn't know, but because He wants you to learn to be honest about your feelings. Now, none of us can expect to be perfect until He has finished forming us into His image. Growing up involves failures. The problem is, when we fail, we tend to be "swallowed up" in our mistakes and don't want to come to Him "one more time." We fear He'd say in disgust, "Not again!" He will never do that.

> *"For as high as the heavens are above the earth, so great is His lovingkindness toward those who fear Him. As far as the east is from the west, so far has He removed our transgressions from us. Just as a father has compassion on his children, so the Lord has compassion on those who fear Him. For He Himself knows our frame; He is mindful that we are but dust"*
> (Ps. 103:11-14 NAS).

Get in touch with your feelings and pour your heart out to the Lord. Then He can help you change them. Remember, He loves **you**! He accepts you as you are. He laid His life down for you. Let your heart fill with joy and burst forth in bloom with this knowledge.

You said You would make my feet like hinds' feet and set me upon mine High Places."

"Well," He answered cheerily, "the only way to develop hinds' feet is to go by the paths which the hinds use—like this one."

Much-Afraid trembled and looked at Him shamefacedly. "I don't think—I want—hinds' feet, if it means I have to go on a path like that," she said slowly and painfully.

The Shepherd was a very surprising person. Instead of looking either disappointed or disapproving, He actually laughed again. "Oh, yes you do," He said cheerfully. "I know you better than you know yourself, Much-Afraid. You want it very much indeed, and I promise you these hinds' feet. Indeed, I have brought you on purpose to this back side of the desert, where the mountains are particularly steep and where there are no paths but the tracks of the deer and of the mountain goats for you to follow, that the promise may be fulfilled. What did I say to you the last time that we met?"

"You said, 'Now shalt thou see what I will do,' " she answered, and then, looking at Him reproachfully, added, "But I never dreamed You would do anything like this! Lead me to an impassable precipice up which nothing can go but deer and goats, when I'm no more like a deer or a goat than is a jellyfish. It's too—it's too—" she fumbled for words, and then burst out laughing. "Why, it's preposterously absurd! It's crazy! Whatever will You do next?"

The Shepherd laughed too. "I love doing preposterous things," He replied. "Why, I don't know anything more exhilarating and delightful than turning weakness into strength, and fear into faith, and that which has been marred into perfection. If there is one thing more than another which I should enjoy doing at this moment it is turning a jellyfish into a mountain goat. That is My special work," He added with the light of a great joy in His face. "Transforming things—to take Much-Afraid, for instance, and to transform her into—" He broke off and then went on laughingly. "Well, we shall see later on what she finds herself transformed into."

# Continual Feast

Is there anything that you are facing that tends to overwhelm you or makes your entire being feel like a jellyfish? Tenderly turn to your Lord and crawl up in His lap. Lay your head on His chest as He holds you, His big, strong, loving arms around you. Look at life from His perspective for a moment. Are you laughing? Looking at ourselves from His perspective enables us to laugh at ourselves rather than despise ourselves because we realize we do not have anything to prove. We are already approved by Him; therefore, we can have a hilarious heart as we watch Him transform us. He is able to turn weakness into strength, fear into faith, and that which has been marred into perfection, thus leading us forth as victorious warriors.

*"A happy heart is a good medicine and a cheerful mind works healing, but a broken spirit dries the bones"*
(Prov. 17:22 AMP).

*"All the days of the desponding afflicted are made evil [by anxious thoughts and foreboding], but he who has a glad heart has a continual feast [regardless of circumstances]"*
(Prov. 15:15 AMP).

Today, Lord, I choose to laugh with You over the absurd things that I do and that You do in return to transform me.

It was a really extraordinary scene. In the place where just a little while before all had been fear and despair were the Shepherd and Much-Afraid, sitting on the rocks at the foot of the impassable precipice, laughing together as though at the greatest joke in the world.

"Come now, little jellyfish," said the Shepherd, "do you believe that I can change you into a mountain goat and get you to the top of the precipice?"

"Yes," replied Much-Afraid.

"Will you let Me do it?"

"Yes," she answered, "if You want to do such a crazy and preposterous thing, why certainly You may."

"Do you believe that I will let you be put to shame on the way up?"

Much-Afraid looked at Him and then said something that she had never been willing to say before. "I don't think I mind so very much if You do; only have Your will and way in me, Shepherd. Nothing else matters."

As she spoke, something lovely happened. A double rainbow appeared above the precipice, arching it completely, so that the zigzag path up which the roe and the doe had gone was framed in the glowing colors. It was such a beautiful and extraordinary sight that Much-Afraid gasped with wonder and delight, but there was something else about it which was almost more wonderful. She saw that Sorrow and Suffering, who had drawn aside while the Shepherd spoke to her, were standing one at either side of the path, and where the ends of the rainbow touched the earth, one touched Suffering and the other Sorrow.

In the shining glory of the rainbow colors, the two veiled figures were so transfigured with beauty that Much-Afraid could only look at them for a moment before being dazzled.

Then she did that which only a short time before had seemed utterly impossible. She knelt down at the foot of the precipice

# Comforting Contemplation

With a heart that is eager to hear His voice and obey His requests, turn to Jesus and rest in His presence. Let Him bring to your memory the ways that you frequently are offended or become resistant to the things He does in your life. Then let your soul be engulfed with the fact that your God is caring, merciful, steadfast, affirming, and holy. Think about these facets of your Lord for a few moments. Ask Him to frame your soul with the glowing colors of His character.

*"His voice and speech are exceedingly sweet; yes, he is altogether lovely—the whole of him delights and is precious. This is my beloved, and this is my friend, O daughters of Jerusalem!"*
(Song 5:16 AMP)

Lord Jesus, I want to walk in Your presence and in Your joy no matter what the outward conditions around me are. Let my life be like a rainbow that receives and reflects Your light as a real rainbow reflects the shining glory of Your colors. Thank You that You are transforming me so I will display Your beauty.

and built an altar and laid on it her will, her dread, and her shrinking, and when the fire had fallen she found among the ashes a larger and rougher-looking stone than any of the others, sharp-edged and dark in color, but otherwise quite ordinary looking.

This she put in her purse and then rose to her feet and waited for the Shepherd to show her what to do. In her heart she was hoping that He would accompany her up the dreadful ascent as He had gone with her down into the desert, but this He did not do.

Instead, He led her to the foot of the precipice and said, "Now, Much-Afraid, you have really come at last to the foot of the High Places, and a new stage of the journey is to begin. There are new lessons for you to learn.

"I must tell you that this precipice to which the path has led you is at the foot of Mount Injury. The whole mountain range stretches a long way beyond this in either direction, and everywhere it is as steep or even steeper than here. There are even more terrible precipices on the sides of Mount Reviling and Mount Hate and Mount Persecution and others besides, but nowhere is it possible to find a way up to the High Places and into the Kingdom of Love, without surmounting at least one of them. This is the one which I have chosen for you to ascend.

"On the way here you have been learning the lesson of acceptance-with-joy, which is the first letter in the alphabet of Love. Now you must learn the B of the alphabet of Love. You have come to the foot of Mount Injury, and I hope and expect that on the way up the precipice you will discover what is this next letter of the alphabet, and that you will learn and practice it as you have the A of Love. Remember that though you must now meet Injury and surmount it, there is nothing on the way up this terrible-looking precipice nor indeed anything that you may meet above and beyond it that can do you the slightest harm or hurt if you will learn and steadfastly practice the second lesson in the Ascent of Love."

# Unconditional Love

With your heart wrapped securely in His love, consider your own "Mount Injury." When hurts came to you recently, what welled up inside your soul? How did you react? Knowing that He loves you unconditionally, regardless of how you reacted to those hurts, pour your heart out to Him. He loves you.

> *"Are not five sparrows sold for two pennies? And*
> *[yet] not one of them is forgotten or uncared for*
> *in the presence of God. But [even] the very hairs of*
> *your head are all numbered. Do not be struck with*
> *fear or seized with alarm; you are of greater worth*
> *than many [flocks] of sparrows"*
> (Lk. 12:6-7 AMP).

It has been said that our Lord takes time to attend the sparrow's funeral. Such a statement certainly portrays His heart. Praise Him for His words concerning His care of those who trust themselves to Him.

Precious Lord, Your loving care for me continually touches my heart. Regardless of what hurts and pain come my way, let me never lose sight of the love You hold for Your children.

When He had said this He put His hands upon her with special solemnity and gentleness and blessed her. Then He called her companions, who immediately stepped forward. Next He took a rope from a crevice in the wall of rock, and with His own hands roped together the three who were to ascend the precipice. Sorrow was in front and Suffering behind, with Much-Afraid in the middle, so that the two who were so strong and sure-footed went before and after. In this way, even if Much-Afraid slipped and fell, they would be able to hold her up and support her by the rope.

Lastly, He put His hand to His side and brought out a little bottle of cordial which He gave to Much-Afraid, telling her to drink a little at once and to make use of it if ever she felt giddy or faint on the way up. The label on the bottle read, "Spirit of Grace and Comfort," and when Much-Afraid had taken a drop or two she felt so revived and strengthened that she was ready to begin the ascent without any feeling of faintness, although there was still a sensation of dread in her heart.

By this time the evening was well advanced, but being summer there were yet two or three hours before it would begin to be dark, and the Shepherd charged them to start at once for, said He, "Although you cannot possibly reach the top before nightfall, there is a cave farther up the cliff which you cannot see from here, and there you can rest and spend the night in perfect safety. If you stay down here at the foot of the precipice your enemies will most certainly steal upon you and seek to do you harm. However, they will not follow you up this track, and while you are going up you will be beyond their reach. Though I doubt not," He added warningly, "that you will meet them again when you have reached the top."

With that He smiled encouragingly upon them and immediately Sorrow put her foot upon the first step of the narrow little track which zigzagged up the face of the cliff. Much-Afraid followed next, and then Suffering, and in a moment or two they were beginning the ascent.

# Gracious Giver

Concentrate today on the truth that your God, your Lord, is a Giver of only good gifts.

*"Every good and perfect gift is from above, coming down from the Father of the heavenly lights, who does not change like shifting shadows"*
(Jas. 1:17 NIV).

*"Or what man is there of you, if his son asks him for a loaf of bread, will hand him a stone? Or if he asks for a fish, will hand him a serpent? If you then, evil as you are, know how to give good and advantageous gifts to your children, how much more will your Father Who is in heaven [perfect as He is] give good and advantageous things to those who keep on asking Him!"*
(Mt. 7:9-11 AMP).

Lord, I stand in awe over Your complete arrangements for every detail of my life. It is wonderful for me to consider that the power of the Creator of heaven and earth is protecting me. I love You and I commit myself to Your ways. Thank You that You always give good gifts.

# CHAPTER 10

# Ascent of the Precipice Injury

Once on the track, Much-Afraid discovered to her surprise and deep thankfulness that it was not nearly so appalling in actual fact as it had seemed in anticipation. Steep, difficult, and slippery it certainly was, and also painfully narrow, but the feeling of being securely roped to her strong companions was very reassuring. Also, the cordial of the Spirit of Grace and Comfort which she had just drunk kept her from feeling giddy and faint when she looked over the edge, the thing she had most dreaded. Moreover, for the first half-hour of their ascent the rainbow still shone above them, and though the Shepherd had disappeared from view Much-Afraid had a lovely sense that He was still close beside them.

She did not look down unless obliged to do so, but once quite soon after they had started she had to wait in a little niche in the rock at one of the difficult places while Sorrow felt her way forward and Suffering waited in the rear.

Just then, she looked down, and felt very thankful indeed that the Shepherd had charged them to start the ascent that evening and not spend the night down below. Sitting on the rocks below were all five of her enemies, gazing up at them and grimacing with fury and spite. Indeed, as she looked she was

# Blessed Obedience

Our Lord's heart is for all to go well with us, but that requires our cooperation and obedience to Him.

*"Oh, that their hearts would be inclined to fear Me*
*and keep all My commands always, so that it might*
*go well with them and their children forever!"*
(Deut. 5:29 NIV)

When we sin, the enemy can use that sin to hold us in bondage. However, when we face that bondage through His Spirit, it loses its power over us and we find it isn't as bad as we anticipated. It is much like being chased by a roaring lion:

*"...your adversary the devil, as a roaring lion, walketh*
*about, seeking whom he may devour"*
(1 Pet. 5:8 KJV).

When we turn and face this lion, we see he is all roar and no power. He is just noise; he has no claws, teeth, or courage when faced with God's strength.

*"... 'Death is swallowed up in victory. O death,*
*where is your victory? O death, where is your sting?'*
*...thanks be to God, who gives us the victory*
*through our Lord Jesus Christ"*
(1 Cor. 15:54-57 NAS).

Lord, help me remember to face my problems and to go through them with You. Thank You that obedience to Your voice releases me from unnecessary pain.

startled to see Self-Pity (who always looked less ugly and dangerous than his companions) stoop down and pick up a sharp stone which he flung at her with all his might. Fortunately they were already practically out of reach of stone-throwing, but the jagged piece did hit the cliff just below her, and Much-Afraid was greatly relieved when she felt Sorrow pull gently on the rope to tell her that she now could move forward.

She remembered the Shepherd's warning that she was likely to meet these enemies again when the precipice was surmounted, though how they would get up onto the Mount Injury she did not know; only that there must be some other way which they could use.

So the three of them climbed higher and higher while the shadows thrown by the cliffs lengthened over the plain below and the sun went down in a blaze of glory beyond the desert and the great sea. From the height which they had now reached they could plainly see the western sea, along the shores of which they had traveled for so long.

The track they followed wound up and ever upward, back and forth across the face of the cliff, and though it was crumbling and even broken in some places, Much-Afraid was tremendously relieved to find that nowhere at all was it too difficult, not even at the spot halfway up the cliff which Craven Fear had so particularly pointed out to her.

On arriving there just as darkness fell, she found that though the path had indeed broken right away, a plank had been laid across the gap and a rope placed through iron rings in the rock face to form a handrail to which she could cling as she walked across the narrow bridge. The hart and the hind, of course, had disdained such unnecessary assistance and had leaped across the chasm, making it look as though there was nothing there. However, even with the handrail to steady her, Much-Afraid was very careful to close her imagination altogether to the picture which Craven Fear had painted. From bitter experience she knew that pictures thrown on the screen

# Greater Love

Jesus did not choose to interrupt our path with sin. Satan, Adam and Eve, and we ourselves made that choice. However, Jesus' love is greater than our wrong choices. He laid down His life as the bridge for us to use to escape sin's power over us.

> *"[Jesus] gave (yielded) Himself up [to atone] for our sins (and to save and sanctify us), in order to rescue and deliver us from this present wicked age and world order, in accordance with the will and purpose and plan of our God and Father"*
> (Gal. 1:4 AMP).

He becomes our "niche in the rock" from all the difficult places of life.

> *"But the Lord has become my high tower and defense, and my God, the rock of my refuge"*
> (Ps. 94:22 AMP).

Father, my "Daddy," *(my way)* I thank You for Your plan of rescue. Thank You for being my defense. Lord Jesus, my Savior, I thank You for Your love. You took my "blows" for me. Oh, how I appreciate You, Lord. Thank You for Your love.

of her imagination could seem much more unnerving and terrible than the actual facts.

When the plank was crossed safely they discovered themselves to be in an exceedingly narrow gorge quite invisible from below. Directly facing them was the very resting place which the Shepherd had spoken of, a little cave where they were to pass the night.

With a sense of great relief and thankfulness she went inside and looked round. Its situation was such that though she could not look down into the dizzy depths beneath, it was possible to look right out over the plateau and the desert to the far-off sea. The moon had just risen and was shedding a pure silver light over everything, and the first stars appeared like faint flickers in the darkening sky. In the cave itself flat rocks had been placed to form rude seats and a table, and on the ground at one side were piled sheepskins on which they could rest.

Not far from the cave entrance a tiny waterfall trickled down the cliff, and they went to it in turn and refreshed themselves. Then Sorrow and Suffering produced two packages of bread and dried fruits and nuts which the Shepherd had given them at the foot of the ascent. With these they gladly satisfied their hunger, and then, overcome by weariness, they laid themselves down in the cave and fell into dreamless slumber.

Much-Afraid woke with the first light of dawn, and getting up, walked to the entrance of the cave. In the cold light of early morning she could not help telling herself that a scene of utter desolation lay before her. As far as the eye could see was nothing but empty plain and sea, with lowering cliffs above her and jagged rock below. The pleasant wooded country which they had left was out of sight, and in all the vast area upon which she looked she saw not a single tree and scarcely a stunted bush. "How desolate," thought Much-Afraid, "and those rocks beneath look very cruel indeed, as if they are waiting to injure and destroy anything which falls upon them. It seems as though nothing can grow anywhere in all this barren waste."

# Higher Way

**D**o you often have pictures thrown on the screen of your imagination that tempt you to be fearful or angry, and thus draw you out of His presence? At such times we must exert ourselves to obey Jesus' instructions.

*"And set your minds and keep them set on what is above— the higher things—not on the things that are on the earth"* (Col. 3:2 AMP).

Keep to His path. Here is God's description of the path He has chosen for us:

*"For the gate is small, and the way is narrow that leads to life, and few are those who find it"* (Mt. 7:14 NAS).

As you walk this path with Him, you find precious resting places of refreshment. You are protected from looking into those things that would entangle you. Choose to set your mind today upon Him and refuse the imaginations of the enemy.

**T**hank You, Lord, for satisfying my hunger and thirst. I enjoy the gifts You have planned along the way. Thank You for making an alternative path from the world's way.

Just then she looked up at the cliffs above her head and started with surprise and delight. In a tiny crevice of the rock, where a few drops from the trickling waterfall could occasionally sprinkle it, was a single plant. It had just two or three leaves, and one fragile stem, almost hairlike in its slenderness, grew out at right angles to the wall. On the stem was one flower, blood red in color, which glowed like a lamp or flame of fire in the early rays of the sun.

Much-Afraid stared at it for some moments, noticing the wall which completely imprisoned it, the minute aperture through which it had forced its way to the light, and the barren loneliness of its surroundings. Its roots were clamped around by sheer rock, its leaves scarcely able to press outside the prison house, yet it had insisted on bursting into bloom, and was holding its little face open to the sun and burning like a flame of joy. As she looked up at it Much-Afraid asked, as she had in the desert, "What is your name, little flower, for indeed I never saw another like you."

At that moment the sun touched the blood-red petals so that they shone more vividly than ever, and a little whisper rustled from the leaves."

"My name is 'Bearing-the-Cost,' but some call me 'Forgiveness.' "

Then Much-Afraid recalled the words of the Shepherd, "On the way up the precipice you will discover the next letter in the alphabet of Love. Begin to practice it at once."

She gazed at the little flower and said again, "Why call you that?"

Once more, a little whispering laugh passed through the leaves, and she thought she heard them say, "I was separated from all my companions, exiled from home, carried here and imprisoned in this rock. It was not my choice, but the work of others who, when they had dropped me here, went away and left me to bear the results of what they had done.

# Everlasting Strength

Once our Lord gives us wisdom into His plan, or a revelation of Himself, we can expect that testings will come. They may seem like "impassable cliffs" or "barren waste lands." However, the Lord wants to use such tests to confirm and solidify the truth in our very beings. Those are the times to apply Isaiah 26:3-4:

*"Thou wilt keep him in perfect peace, whose mind is stayed on Thee: because he trusteth in Thee. Trust ye in the Lord for ever: for in the Lord JEHOVAH is everlasting strength"*
(KJV).

Be comforted, for He understands all that you are, or ever will, experience:

*"Since then the children share in flesh and blood, He Himself likewise also partook of the same, that through death He might render powerless him who had the power of death, that is, the devil; and might deliver those who through fear of death were subject to slavery all their lives"*
(Heb. 2:14-15 NAS).

Lord Jesus, I trust You to take care of what looks desolate, cruel, and destructive. I commit myself to You, the Rock of Ages. Thank You for the confident hope You give.

"I have borne and have not fainted; I have not ceased to love, and Love helped me push through the crack in the rock until I could look right out onto my Love the sun himself. See now! There is nothing whatever between my Love and my heart, nothing around to distract me from him. He shines upon me and makes me to rejoice, and has atoned to me for all that was taken from me and done against me. There is no flower in all the world more blessed or more satisfied than I, for I look up to him as a weaned child and say, 'Whom have I in heaven but thee, and there is none upon earth that I desire but thee.'"

Much-Afraid looked at the glowing flame above her head, and a longing which was almost envy leaped into her heart. She knew what she must do. Kneeling on the narrow path beneath the imprisoned flower, she said, "O my Lord, behold me—I am Thy little handmaiden Bearing-the-Cost."

At that moment a fragment of the rock which imprisoned the roots of the flower above her loosened and fell at her feet. She picked it up and put it very gently with the other seven stones in her purse, then returned to the cave. Sorrow and Suffering were waiting for her with a further supply of bread and raisins and nuts, and after they had given thanks and had eaten, they roped themselves together again and continued up the precipice.

After a little they came to a place which was very steep and slippery. Suddenly Much-Afraid had her first fall and cut herself quite badly on the pieces of jagged rock which had tripped her. It was a good thing she was so securely roped, for a great terror came upon her and she became so giddy and faint that had she not been tied she might have slipped over the edge of the path and been dashed to pieces on the rocks below. As this thought struck her she was so overcome with panic and trembling that all she could do was to crouch against the wall of rock and cry out to her companions that she was fainting and was in terror of falling.

Immediately Sorrow, who was in front, tightened the rope, then Suffering came up to her, put her arms around her and

# Forgiving Grace

Forgiveness is a choice, not a feeling. Our Lord does not say that we are to feel forgiveness, but to simply forgive.

*"For if you forgive men when they sin against you, your heavenly Father will also forgive you"*
(Mt. 6:14 NIV).

Have you experienced situations that were not your choice, or works of others toward you that were painful? Remember, forgiveness is the door to love's flowing freely to us and others. The enemy would like us to harbor bitterness and resentment. Then he would be able to cause more damage.

*"Watch out that no bitterness takes root among you, for as it springs up it causes deep trouble, hurting many in their spiritual lives"*
(Heb. 12:15b TLB).

If you are still hesitant about forgiving your offender, consider this verse:

*"But if you do not forgive men their sins, your Father will not forgive your sins"*
(Mt. 6:15 NIV).

What is your choice?

Lord Jesus, I choose to forgive _____ Thank You for giving me the grace to forgive.

*Amen*

said urgently, "Drink some of the cordial which the Shepherd gave you."

Much-Afraid was so faint and frightened that she could only lie in the arms of Suffering and gasp, "I don't know where the bottle is—I can't move even to fumble for it."

Then Suffering herself put her hand into the bosom of the fainting girl, drew out the bottle, and poured a few drops between her lips. After a few moments the color returned to Much-Afraid's cheeks, and the faintness began to pass off, but still she could not move. She took more of the Spirit of Grace and Comfort and began to feel strengthened.

Then Sorrow, who had come back to the place where she was crouching, gently shortened the rope so that Much-Afraid could take her hand and again they started to climb. In the fall, however, Much-Afraid had cut both knees so severely that she could only limp forward very painfully, moaning continually and halting constantly. Her companions were very patient, but progress was so slow that finally it became necessary to make greater speed, or they would not reach the top of the precipice before nightfall, and there was no other cave where they could rest.

At last Suffering stooped over her and asked, "Much-Afraid, what were you doing when you left the cave this morning and went off by yourself?"

Much-Afraid gave her a startled look, then said with a painful flush, "I was looking at a flower which I had not seen before, growing in the rock by the waterfall."

"What flower was that?" persisted Suffering very gently.

"It was the flower of Bearing-the-Cost," replied Much-Afraid in a very low voice, "but some call it Forgiveness." For a few moments she was silent, remembering the altar she had built and realizing that she was not practicing this new and difficult letter of the alphabet of Love. Then said she, "I wonder if it would help my knees if we put a few drops of the cordial on them."

# Upholding Hands

We will all fall at times in our journey to the High Places. That is part of the process. To suffer or not to suffer is not a choice we can make, either. Reality dictates that our sin-contaminated world carries pain with it. However, we are not to suppress, deny, or conceal the pain of our mistakes.

*"To You I call, O Lord my Rock; do not turn a deaf ear to me....Hear my cry for mercy as I call to You for help, as I lift up my hands toward Your Most Holy Place"*
(Ps. 28:1-2 NIV).

Just as a loving parent would never reprimand her one-year-old child's first stumbling steps, neither does your loving heavenly Father. Listen to His promise:

*"Though he fall, he shall not be utterly cast down, for the Lord grasps his hand in support and upholds him"*
(Ps. 37:24 AMP).

If you have fallen, forgive yourself. Release any pain you have hidden in your soul, and walk forward in His presence.

"Let us try," said Sorrow and Suffering both together. "It is an excellent suggestion."

As they dropped a little of the cordial on both knees, almost at once the bleeding ceased, and the worst of the smart and pain died away. Her legs remained very stiff and she was still obliged to limp quite badly, but they did go forward at a much better pace. By late afternoon they were right at the top of the awful ascent, and found themselves in a forest of young pine trees with moss and blueberries growing on the banks beside the path, and the precipice which had looked so impassable actually behind them. They sat down on one of the mossy banks in the wood to rest, then heard a voice singing quite close at hand.

> *Thou art all fair, my dearest love,*
> *There is no spot in thee.*
> *Come with me to the heights above,*
> *Yet fairer visions see.*
> *Up to the mount of Myrrh and thence*
> *Across the hills of Frankincense,*
> *To where the dawn's clear innocence*
> *Bids all the shadows flee.*
>
> *Come with me, O my fairest dear,*
> *With me to Lebanon,*
> *Look from the peaks of grim Shenir,*
> *Amana and Hermon.*
> *The lions have their dens up there—*
> *The leopards prowl the glens up there,*
> *But from the top the view is clear*
> *Of land yet to be won.*

(Cant. 4:7,8)

There, coming toward them through a clearing in the trees, was the Shepherd Himself.

# Grace Released

Practicing forgiveness does not come naturally—but its fruits are rich. When we forgive, we release the flow of God's grace. That's why forgiveness is one of the greatest tools of warfare. When we forgive, it releases us and others from the ground or footholds that the enemy gains when we hold on to unforgiveness.

*"If you forgive anyone, I also forgive him. And*
*what I have forgiven—if there was anything to*
*forgive—I have forgiven in the sight of Christ for*
*your sake, in order that Satan might not outwit us.*
*For we are not unaware of his schemes"*
(2 Cor. 2:10-11 NIV).

I choose, my Lord, to forgive my offenders quickly, so the enemy might not have an advantage in my life or in theirs. I do not want to hinder Your progress in our lives. I do not want to frustrate, nullify, or insult the Spirit of grace. Thank You for Your gift of grace to forgive. I freely release this grace today to all I meet. Let Your healing power be released.

If there are people in your past whom God brings to mind as you wait before Him, forgive and release them also.

# CHAPTER 11

# In the Forests of Danger and Tribulation

With what joy they welcomed the Shepherd as He sat down in the midst, and after cheerfully congratulating them on having surmounted the precipice, He laid His hands gently on the wounds which Much-Afraid had received when she fell, and immediately they were healed. Then He began to speak to them about the way which lay ahead.

"You have now to go through the forests which clothe the sides of these mountains almost up to the snowline. The way will be steep, but you will come to resting places here and there. These are the Forests of Danger and Tribulation, and often the pine trees grow so tall and so closely together that the path may seem quite dark. Storms are very frequent up here on these slopes, but keep pressing forward, for remember that nothing can do you any real harm while you are following the path of My will."

It did seem strange that even after safely surmounting so many difficulties and steep places, including the "impassable precipice" just below them, Much-Afraid should remain so like her name. But so it was! No sooner did the Shepherd pronounce the words "danger and tribulation" than she began to shake and tremble all over again.

# Winner's Prize

Our Lord is training us to face hardships with His strength and to emerge as winners. As we press forward, the vile, evil things in life lose their hold on us and we walk in strength and dignity regardless of the circumstances. However, to walk in such a way requires co-operation and perseverance on our part. Paul describes the process:

> *"...I press on in order that I may lay hold of that for which also I was laid hold of by Christ Jesus... forgetting what lies behind and reaching forward to what lies ahead, I press on toward the goal for the prize of the upward call of God in Christ Jesus"*
> (Phil. 3:12-14 NAS).

If you are unwilling to face what lies ahead of you, then remember that the Father sent Jesus

> *"...to bring good news to the afflicted...to bind up the brokenhearted, to proclaim liberty to captives, and freedom to prisoners...to comfort all who mourn.... So they will be called oaks of righteousness, the planting of the Lord, that He may be glorified"*
> (Is. 61:1-3 NAS).

Lord Jesus, thank You that Your paths are always divinely designed to release me from being captured by evil and to allow me to be free to live as You created me to live. Thank You that You will use what lies before me to strengthen my walk with You.

"The Forests of Danger and Tribulation!" she repeated with a piteous quaver in her voice. "O Shepherd, wherever will You lead me next?"

"To the next stage on the way to the High Places," He answered promptly, smiling at her as nicely as possible.

"I wonder if You will ever be able to get me there!" groaned poor foolish little Much-Afraid. "I wonder You continue to bother with me and don't give up the job altogether. It looks as though I never shall have anything but lame feet, and that even You won't be able to make them like hinds' feet." She looked disconsolately at her feet as she spoke. Certainly at the moment they did look even more crooked than ever.

"I am not a man that I should lie," said the Shepherd gravely. "Look at Me, Much-Afraid. Do you believe that I will deceive you? Have I said, and shall I not do it? Or have I spoken, and shall I not make it good?"

Much-Afraid trembled a little, partly at the tone of His voice and partly because she was still Much-Afraid by nature and was already trying to picture what the Forests of Danger and Tribulation would be like. That always had a disastrous effect upon her, but she answered penitently, "No—I know that You are not a man who would lie to me; I know that You will make good what You have said."

"Then," said the Shepherd, speaking very gently again, "I am going to lead you through danger and tribulation, Much-Afraid, but you need not be the least bit afraid, for I shall be with you. Even if I lead you through the Valley of the Shadow itself you need not fear, for My rod and My staff will comfort you."

Then He added, "Thou shalt not be afraid for the terror by night; nor for the arrow that flieth by day; nor for the pestilence that walketh in darkness; nor for the destruction that wasteth at noonday. Though a thousand fall at thy side, and ten thousand at thy right hand, it shall not come nigh thee...For I will cover thee with My feathers, and under My wings shalt thou trust" (Psa. 91:4-7). The gentleness of His voice as He said these things was indescribable.

# Courage Renewed

Do you have "what ifs" that haunt your mind and make you easy prey for the enemy? All of us tend to set our minds on what is below rather than on what is above–thus getting ourselves into trouble. However, Jesus specifically said:

*"So do not worry or be anxious about tomorrow,*
*for tomorrow will have worries and anxieties of its own.*
*Sufficient for each day is its own trouble"*
(Mt. 6:34 AMP).

When times of danger or tribulation do approach and you are worried over things, then that is the time to boost your courage with this promise of God:

*"So shall My word be that goes forth out of My mouth;*
*it shall not return to Me void—without producing*
*any effect, useless—but it shall accomplish that*
*which I please and purpose, and it shall prosper*
*in the thing for which I sent it"*
(Is. 55:11 AMP).

Praise God!

Lord Jesus, I confess my worry and anxiety over _____ as sin. Thank You for cleansing it. I choose to set my mind on You today and live by the power and strength You have set aside for me. Thank You that the truth You have spoken has the power of the universe behind it.

Then Much-Afraid knelt at His feet and built yet another altar and said, "Yea, though I walk through the Valley of the Shadow of Death, I will fear no evil: for Thou art with me." Then, because she found that even as she spoke her teeth were chattering with fright and her hands had gone quite clammy, she looked up into His face and added, "For Thou art not a man that Thou shouldest lie, nor the Son of man that Thou shouldest repent. Hast Thou said, and shalt Thou not do it? And has Thou spoken and shalt Thou not make it good?"

Then the Shepherd smiled more comfortingly than ever before, laid both hands on her head and said, "Be strong, yea, be strong and fear not." Then He continued, "Much-Afraid, don't ever allow yourself to begin trying to picture what it will be like. Believe Me, when you get to the places which you dread you will find that they are as different as possible from what you have imagined, just as was the case when you were actually ascending the precipice. I must warn you that I see your enemies lurking among the trees ahead, and if you ever let Craven Fear begin painting a picture on the screen of your imagination, you will walk with fear and trembling and agony, where no fear is."

When He had said this, He picked up another stone from the place where she was kneeling, and gave it to her to put with the other memorial stones. Then He went His way, and Much-Afraid and her companions started on the path which led up through the forests.

Almost as soon as they had reached the trees they saw the face of mean, sickly Self-Pity, looking out from behind one of the trunks. He gabbled ever so quickly before he dodged back into hiding, "I say, Much-Afraid, this really is a bit too thick. I mean, whatever will He do next, forcing a poor little lame, frightened creature like yourself to go through dangers which only brave, strong men ought to be expected to face. Really, your Shepherd is almost more of a bully than Craven Fear himself."

Hardly had he stopped before Resentment put his head out and said crossly, "There's absolutely no reason for it either, because there's another perfectly good path which skirts the forest

# Heavenward Gaze

We become like whatever we behold or set our gaze upon because that thing becomes our "god" or life source.

*"Those who make idols are like them; so is every one who trusts and relies on them"*
(Ps. 135:18 AMP).

These "gods" are anything that we spend our time dwelling upon. Such "idols" are not just bad things. They can be good things that we try to accomplish in our own strength and energy. God, and God alone, is to be our motivation and power for everything we do and say.

*"And now, Israel, what does the Lord your God require of you, but (reverently) to fear the Lord your God: [that is,] to walk in all His ways, and to love Him, and to serve the Lord your God with all your [mind and] heart and with your entire being"*
(Deut. 10:12 AMP).

Lord Jesus, I commit to walking with You alone, beholding only You, regardless of the diversions going on around me. You and You alone are my God, now and forever!

altogether and brings you right up to the snowline without going anywhere near these unnecessary dangers. Everybody else goes that way, so why shouldn't you? Tell Him you won't go this way, Much-Afraid, and insist on being taken by the usual path. This way is for martyrs only, and you, my dear, don't fit into the picture at all."

Then Craven Fear leered at her for a moment and said contemptuously, "So you think you're going to become a little heroine, do you? and go singing through the Forest of Danger! What will you bet, Much-Afraid, that you won't end up shrieking and screaming like a maniac, maimed for the rest of your life?"

Bitterness was next to speak, and sneered from behind another tree, "He would do this. It's just as I told you. After you have dutifully gone through one terrifying experience He's always got something still worse lying ahead of you."

Then Pride (who was still limping badly and seemed extra venomous as a result) said, "You know, He won't be able to rest content until He has put you to complete shame, because that's the way He produces that precious humility He's so crazy about. He'll humble you to the dust, Much-Afraid, and leave you a groveling idiot in front of everyone."

Much-Afraid and her companions walked on without answering and without taking any notice, but as before, Much-Afraid discovered that she limped more painfully whenever she heard what they said. It was really terribly perplexing to know what to do. If she listened, she limped, and if she put her fingers in her ears, she couldn't accept the hands of her two guides, which meant that she stumbled and slipped.

So they stopped for a moment or two and discussed the matter, and then Suffering opened the little First Aid kit hanging at her girdle, took out some cotton and firmly plugged the ears of Much-Afraid. Although this was uncomfortable, it did seem to have the desired effect, at least temporarily, for when the five sulkers saw that they could not make her hear them

# Righteous Boast

When any thought or statement comes to you that attacks the character or motives of God, immediately respond with the postal message, "Return to Sender"! When any taunt comes to you from the enemy that attacks your own character or motives, act as a mirror and reflect those thoughts to God. He then takes what was designed to destroy you and uses it to strengthen you. He takes the enemy's jagged, life-threatening boulders and turns them into building blocks of godly character. So shout your victory over the enemy!

*"We will (shout in) triumph at your salvation and victory, and in the name of our God we will set up our banners....Some trust in and boast of chariots, and some of horses; but we will trust in and boast of the name of the Lord our God"* (Ps. 20:5,7 AMP).

The enemy has no choice but to flee when faced with God's Word!

Lord, I proclaim Your Lordship over my life. All the negative things the enemy tells me about myself I reflect upward to Your care. Thank You for Your victory!

they soon tired of bawling at her and left her alone until another opportunity should occur for badgering her again.

At first the forest did not really seem too dreadful. Perhaps it was that up there on the mountains the air was so fresh and strong that it made those who breathed it fresh and strong too. Also, the sun was still shining, and Much-Afraid began to feel a sensation which was completely new to her, a thrill of excitement and, incredible as it seemed, of almost pleasurable adventure.

Here she was, lame Much-Afraid, actually walking through the Forest of Danger and not really minding. This lasted for quite a time until huge black clouds gradually rolled over the sky, and the sun went in. In the distance thunder rolled and the woods became dark and very still. Suddenly a bolt of lightning scorched across the sky, and somewhat ahead of them was a rending crash as a great forest tree fell to the earth, then another and another. Then the storm in all its fury was bursting around them, thunder rolling, lightning sizzling and crackling in every direction until the whole forest seemed to be groaning and shaking and falling about them.

The strangest thing was that though Much-Afraid felt a shuddering thrill go through her at every crash she was not really afraid. That is, she felt neither panic nor desire to run, nor even real dread, for she kept repeating to herself, "Though a thousand shall fall at thy side and ten thousand at thy right hand, it shall not come nigh thee....For I will cover thee with My feathers, and under My wings shalt thou trust." So throughout the whole storm she was filled with a strange and wonderful peace such as she had never felt before, and walked between her two companions saying to herself, "I shall not die, but live and declare the works of the Lord."

At last the storm began to rumble off into the distance, the crashes died down, and there was a quiet lull. The three women stopped to wring the water out of their clothes and hair and try to tidy themselves. As they did this, Craven Fear

# Total Trust

The path to the High Places is not found with "pat" answers, processed steps, or precise formulas. On the contrary, in order to arrive at the High Places, we must make Jesus our very life—our all in all! If a perplexing question or situation is blocking your way, then you must

> *"Trust in the Lord with all your heart, and do*
> *not lean on your own understanding"*
> (Prov. 3:5 NAS).

We must be at rest in Him.

> *"Let us therefore be diligent to enter that rest..."*
> (Heb. 4:11 NAS).

Have you ever heard the godly advice, "Stay alert, and rest in Him"? It's not really contradictory; it's just two sides of the same coin. We are to stay alert to our responsibilities, but also to rest in His ability to care for His responsibilities. He will guide us on the path to the High Places.

Lord Jesus, as I walk through the Forest of Danger today, clearly expose the areas where I am to be alert to obey and where I am to rest and watch You. Thank You for this confidential communion and counsel. It is so satisfying to my soul, and it always provides what I need when I need it.

appeared near them again and yelled at the top of his voice, "I say, Much-Afraid, the storm has only gone round the mountains for a short time. Already it is beginning to approach again and will be worse than before. Make a bolt back down the path as quickly as you can and get away from these dangerous trees before it starts again or you will be killed. There is just time for you to make good your escape."

"Look here," exclaimed Much-Afraid most unexpectedly, water still dripping from her hair and her sodden skirts clinging like wet rags around her legs, "I can't stand that fellow shouting at me any longer. Please help me—both of you," and setting the example, she stooped down, picked up a stone and flung it straight at Craven Fear.

Her two companions actually laughed for the very first time and started hurling a barrage of stones among the trees where the five were lurking. In a moment or two none of their enemies were visible. Then, just ahead of them, through the trees, they saw a log hut which seemed to offer a promise of shelter and protection from the storm, which certainly was again drawing nearer. Hurrying toward the cabin, they found that it stood in a clearing well away from the trees, and when they tried the door latch, to their joy it opened and they thankfully slipped inside. With great presence of mind, Suffering immediately closed the door and bolted it behind them, and none too soon!

Next minute their enemies were banging on the door and shouting, "Hi! I say—open the door and let us in. The storm is starting again. You can't be so inhuman as to shut us outside and leave us to our fate."

Much-Afraid went to the door and shouted through the keyhole the advice they had offered her, "Make a bolt down the path as quickly as you can and get away from these dangerous trees, or you will be killed. You have just time to make good your escape before the storm starts again."

There was a sound of muttered curses outside, then of hurrying feet fading away into the distance, and it seemed as

# Standing Firm

There are times in our lives when we retreat into Jesus' arms and He fights for us.

*"... Fear not, stand still (firm, confident, undismayed)*
*and see the salvation of the Lord, which He will work*
*for you today.... The Lord will fight for you, and*
*you shall hold your peace and remain at rest"*
(Ex. 14:13-14 AMP).

There are times when we simply stand in His power.

*"Finally, be strong in the Lord, and in the strength*
*of His might. Put on the full armor of God, that you*
*may be able to stand firm against the schemes of the devil"*
(Eph. 6:10-11 NAS).

There are other times when we are to attack the enemy head on and resist him!

*"So be subject to God.—Stand firm against the devil;*
*resist him and he will flee from you"*
(Jas. 4:7 AMP).

Thank You that the covering of Your shed blood guarantees that nothing the enemy can do shall in any way harm me. I love You.

though this time the advice was being acted upon. Back rolled the storm, fiercer and more terrible than before, but they were safely sheltered in the hut out of range of the crashing trees, and their shelter proved perfectly weatherproof, for not a drop came through the roof.

They found in the room a supply of firewood stacked beside a small kitchen range with a kettle and some saucepans on it. While Suffering busied herself lighting the fire, Sorrow held the kettle under a spout outside the window and filled it with rain water. Much-Afraid went to a cupboard on the wall to see if it would yield any treasure. Sure enough, there was crockery on the shelves and a supply of tinned foods, as well as a big tin of unleavened biscuits.

So in a very little time, while the storm still furiously raged and rattled outside, there they were, sitting around a crackling fire, warming themselves and drying their sopping garments while they drank comforting hot cocoa and satisfied their hunger. Though the uproar of the tempest without was almost deafening and the hut shuddered and shook in every blast, yet inside was nothing but peace and thanksgiving and cheerful contentment.

Much-Afraid found herself thinking with astonished awe that it was really the happiest and the most peaceful experience during the whole of her journey up till that time. As they lay down on the mattresses which they discovered piled in another part of the hut, she repeated again to herself very softly: "He has covered me with His feathers, and under His wings I do trust."

The storm continued with great violence for two or three days, but while it lasted the three travelers rested quietly in the shelter of the hut, going outside only during the brief lulls to gather wood. This they dried in the oven to replenish the stock they were using, so that others, following on behind, might not be left without fuel. There seemed to be a good store of tinned foods and unleavened biscuits and they supposed

# Unshakable Bounty

Tenderly turn to your Lord today and enter into His presence as your "ark," your shelter from all storms and harm. Contemplate this truth: No matter how fierce the storm–the bolts of lightning, the crashing of trees, or torrential downpours–you are protected because you are "in Him." Examine your bounty: peace regardless of circumstances, grace to match the situation, and nourishment for all of your needs. Where did you get all of these gifts? They are from your inheritance!

> *"And if we are [His] children, then we are [His] heirs also: heirs of God and fellow heirs with Christ— sharing His inheritance with Him; only we must share His suffering if we are to share His glory"* (Rom. 8:17 AMP).

I thank You, dear Lord Jesus, that no matter how violent and stormy my circumstances become, You have provided grace and peace! Thank You for making me a joint heir with You.

that some of the Shepherd's servants must visit the hut from time to time with a new supply.

During those quiet days in the midst of the raging tempest Much-Afraid came to know her two companions in a new way and also to understand more of the mountain dialect which they spoke. In some strange way she began to feel that they were becoming real friends, and not just attendants whom the Shepherd had commanded to go with her as guides and helpers. She found, too, that now she was accepting their companionship in this way she seemed more alive than ever before to beauty and delight in the world around her.

It seemed as though her senses had been quickened in some extraordinary way, enabling her to enjoy every little detail of her life; so that although her companions actually were Sorrow and Suffering, she often felt an almost inexplicable joy and pleasure at the same time. This would happen when she looked at the bright, crackling flames in the log fire, or listened to the sound of lashing rain overhead emphasizing the safety and peace within the hut, or when she saw through the window the tossing trees waving their arms against a background of scurrying clouds or lightning-rent sky. Or again, very early before daybreak, when she saw the morning star shining serenely through a rift in the clouds or heard the clear, jubilant note of a bird during a lull in the storm.

All these things seemed to be speaking to her in the mountain dialect, and to her growing astonishment, she found it an incredibly beautiful language, so that sometimes her eyes filled with tears of pure joy and her heart seemed so full of ecstasy that she could hardly bear it.

One morning when the storm was rattling and raging through the forest louder than ever, she noticed Sorrow sitting by the fire singing quietly to herself, the words, of course, being in the mountain dialect, which Much-Afraid was learning to understand. This is the best translation that I can give,

# Serene Guardian

Much-Afraid applied the truth set forth in Philippians 4:8 and saw the results described in verse 7.

*"Finally, brothers, whatever is true, whatever is noble, whatever is right, whatever is pure, whatever is lovely whatever is admirable—if anything is excellent or praiseworthy—think about such things"*
(4:8 NIV).

*"And the peace of God, which transcends all understanding, will guard your hearts and your minds in Christ Jesus"*
(4:7 NIV).

As we think His thoughts and obey Him, not only do we find peace, but we also begin to like who we are. It is the same situation when the knowledge of Jesus' Lordship over all things settles into our inner beings. Then all of life becomes a priceless exhibit in God's art gallery. No longer can we view another or ourselves with contempt or indifference. Instead we see others and ourselves as products of our Lord's craftsmanship.

Thank You, Lord, for providing peace and serenity when I settle my mind on Your thoughts of myself and others.

but you will realize that the original was much more beautiful and full of forest sounds and music.

> *How lovely and how nimble are thy feet,*
> *O prince's daughter!*
> *They flash and sparkle and can run more fleet*
> *Than running water.*
> *On all the mountains there is no gazelle,*
> *No roe or hind,*
> *Can overtake thee nor can leap as well—*
> *But lag behind.*

(Cant. 7:1)

"Why, Sorrow," exclaimed Much-Afraid, "I didn't know that you could sing, nor even that you knew any songs."

Sorrow answered quietly, "Neither did I, but on the way up here through the forest I found the words and tune coming into my head just as I am singing them now."

"I like it," said Much-Afraid. "It makes me think of the time when I shall have hinds' feet myself, and so it is comforting and the tune is so nice and springy. It makes me want to jump." She laughed at the thought of her crooked feet being able to jump, then coaxed, "Teach me the song—please do."

So Sorrow sang it over several times until Much-Afraid knew it perfectly and went about the hut humming it to herself, trying to picture what it would be like to be a gazelle leaping on the mountains, and able to jump from crag to crag, just as the Shepherd did. When the day came for her to receive her hinds' feet, she would be able to follow Him wherever He went. The picture was so lovely she could hardly wait for it to come true.

# Peaceful Rule

Letting the peace of God rule in our hearts is a choice. We can let our hearts be upset or worried, or we can choose to let God fill us with peace.

*"And let the peace (soul harmony which comes) from the Christ rule (act as umpire continually) in your hearts—deciding and settling with finality all questions that arise in your minds—[in that peaceful state] to which [as members of Christ's] one body you were also called [to live]. And be thankful—appreciative, giving praise to God always"* (Col. 3:15 AMP).

If you do not have peace, could it be because you fear you are of little worth or value? Do you not feel deeply loved, fully pleasing, totally forgiven, accepted and complete in Christ? Run into the secret place of the Most High God and sit for a while under the shadow of the Almighty.

Lord, I choose to allow Your peace rule my heart today! Thank You for the value You have placed on me by shedding Your blood for my salvation.

# CHAPTER 12

# In the Mist

At last the storm gradually died down, the clamor on the mountains ceased, and it was time to resume the journey. However, the weather had broken completely, and though the storm itself was over, thick mist and cloud remained, shrouding everything on the heights.

When they started the mist was so thick that they could see only the trees on either side of the narrow path, and even they looked ghostly and unreal. The rest of the forest was simply swallowed up and entirely lost to sight, veiled in a cold and clammy white curtain. The ground was dreadfully muddy and slippery, and although the path did not climb nearly so steeply as before, after some hours Much-Afraid found to her amazement that she was missing the rolling thunder of the storm and even the sickening crash of the trees as the lightning splintered them.

She began to realize that, cowardly though she was, there was something in her which responded with a surge of excitement to the tests and difficulties of the way better than to easier and duller circumstances. It was true that fear sent a dreadful shuddering thrill through her, but nevertheless it was a thrill, and she found herself realizing with astonishment that even the dizzy precipice had been more to her liking than this dreary plodding on and on through the bewildering mist. In some way the dangers of the storm had stimulated her;

# Passing Through

On ordinary, mundane days it is often easier to be distracted from our Lord than on pressure-packed days when we are aware of our helplessness. Don't be drawn into the trap or noose of boredom that often comes with dull circumstances. On the other hand, when the subtlety of the enemy comes in like a fog, remember that the fog has no power to destroy the road ahead. It just rolls in. That's all. You are passing through.

*"When you pass through the waters, I will be with you;*
*and through the rivers, they will not overflow you.*
*When you walk through the fire, you will not be*
*scorched, nor will the flame burn you"*
(Is. 43:2 NAS).

Jesus didn't stay on the cross; He passed through. So the road Jesus has for you is not affected by the mist threatening your view.

Lord Jesus, I let You set my feet firmly upon the path. I look to You to guide me even during the ordinary, unexciting days.

now there was nothing but tameness, just a trudge, trudge forward, day after day, able to see nothing except for white, clinging mist which hung about the mountains without a gleam of sunshine breaking through.

At last she burst out impatiently, "Will this dull, dreary mist never lift, I wonder?" And would you believe it! A voice she knew all too well immediately answered from beyond the trees.

"No, it won't," replied Resentment. "Moreover you might just as well know now that this is going to continue for no one knows how long. Higher up the mountains the mist hangs thicker and thicker still. That's all you can expect for the rest of the journey."

Much-Afraid pretended not to hear, but the voice went on again almost at once.

"Have you noticed, Much-Afraid, that the path which you are following isn't going up the mountain at all, but is almost level? You've missed the upward way, and you are just going round and round the mountain in circles."

Much-Afraid had not exactly noticed this fact, but now she could not help realizing that it was true. They were not climbing at all, but simply moving along the mountainside with constant ups and downs, and the downs seemed to be getting more frequent. Could it be possible that they were really gradually descending the mountain instead of going up? In the bewildering mist one simply could not see anything, and she found she had lost all sense of direction. On asking her companions what they thought about it they answered rather shortly (because, of course, she ought not to have listened to any suggestion from Resentment) that they were on the path which the Shepherd had pointed out, and would certainly not allow anyone to persuade them to leave it.

"But," persisted Much-Afraid petulantly, "don't you think that we may have missed the way in this mist? The Shepherd said the path led upward, and as you see, this one doesn't. It

# Patient Progression

Have you ever thought, "I'm making absolutely no progress spiritually"? Why did you feel that way? That feeling comes when we do what Paul described in Second Corinthians 10:12:

*"However, when they measure themselves with themselves and compare themselves with one another, they are without understanding and behave unwisely"*
(2 Cor. 10:12b AMP).

When we become impatient and rash in our slow progress, we are likely to give ground to the enemy. It is easier to give such ground to the enemy than to take it back.

Lord Jesus, I see that one burst of impatience or any other seemingly we "small" thing can open the door to the "floodgates of hell." Let me look only to You to help me progress in both my spiritual growth and in the establishment of my earthly path.

Is there any area in your life where you are questioning His leadership? If so, realize the futility of such actions and release that area back to Him.

runs along the side of the mountain. There may easily have been a more direct way up which we didn't notice in the mist."

Their only answer was that they knew better than to listen to any suggestion made by Resentment.

At that the voice of Bitterness broke in quite clearly, "You might at least be willing to go back a little way and look, instead of insisting on going on and on along what may prove to be a wrong path leading you round in circles."

Sorrow and Suffering took absolutely no notice, but unfortunately Much-Afraid did, and said with still greater petulance, "I think you ought to consider the suggestion. Perhaps it would be better to go back a little way and see if we have missed the right path. Really, it is no use going on and on in circles, getting nowhere."

To this they replied, "Well, if we are going round in circles, we shall eventually arrive back where we went wrong, and if we keep our eyes open we shall be able to see the path we missed—always provided that it does exist and is not just a bit of imagination on the part of Bitterness."

"You poor little thing," came the whisper of Self-Pity through the mist. "It is too bad that you have been put in the charge of such obstinate mule-like creatures. Just think of the time you are wasting, getting nowhere at all. Trudge, trudge, day after day, nothing to show for it, and you ought to be getting up onto the High Places."

So they went on, whispering and talking at her through the clinging mist, which shrouded everything and made it all seem so ghostly and dreary. Of course, she ought not to have listened to them, but the mist was so bewildering and the path so unspeakably tame that she found something in her heart responding to them almost against her will.

Suffering doggedly led the way, and Sorrow just as doggedly was her rearguard, so that there was no possibility of turning back, but Much-Afraid found herself limping and slipping and stumbling far more often and badly than at any other stage of

# Obedience Rewarded

The degree to which we resist the guidance of those placed by God in our lives reveals the degree of resistance we have toward God Himself. That may seem like a hard word, but read what God says:

*"Obey your spiritual leaders and be willing to do what they say. For their work is to watch over your souls, and God will judge them on how well they do this. Give them reason to report joyfully about you to the Lord and not with sorrow, for then you will suffer for it too"*
(Heb. 13:17 TLB).

When by disobedience and resistance we allow ourselves to be drawn out of His presence, then our strength, dignity, and peace begins to be drained. We end up hurting ourselves.

Lord Jesus, I did not realize how serious my response to others was, especially to those whom You have given to guide, bless, and protect me. I repent of my attitude toward _____ . Show me how I can bless them instead. Thank You for Your grace that enables me to do so.

the journey. It made her very disagreeable and difficult to deal with. It is true that after every stumble her conscience smote her and she apologized sorrowfully and abjectly to her companions, but that did not prevent her slipping again almost directly afterwards. Altogether it was a miserable time, and the mist, instead of clearing, seemed to get thicker and colder and drearier than ever.

At last, one afternoon, when the only word which at all described her progress is to say that she was slithering along the path, all muddy and wet and bedraggled from constant slips, she decided to sing.

It has not been mentioned before, but Much-Afraid did not possess the gift of a sweet voice any more than a pretty face. It is true that she was fond of singing and that if the Shepherd sang with her she could keep in tune and manage quite nicely, but if she tried alone the results were by no means so good. However, the mist was so thick and clammy that she was nearly stifled, and she felt she must do something to try to cheer herself and to drown the ghostly voices which kept whispering to her through the trees.

It was not pleasant to think of her relatives now having the opportunity to entertain themselves at the expense of her very unmelodious voice, but she decided to risk their ribald comments. "If I sing quite loudly," she told herself, "I shall not be able to hear what they say." The only song which she could think of at the moment was the one which Sorrow had taught her in the hut, and though it seemed singularly inappropriate she lifted up her voice and sang quaveringly:

> *How lovely and how nimble are thy feet,*
> *O prince's daughter!*
> *They flash and sparkle and can run more fleet*
> *Than running water.*
> *On all the mountains there is no gazelle,*
> *No roe or hind,*
> *Can overtake thee nor can leap as well—*
> *But lag behind.*

(Cant 7:1)

194

# Powerful Praise

Which voice most easily drags you out of His presence—Resentment, Bitterness, Self-Pity, Pride, Fear, or Anger? A wonderful method of frontal attack that routs these enemies, which is also a means of building up ourselves, is singing praises to Jesus. To decide to sing in the face of an attack is also an important choice that we make.

> *"And now shall my head be lifted up above my enemies round about me; in His tent I will offer sacrifices and shouting of joy; I will sing, yes, I will sing praises to the Lord"*
> (Ps. 27:6 AMP).

Enter into His "tent" or presence today and quietly think about Him. Sing a song to Him. If you don't know a song, use a hymnbook or turn to a Psalm and sing it to Him.

> *"Praise the Lord! Praise God in His sanctuary; praise Him in the heavens of His power! Praise Him for His mighty acts; praise Him according to the abundance of His greatness!"*
> (Ps. 150:1-2 AMP)

Continue until you break through any awkwardness you might feel.

There was perfect silence as she sang. The loud, sneering voices of her enemies had died away altogether. "It is a good idea," said Much-Afraid to herself jubilantly. "I wish I had thought of it before. It is a much better way to avoid hearing what they are saying than putting cotton in my ears, and I believe, yes, I really do believe, there is a little rift in the mist ahead. How lovely, I shall sing the verse again." And she did so.

"Why, Much-Afraid," said a cheery voice close beside her, "I have not heard that song before. Where did you learn it?"

There, striding toward her with a particularly pleased smile on His face, was the Shepherd Himself. It is just impossible to describe in words the joy of Much-Afraid when she saw Him really coming toward them on that dreary mountain path, where everything had been swallowed up for so long in the horrible mist and everything one touched had been so cold and clammy. Now with His coming the mist was rapidly clearing away and a real gleam of sunshine—the first they had seen for days—broke through at last.

"O Shepherd," she gasped, and caught hold of His hand and could say no more. It really had seemed as though she would never see Him again.

"Tell me," He repeated cheerily as He smiled at them all, "where did you learn that song, Much-Afraid?"

"Sorrow taught it to me," she replied. "I didn't think that she knew any songs, Shepherd, but she said the words and the music came to her as we were climbing up through the forest. I asked her to teach it to me because—I know I am a goose, but it makes me think of the time when You will have made my feet like hinds' feet and I won't ever have to slither along again," and she looked shamefacedly at her bedraggled and muddy condition.

"I am glad you sing it," said the Shepherd more pleasantly than ever. "I think it is a particularly nice song. Indeed," He added smiling, "I think I will add another verse to it Myself," and at once He began to sing these words to the same tune:

# Joy Unspeakable

Much-Afraid laid aside the "fear of man" when she sang. She risked hearing ribald comments from her enemies with her unmelodious singing. Her reward for serving God rather than man was a joy impossible to describe. The blinding mist was cleared away and the sunshine broke through.

*"Now, therefore, fear the Lord and serve Him in sincerity and truth; and put away the gods which your fathers served...and serve the Lord"*
(Josh. 24:14 NAS).

*"Only fear the Lord and serve Him in truth with all your heart; for consider what great things He has done for you"*
(1 Sam. 12:24 NAS).

Look into Jesus' smiling face and take Him by the hand. Ask Him to show you an area in which you easily give in to fleshly approval. Wait before Him patiently.

Lord, I desire to follow You regardless of what others may think or say. Teach me to unabashedly rejoice before You!

*Thy joints and thighs are like a supple band*
*On which are met*
*Fair jewels which a cunning master hand*
*Hath fitly set.*
*In all the palace, search where'er you please,*
*In every place*
*There's none that walks with such a queenly ease,*
*Nor with such grace.*

(Cant. 7:1)

"O Shepherd," exclaimed Much-Afraid, "where did You find that verse to fit in so nicely to the tune which Sorrow taught me?"

Again He smiled at her in the nicest possible way and answered, "The words came to Me just now as I followed you along the path."

Poor Much-Afraid, who knew that she had been slipping and stumbling in the most dreadful way, indeed worse than at any other time, flushed painfully all over her face. She said nothing, only looked at Him almost reproachfully.

"Much-Afraid," said He very gently in answer to that look, "don't you know by now that I never think of you as you are now but as you will be when I have brought you to the Kingdom of Love and washed you from all the stains and defilements of the journey? If I come along behind you and notice that you are finding the way especially difficult, and are suffering from slips and falls, it only makes Me think of what you will be like when you are with Me, leaping and skipping on the High Places. Wouldn't you like to learn and sing My verse just as much as the one which Sorrow taught you?"

"Yes," said Much-Afraid thankfully, and taking His hand again, "certainly I will learn it and sing about the cunning master hand which takes such pains with me."

By this time the mist had actually melted right away and the sun, shining brilliantly, was making the dripping trees

# Glorious Inheritance

Are there any traces of shame on your face or in your soul today because you were caught in a bedraggled or muddy condition? Make the Lord God your refuge. Snuggle under His wings and allow Him to soothe you.

> *"How precious is Your steadfast love, O God!*
> *The children of men take refuge and put their*
> *trust under the shadow of Your wings"*
> (Ps. 36:7 AMP).

Realize that He sees you as mature and perfected. Apply Second Corinthians 5:7 to yourself:

> *"For we walk by faith, not by sight"*
> (2 Cor. 5:7 NKJ).

Lord, my allegiance is to You, not to what I see. I rejoice with You over the results that *You* see.

This is easier to do when you realize that you are God's inheritance. Ask Him to enlighten the eyes of your heart to grasp this awesome truth.

> *"By having the eyes of your heart flooded with light,*
> *so that you can know and understand the hope to*
> *which He has called you and how rich is His*
> *glorious inheritance in the saints—His set-apart ones"*
> (Eph. 1:18 AMP).

and grass sparkle with joy and brightness. All three thankfully accepted the suggestion of the Shepherd that they should sit down for a short time and rest and rejoice in the sunshine. Sorrow and Suffering withdrew a little, as they always did when the Shepherd was present, leaving Him to talk with Much-Afraid alone. She told Him all the dismal tale of their long wanderings in the mist, the way Resentment, Bitterness, and Self-Pity had been bothering her and her fear that perhaps, after all, they had wandered from the path and lost their way.

"Did you really think that I would let you stray from the right path to the High Places without doing anything to warn you or to prevent it?" asked the Shepherd quietly.

She looked at him sorrowfully and said with a sigh, "When Resentment and the others are shouting at me I am almost ready to believe anything, no matter how preposterous."

"You had better become a singer," said He, smiling. "Then you won't hear what they say to you. Ask Sorrow and Suffering if they have any more songs which they can teach you. Do you find them good guides, Much-Afraid?"

She looked at Him earnestly and nodded her head. "Yes, very good. I never could have believed it possible, Shepherd, but in a way, I have come to love them. When I first saw them they looked so terrifyingly strong and stern, and I was sure that they would be rough with me and just drag me along without caring how I felt. How I dreaded it, but they have dealt with me very, very kindly indeed. I think they must have learned to be so gentle and patient with me by seeing Your gentleness.

"I never could have managed without them," she went on gratefully, "and the queer thing is I have a feeling that they really like helping an ugly little cripple like me in this way. They do truly want to get me up to the High Places, not just because it is the commandment which You have given them, but also because they want a horrid coward like myself to get there and be changed. You know, Shepherd, it makes a great difference in

# Humble Confession

Humbly turn to your Lord today and tell Him all that is on your heart. He loves to hear it. You will be edified also—such a release is healthy for your emotional well-being. Thank Him that His leading is always perfect.

> *"...Listen to and obey My voice, and I will be*
> *your God, and you shall be My people; and*
> *walk in the whole way that I command*
> *you, that it may be well with you"*
> (Jer. 7:23 AMP).

Has He warned you lately of an upcoming threat and you failed to listen? If so, repent and ask His forgiveness. Thank Him for the promise in His Word:

> *"The Lord upholds all those [of His own]*
> *who are falling, and raises up all those*
> *who are bowed down"*
> (Ps. 145:14 AMP).

> *"If we confess our sins, He is faithful and just*
> *and will forgive us our sins and purify*
> *us from all unrighteousness"*
> (1 John 1:9 NIV).

Lord, I ask that You use the consequences of my disobedience to press out of me all that caused me to not listen and obey.

my feelings toward them not to look upon them any longer with dread, but as friends who want to help me. I know it seems ridiculous, but sometimes I get the feeling that they really love me and want to go with me of their own free will."

As she finished speaking she looked up in His face and was surprised to see that He actually looked as though He were trying not to laugh. He said nothing for a moment or two, but turned slightly so that He could look round at the two guides. Much-Afraid looked too.

They were sitting apart in the background and were unaware that they were being watched. They sat close to one another and were looking away up to the mountains toward the High Places. Their veils had been thrown back, although she still could not see their faces because their backs were toward the Shepherd and herself. She was struck by the fact that they seemed even taller and stronger than when she had first seen them waiting for her at the foot of the mountains.

There was something almost indescribably majestic about them at that moment, a sort of radiant eagerness expressed in their attitude. They were talking quickly to one another, but their voices were so low that she could not catch what they were saying. Was it possible—yes it was! They were actually laughing! That they were talking about something which thrilled them with eagerness and expectation, she felt quite sure.

The Shepherd watched them for a few moments without speaking, then He turned back to Much-Afraid. His eyes were laughing at her, but He said quite gravely, "Yes, I really believe you are right, Much-Afraid. They do look to Me as though they really enjoy their task, and perhaps even feel a little affection for the one they serve." Then He really did laugh out loud.

Sorrow and Suffering dropped the veils back over their faces and looked round to see what was happening, but the Shepherd had something more to say before He sped them farther on the journey.

# Trusting Embrace

Have there been people, circumstances, or things in your life that you have been reluctant to embrace because they seemed hard and completely unbeneficial, even in the hands of your God? If so, could you be questioning God's ways, His methods, or His vessels? If something does not look honorable or usable, we tend to criticize or assume the responsibility for the situation rather than say:

*"And we know that God causes all things to work*
*together for good to those who love God,*
*to those who are called according to His purpose"*
(Rom. 8:28 NAS).

To embrace things like Sorrow and Suffering as Much-Afraid did, we must rise above our perspective and accept what is difficult, trusting Jesus to work things together for good.

*"Let not your heart be troubled: ye believe*
*in God, believe also in Me"*
(Jn. 14:1 KJV).

Lord, I embrace what You have for me. Thank You for helping me to do so.

The laughter died out of His face, and very seriously He asked, "Do you love Me enough to be able to trust Me completely, Much-Afraid?"

She looked at Him in the usual startled fashion so natural to her whenever she sensed that He was preparing her for a new test, then faltered, "You know that I do love You, Shepherd, as much as my cold little heart is capable. You know that I love You and that I long to trust You as much as I love You, that I long both to love and trust You still more."

"Would You be willing to trust Me," He asked, "even if everything in the wide world seemed to say that I was deceiving you—indeed, that I had deceived you all along?"

She looked at Him in perplexed amazement. "Why, yes," she said, "I'm sure I would, because one thing I know to be true, it is impossible that You should tell a lie. It is impossible that You should deceive me. I know that I am often very frightened at the things which You ask me to do," she added shamefacedly and apologetically, "but I could never doubt You in that way. It's myself I am afraid of, never of You, and though everyone in the world should tell me that You had deceived me, I should know it was impossible.

"O Shepherd," she implored, "don't tell me that You think I really doubt You, even when I am most afraid and cowardly and despicably weak. You know—You know I trust You. In the end I know I shall be able to say Thy gentleness hath made me great."

He said nothing for a little, only looked down very tenderly, almost pitifully at the figure now crouching at His feet. Then, after a time, He said very quietly, "Much-Afraid, supposing I really did deceive you? What then?"

It was then her turn to be quite silent, trying to grasp this impossible thing He was suggesting and to think what her answer would be. What then? Would it be that she could never trust, never love Him again? Would she have to be alive in the

# Deepest Desire

With gratefulness welling up in your soul for who your God is, sit in Jesus' presence and allow Him to draw you to Himself. Listen to Him carefully. If He were to specifically ask you, "Would you be willing to trust Me even if everything in the wide world seemed to say that I was deceiving you—indeed, that I had deceived you all along," what would you say? Take a moment before coming to a conclusion. Could you say with the psalmist:

*"Whom have I in heaven but You? And earth has nothing I desire besides You"*
(Ps. 73:25 NIV).

Could you say:

*"…You are my Lord; apart from You I have no good thing"*
(Ps. 16:2 NIV).

Express your conclusion to Him in complete honesty, knowing that He already knows anyway. His love for you is not affected by your answer. Give Him your heart—whatever place or condition it is in.

Lord, I thank You for receiving me as I am. I bare my heart before You.

world where there was no Shepherd, only a mirage and a broken lovely dream? To know that she had been deceived by One she was certain could not deceive? To lose Him?

Suddenly she burst into a passion of weeping, then after a little while looked straight up into His face and said, "My Lord—if You can deceive me, You may. It can make no difference. I must love You as long as I continue to exist. I cannot live without loving You."

He laid His hands on her head, then with a touch more tender and gentle than anything she had ever felt before, repeated as though to Himself, "If I can, I may deceive her." Then without another word He turned and went away.

Much-Afraid picked up a little icy-cold pebble which was lying on the ground where He had stood, put it in her bag, then tremblingly rejoined Sorrow and Suffering, and they continued their journey.

# Unwavering Trust

If your world did not have your Shepherd, the Lord Jesus, in it, how would it be different? Or stated another way, if Jesus was suddenly removed from your life, what would be different? Think before you answer. Be honest. Can you say with Much-Afraid, "My Lord, if You deceive me, You may. It can make no difference. I must love You as long as I continue to exist. I cannot live without loving You." Can you say with Esther:

*"...if I perish, I perish"*
(Esther 4:16 KJV).

Or does it sound better to say, "I could never doubt You. It's myself I am afraid of, never You." It is true that we are not to trust ourselves and to continually rely upon Jesus. But it is easy to cross over into unbelief by thinking He is not capable of directing us. That is not a lack of trusting in ourselves; it is not trusting Him. Jesus cannot and will not deceive you because He is holy and pure. We may feel deceived because of our lack of perspective. The issue is, will we trust Him no matter what?

# CHAPTER 13

# In the Valley of Loss

The mist had cleared from the mountains and the sun was shining, and as a consequence the way seemed much more pleasant and easy than it had for a very long time. The path still led them along the side of the mountain rather than upward, but one day, on turning a corner, they found themselves looking down into a deep valley. To their surprise, their path actually plunged straight down the mountainside toward it, exactly as at the beginning of the journey when Much-Afraid had been led down into Egypt.

All three halted and looked first at one another, then down into the valley and across to the other side. There the ascent was as steep and even higher than the Precipice of Injury and they saw that to go down and then ascend again would not only require an immense amount of strength and effort, but also take a very long time.

Much-Afraid stood and stared, and at that moment experienced the sharpest and keenest test which she had yet encountered on the journey. Was she to be turned aside once again, but in an even more terrible way than ever before? By now they had ascended far higher than ever before. Indeed, if only the path they were following would begin to ascend, they could not doubt that they would soon be at the snowline and approaching the real High Places, where no enemies could follow and where the healing streams flowed.

# Righteousness Revealed

In the quietness of the moment, gently turn to your Lord. Ponder the fact that you are as righteous as Jesus. No matter what happened in the past, is happening now, or will ever happen, your righteousness does not depend on it! Let the Word convince you:

*"For our sake He made Christ [virtually] to be sin Who knew no sin, so that in and through Him we might become [endued with, viewed as in and examples of] the righteousness of God—what we ought to be, approved and acceptable and in right relationship with Him, by His goodness"*
(2 Cor. 5:21 AMP).

What reservations or questions do you have? Ask the Father to enlighten the eyes of your understanding so you can enjoy your righteousness today.

Lord, enable me to comprehend the wonderful truth that You are my righteousness! Let it sink down into the depths of my spirit.

Expect Him, by faith, to answer you. Perhaps He will reply in a way you do not expect or even think about.

Now instead of that the path was leading them down into a valley as low as the Valley of Humiliation itself. All the height which they had gained after their long and toilsome journey must now be lost and they would have to begin all over again, just as though they had never made a start so long ago and endured so many difficulties and tests.

As she looked down into the depths of the valley the heart of Much-Afraid went numb. For the first time on the journey she actually asked herself if her relatives had not been right after all and if she ought not to have attempted to follow the Shepherd. How could one follow a person who asked so much, who demanded such impossible things, who took away everything? If she went down there, as far as getting to the High Places was concerned she must lose everything she had gained on the journey so far. She would be no nearer receiving the promise than when she started out from the Valley of Humiliation.

For one black, awful moment Much-Afraid really considered the possibility of following the Shepherd no longer, of turning back. She need not go on. There was absolutely no compulsion about it. She had been following this strange path with her two companions as guides simply because it was the Shepherd's choice for her. It was not the way which she naturally wanted to go. Now she could make her own choice. Her sorrow and suffering could be ended at once, and she could plan her life in the way she liked best, without the Shepherd.

During that awful moment or two it seemed to Much-Afraid that she was actually looking into an abyss of horror, into an existence in which there was no Shepherd to follow or to trust or to love—no Shepherd at all, nothing but her own horrible self. Ever after, it seemed that she had looked straight down into Hell. At the end of that moment Much-Afraid shrieked—there is no other word for it.

"Shepherd," she shrieked, "Shepherd! Shepherd! Help me! Where are You? Don't leave me!" Next instant she was clinging to Him, trembling from head to food, and sobbing over and over again, "You may do anything, Shepherd. You may ask anything— only don't let me turn back. O my Lord, don't let me leave You.

# Buried Treasure

Have you ever been in a place that felt like "the valley of the shadow of death" or stared into a future where all of your dreams and hopes appeared to be dashed into a zillion little pieces? Have you ever been accused of being a "turkey" for following God, when He says you are an "eagle"? We never anticipate such times, and we never ask for them, but to one degree or another they come to all of us. At those moments it is hard to accept with our minds that we need to lay down our lives for Jesus. But to have that truth worked out through our emotions, in actual experience, makes it feel like a whole new truth.

*"He who has found his life shall lose it, and he who has lost his life for My sake shall find it"*
(Mt. 10:39 NAS).

When these times come, knowing that God is working a truth through your entire being often makes the death to self less frightening. So release your emotions to Jesus. Let Him be your courage. He is with you even when it seems that He's not.

Lord Jesus, my emotions are numb. It seems like You are really requiring too much this time! Nevertheless, I give You my entire being.

Entreat me not to leave Thee nor to return from following after Thee." Then as she continued to cling to Him she sobbed out, "If You can deceive me, my Lord, about the promise and the hinds' feet and the new name or anything else, You may, indeed You may; only don't let me leave You. Don't let anything turn me back. This path looked so wrong I could hardly believe it was the right one," and she sobbed bitterly.

He lifted her up, supported her by His arm, and with His own hand wiped the tears from her cheeks, then said in His strong, cheery voice, "There is no question of your turning back, Much-Afraid. No one, not even your own shrinking heart, can pluck you out of My hand. Don't you remember what I told you before? 'This delay is not unto death but for the glory of God.' You haven't forgotten already the lesson you have been learning, have you?

"It is no less true now that 'what I do thou knowest not now, but thou shalt know hereafter.' My sheep hear My voice, and they follow Me. It is perfectly safe for you to go on in this way even though it looks so wrong, and now I give you another promise: Thine ears shall hear a word behind thee saying, 'This is the way, walk ye in it,' when ye turn to the right hand or to the left."

He paused a moment, and she still leaned against Him, speechless with thankfulness and relief at His presence. Then He went on. "Will you bear this too, Much-Afraid? Will you suffer yourself to lose or to be deprived of all that you have gained on this journey to the High Places? Will you go down this path of forgiveness into the Valley of Loss, just because it is the way that I have chosen for you? Will you still trust and still love Me?"

She was still clinging to Him, and now repeated with all her heart the words of another woman tested long ago. "Entreat me not to leave Thee, or to return from following after Thee: for whither Thou goest I will go; Thy people shall be my people and Thy God my God." She paused and faltered a moment, then went on in a whisper, "And where Thou diest, will I die, and there will I be buried. The Lord do so to me, and more also, if aught but death part Thee and me" (Ruth 1:16,17).

# Reassuring Rest

What is hell? Is it not the absence of God? There is, of course, a literal hell, but partly what makes it hell is the absence of God's presence. Ask God to give you a glimpse into a life where there is nothing except your own horrible self apart from Him. Then run into His welcoming, loving arms and rest for a while. Meditate upon the following words of Jesus to you:

> "All whom My Father has given (entrusted) to Me
> will come to Me; and him who comes to Me I will
> most certainly not cast out—I will never, no never
> reject one of them who comes to Me. For I have come
> down from heaven, not to do My own will and purpose;
> but to do the will and purpose of Him Who sent Me.
> And this is the will of Him Who sent Me, that I should
> not lose any of all that He has given Me…"
> (Jn. 6:37-39 AMP).

Praise Him for

> "…the glorious riches of this mystery, which is
> Christ in you, the hope of glory"
> (Col. 1:27 NIV).

Lord Jesus, life apart from You is the most frightening thing in all the world. Entreat me not to leave You nor to return from following after You.

So another altar was built at the top of the descent into the Valley of Loss and another stone added to those in the bag she still carried in her bosom. After that they began the downward journey, and as they went she heard her two guides singing softly:

> *O whither is thy Beloved gone,*
> *Thou fairest among women?*
> *Where dost thou think he has turned aside?*
> *That we may seek him with thee.*

The Shepherd Himself sang the next verse:

> *He is gone down into his garden,*
> *To the beds of spices sweet,*
> *For he feedeth among the lilies,*
> *'Tis there we are wont to meet.*

Then Much-Afraid herself sang the last two verses, and her heart was so full of joy that even her unmelodious voice seemed changed and sounded as sweet as the others.

> *So I went down into the garden,*
> *The valley of buds and fruits,*
> *To see if the pomegranates budded,*
> *To look at the vinestock shoots.*
>
> *And my soul in a burst of rapture,*
> *Or ever I was aware,*
> *Sped swifter than chariot horses,*
> *For lo! he was waiting there.*

(Cant. 6:1-3)

Considering how steep it was, the descent down into the valley seemed surprisingly easy, but perhaps that was because Much-Afraid desired with her whole will to make it in a way that would satisfy and please the Shepherd. The awful glimpse down into the abyss of an existence without Him had so staggered and appalled her heart that she felt she could never be quite the same again. However, it had opened her eyes to the

# Inseparable Love

Are you facing a delay today, or what looks like a Valley of Loss? Are you willing to forgive Jesus for choosing a path that you do not understand or that brings pain with it? Consider its purpose, which the Lord spoke through Paul in Philippians 3:10:

> *"That I may know Him, and the power of His resurrection and the fellowship of His sufferings, being conformed to His death"*
> (NAS).

As you keep a listening ear and an open heart tuned toward Him, say with Ruth:

> *"...Don't urge me to leave you or to turn back from you. Where you go I will go, and where you stay I will stay. Your people will be my people and your God my God. Where you die I will die, and there I will be buried. May the Lord deal with me, be it ever so severely, if anything but death separates you and me"*
> (Ruth 1:16-17 NIV).

O Lord, I embrace my present disappointment as a delay that is not unto death, but is for the glory of God. I will bear the pain involved, knowing that life is being brought forth.

fact that right down in the depths of her own heart she really had but one passionate desire, not for the things which the Shepherd had promised, but for Himself. All she wanted was to be allowed to follow Him forever.

Other desires might clamor strongly and fiercely nearer the surface of her nature, but she knew now that down in the core of her own being she was so shaped that nothing could fit, fill, or satisfy her heart but He Himself. "Nothing else really matters," she said to herself, "only to love Him and to do what He tells me. I don't know quite why it should be so, but it is. All the time it is suffering to love and sorrow to love, but it is lovely to love Him in spite of this, and if I should cease to do so, I should cease to exist." So, as has been said, they reached the valley very quickly.

The next surprising thing was that though the valley did seem at first a little like a prison after the strong bracing air of the mountains, it turned out to be a wonderfully beautiful and peaceful place, very green and with flowers covering the fields and the banks of the river which flowed quietly through it.

Strangely enough, down there in the Valley of Loss, Much-Afraid felt more rested, more peaceful, and more content than anywhere else on the journey. It seemed, too, that her two companions also underwent a strange transformation. They still held her hands, but there was neither suffering nor sorrow in the touch. It was as though they walked close beside her and went hand in hand simply for friendship's sake and for the joy of being together.

Also, they sang continually, sometimes in a language quite different from the one which she had learned from them, but when she asked the meaning of the words they only smiled and shook their heads. This is one of the many songs which all three sang down in the Valley of Loss, and it was another from the collection in the old songbook which Much-Afraid so loved.

# Abiding Adoration

Saint Augustine, a church leader in the first century, correctly stated, "Thou hast formed us for Thyself, O Lord, and our hearts are restless until they find their rest in Thee." How can we rest, though, if our attention is pulled in different directions? Suffering and Sorrow proved their friendship to us by stripping away all that would distract us from our Lord to show us what is truly important to us and what god we are serving. Then we can say with David, the psalmist:

> *"One thing have I asked of the Lord, that will I seek after, inquire for and [insistently] require, that I may dwell in the house of the Lord [in His presence] all the days of my life, to behold and gaze upon the beauty [the sweet attractiveness and the delightful loveliness] of the Lord, and to meditate, consider and inquire in His temple"*
> (Ps. 27:4 AMP).

Using words from this verse, pray to Jesus what's on your heart.

*I am my Love's and he is mine,*
*And this is his desire,*
*That with his beauty I may shine*
*In radiant attire.*
*And this will be—when all of me*
*Is pruned and purged with fire.*

*Come, my Beloved, let us go*
*Forth to the waiting field;*
*And where thy choicest fruit trees grow,*
*Thy pruning knife now wield*
*That at thy will and through thy skill*
*Their richest store may yield.*

*And spices give a sweet perfume,*
*And vines show tender shoots,*
*And all my trees burst forth in bloom,*
*Fair buds from bitter roots.*
*There will not I my love deny,*
*But yield thee pleasant fruits.*

(Cant. 7:10-13)

It is true that when Much-Afraid looked at the mountains on the other side of the valley she wondered how they would ever manage to ascend them, but she found herself content to wait restfully and to wander in the valley as long as the Shepherd chose. One thing in particular comforted her; after the hardness and slipperiness of the way on the mountains, where she had stumbled and limped so painfully, she found that in those quiet green fields she could actually walk without stumbling, and could not feel her wounds and scars and stiffness at all.

All this seemed a little strange because, of course, she really was in the Valley of Loss. Also, apparently, she was farther from the High Places than ever before. She asked the Shepherd about it one day, for the loveliest part of all was that

# Thankful Contentment

Turn to your Lord today with a patience that waits for His sure deliverance. Set your mind to embrace whatever today brings as a gift from Him. Decide not to resist, resent, or rebel no matter what comes your way. As you rest with Him in the "fields" of refreshment He provides, thank Him for the contentment His Lordship produces.

*"[And it is, indeed, a source of immense profit, for] godliness accompanied with contentment—that contentment which is a sense of inward sufficiency—is great and abundant gain"*
(1 Tim. 6:6 AMP).

Like Paul, we need to learn to be content wherever and however we find ourselves.

*"Not that I am implying that I was in any personal want, for I have learned how to be content (satisfied to the point where I am not disturbed or disquieted) in whatever state I am"*
(Phil. 4:11 AMP).

Thank You, Jesus, for the contentment that comes when I cease wrestling with You and flow with Your leadership.

He often walked with them down there, saying with a beautiful smile that it was one of His favorite haunts.

In answer to her question, He said, "I am glad that you are learning to appreciate the valley too, but I think it was the altar which you built at the top, Much-Afraid, which has made it so easy for you."

This also rather puzzled her, for she said, "But I have noticed that after the other altars which You told me to build, the way has generally seemed harder and more testing than before."

Again He smiled, but only remarked quietly that the important thing about altars was that they made possibilities of apparent impossibilities, and that it was nice that on this occasion it had brought her peace and not a great struggle. She noticed that He looked at her keenly and rather strangely as He spoke, and though there was a beautiful gentleness in the look, there was also something else which she had seen before, but still did not understand. She thought it held a mixture of two things, not exactly pity—no, that was the wrong word, but a look of wonderful compassion together with unflinching determination.

When she realized that, she thought of some words which one of the Shepherd's servants had spoken down in the Valley of Humiliation before ever the Shepherd had called her to the High Places. He had said, "Love is beautiful, but it is also terrible—terrible in its determination to allow nothing blemished or unworthy to remain in the beloved."

When she remembered this, Much-Afraid thought with a little shiver in her heart, "He will never be content until He makes me what He is determined that I ought to be," and because she was still Much-Afraid and not yet ready to change her name, she added with a pang of fear, "I wonder what He plans to do next, and if it will hurt very much indeed?"

# Conforming Image

Come into Jesus' presence and at once gently sink down before God, embracing His wonderful compassion together with His unflinching determination to make you like Himself. Thank Him that His Word assures us He chose us before time began because He knew He could make us holy and blameless.

> *"Even as [in His love] He chose us—actually picked us out for Himself as His own—in Christ before the foundation of the world; that we should be holy (consecrated and set apart for Him) and blameless in His sight, even above reproach, before Him in love"*
> (Eph. 1:4 AMP).

Consider the insults, threats, and injustices that Jesus endured. Yet He continually entrusted Himself to the Father. Micah 7:18 assures us that we can trust God as much as Jesus did.

> *"Who is a God like You, Who forgives iniquity and passes over the transgression of the remnant of His heritage? He retains not His anger for ever, because He delights in mercy and loving-kindness"*
> (AMP).

My Lord, I rest in Your love and I put my confidence in Your determination to remove all my blemishes, that I might be Your beloved forever!

# CHAPTER 14

# The Place of Anointing

As it happened, the next thing which the Shepherd had planned was very beautiful indeed. Not long after this conversation the path finished its winding way through the valley and led them to the foot of the mountains on the other side to a place where they rose up like a wall, far higher and steeper than the Precipice of Injury.

However, when Much-Afraid and her two companions reached this place they found the Shepherd waiting for them beside a little hut, and lo! just where the cliffs were steepest and highest was an overhead cable suspended between that spot and the summit far above. On this cable hung chairs, in which two could sit side by side and be swung right up to the top without any effort on their part at all. It is true that at first the very sight of these frail-looking aerial chairs swinging along so high above the ground made Much-Afraid feel giddy and panicky. She felt she could never voluntarily place herself in one of them and be swung up that frightful-looking precipice, with only a little foot-rest and nothing to prevent her casting herself out of the chair if the urge should come upon her.

However, that passed almost at once, for the Shepherd smiled and said, "Come, Much-Afraid, we will seat ourselves in the first two chairs and Sorrow and Suffering will follow in the next. All you have to do is to trust yourself to the chair and be carried

# Righteous Rest

My Lord, what beautiful places of refreshment You provide for me as I rest under Your nurturing wing. I'm just going to bask for a while and rest upon the truth that my righteousness is based on a relationship with You—not on whether I still have a pang of fear now and then, feel righteous, or do the right thing.

*"This is the heritage of the servants of the Lord, and their righteousness is of Me, saith the Lord"*
(Is. 54:17b KJV).

I am beginning to know You; that You are loving, faithful, and in control. I thank You that You *never* ask me to do anything You are not doing with and in me. When You require something of me, You are really requiring it of Yourself in me and You can and will do it. All You need is my agreement and cooperation. So, Lord, I choose to enter the place of rest You have for me today.

It may be hard to comprehend, but you don't have inferior righteousness. Receive and rest in the righteousness He has put to your account.

in perfect safety up to the place to which I wish to take you and without any struggling and striving on your part."

Much-Afraid stepped into one of the seats, and the Shepherd sat beside her while the two companions occupied the next pair. In a minute they were moving smoothly and steadily toward the High Places which had looked so impossibly out of reach, supported entirely from above, and with nothing to do but rest and enjoy the marvelous view. Though the chairs swung a little in places, they felt no giddiness at all, but went upward and still upward until the valley below looked like a little green carpet and the gleaming white peaks of the Kingdom of Love towered around and above them. Soon they were far above the place to which they had climbed on the mountains opposite, and still they swung along.

When at last they stepped out of the aerial chairs they were in a place more beautiful than anything Much-Afraid had seen before, for though these were not the real High Places of the Kingdom of Love, they had reached the borderland. All around were alps with grassy meadows almost smothered in flowers. Little streams gurgled and splashed between banks of kingcups, while buttercups and cowslips, violets and pink primulae carpeted the ground. Clumps of delicate purple soldanella grew in vivid clusters, and all over the fields, glowing bright as gems, were gentians, more blue than the sky at midday, looking like jewels on a royal robe.

Above were peaks of pure white snow which towered up into a cloudless sky like a roof of sapphire and turquoise. The sun shone so brilliantly it almost seemed that one could see the flowers pushing their way up through the earth and unfolding themselves to receive the glory of its rays. Cowbells and goatbells sounded in every direction, and a multitude of bird notes filled the air, but above the rest was one voice louder and more dominant than them all, and which seemed to fill the whole region.

It was the voice of a mighty waterfall, leaping down another great cliff which towered above them, and whose rushing waters

# Far Above

Let Jesus lift you to a place far above the things that normally tend to rob you of strength and dignity. As the flowers push their way up through the earth and unfold themselves to receive the glory of the sun's rays, so are we to enjoy the life, the eternal life, that our Lord bestows upon us. Eternal life does not begin when we arrive in Heaven; it is the life of Jesus to be lived and enjoyed now, as a way of life. His life is to be our life, 24 hours a day, moment by moment.

> *"And this is what He promised us—even eternal life"*
> (1 John 2:25 NIV).

> *"Now this is eternal life: that they may know You, the only true God, and Jesus Christ, whom You have sent"*
> (Jn. 17:3 NIV).

Lord Jesus, I accept today's happenings as a platform from which You will reveal Yourself. My hands are outstretched to whatever lies ahead. Thank You for Your life, eternal life, flowing through me.

sprang from the snows in the High Places themselves. It was so unspeakably lovely that neither Much-Afraid nor her companions could utter a word, but stood, drawing deep breaths and filling their lungs with the spicy, pine-scented mountain air.

As they wandered forward, they stooped down at every other step, gently touching the jewel-like flowers or dabbling their fingers in the splashing brooks. Sometimes they just stood still amid the profusion of shining beauty around them and laughed aloud with pure joy. The Shepherd led them across meadows where the warm, scented grass grew nearly waist high, toward the mighty waterfall.

At the foot of the cliffs they found themselves standing in cool shadows with a light spray sometimes splashing their faces, and there the Shepherd bade them stand and look up. There stood Much-Afraid, a tiny figure at the foot of the mighty cliffs, looking up at the great, never-ending rush of waters as they cast themselves down from the High Places. She thought that never before had she seen anything so majestic or so terrifyingly lovely. The height of the rocky lip, over which the waters cast themselves to be dashed in pieces on the rocks below, almost terrified her. At the foot of the fall, the thunderous voice of the waters seemed almost deafening, but it seemed also to be filled with meaning, grand and awesome, beautiful beyond expression.

As she listened, Much-Afraid realized that she was hearing the full majestic harmonies, the whole orchestra as it were, playing the original of the theme song which all the little streamlets had sung far below in the Valley of Humiliation. Now it was uttered by thousands upon thousands of voices, but with grander harmonies than anything heard down in the valleys, yet still the same song.

*From the heights we leap and go*
*To the valleys down below,*
*Always answering to the call,*
*To the lowest place of all.*

# Joyous Abandon

Have your eyes feasted recently upon any breath-taking beauty like the mighty waterfall that Much-Afraid gazed upon? Can you see your relation to the creation that you viewed? The waterfall joyfully abandoned itself, but the thought of "casting ourselves down" or humbling ourselves is repulsive to our fleshly nature. A fallen nature desires to promote one's self, not lay down or crucify its self-centered desires. However, God says just the opposite.

*"Humble yourselves before the Lord,*
*and He will lift you up"*
(Jas. 4:10 NIV).

Lord Jesus, it is terrifying to turn loose of self-promotion and let my ways be dashed upon the rocks of life. But there is an underlying beauty and excitement that says this is the path of life. I choose today to take the risk of doing it Your way.

Ponder the beauty in a waterfall's casting itself down. See yourself abandoning your self life just as joyously.

"Much-Afraid," said the Shepherd's voice in her ear, "what do you think of this fall of great waters in their abandonment of self-giving?"

She trembled a little as she answered. "I think they are beautiful and terrible beyond anything which I ever saw before."

"Why terrible?" He asked.

"It is the leap which they have to make, the awful height from which they must cast themselves down to the depths beneath, there to be broken on the rocks. I can hardly bear to watch it."

"Look closer," He said again. "Let your eye follow just one part of the water from the moment when it leaps over the edge until it reaches the bottom."

Much-Afraid did so, and then almost gasped with wonder. Once over the edge, the waters were like winged things, alive with joy, so utterly abandoned to the ecstasy of giving themselves that she could almost have supposed that she was looking at a host of angels floating down on rainbow wings, singing with rapture as they went.

She gazed and gazed, then said, "It looks as though they think it is the loveliest movement in all the world, as though to cast oneself down is to abandon oneself to ecstasy and joy indescribable."

"Yes," answered the Shepherd in a voice vibrant with joy and thanksgiving, "I am glad that you have noticed that, Much-Afraid. These are the Falls of Love, flowing from the High Places in the Kingdom above. You will meet with them again. Tell Me, does the joy of the waters seem to end when they break on the rock below?"

Again Much-Afraid looked where He pointed, and noticed that the lower the water fell, the lighter it seemed to grow, as though it really were lighting down on wings. On reaching the rocks below, all the waters flowed together in a glorious host,

# Divine Humility

Jesus never asks us to do anything that He has not experienced, and thereby sets our example. Before asking us to humble ourselves in abandoning ourselves to Him, He first humbled Himself.

*"Have this attitude in yourselves which was also in Christ Jesus, who, although He existed in the form of God, did not regard equality with God a thing to be grasped, but emptied Himself, taking the form of a bondservant, and being made in the likeness of men. And being found in appearance as a man, He humbled Himself by becoming obedient to the point of death, even death on a cross"*
(Phil. 2:5-8 NAS).

Jesus stooped even lower than man fell. He laid down His Kingship so we might be released from our sins to live life with Him as we were created to live.

*"And He Himself bore our sins in His body on the cross, that we might die to sin and live to righteousness; for by His wounds you were healed"*
(1 Pet. 2:24 NAS).

Lord Jesus, I choose to answer the call to go to the lowest place of all–the call to abandonment of self-giving.

forming an exuberant, rushing torrent which swirled triumphantly around and over the rocks.

Laughing and shouting at the top of their voices, they hurried still lower and lower, down through the meadows to the next precipice and the next glorious crisis of their self-giving. From there they would again cast themselves down to the valleys far below. Far from suffering from the rocks, it seemed as though every obstacle in the bed of the torrent was looked upon as another object to be overcome and another lovely opportunity to find a way over or around it. Everywhere was the sound of water, laughing, exulting, shouting in jubilation.

"At first sight perhaps the leap does look terrible," said the Shepherd, "but as you can see, the water itself finds no terror in it, no moment of hesitation or shrinking, only joy unspeakable, and full of glory, because it is the movement natural to it. Self-giving is its life. It has only one desire, to go down and down and give itself with no reserve or holding back of any kind. You can see that as it obeys that glorious urge the obstacles which look so terrifying are perfectly harmless, and indeed only add to the joy and glory of the movement." When He had said this, He led them back to the sunny fields, and gently told them that for the next few days they were to rest themselves there in preparation for the last part of their journey.

On hearing these words, "the last part of the journey," Much-Afraid felt almost as though she would sink to the ground with happiness. Moreover, the Shepherd Himself remained there with them the whole time. Not for a single hour was He apart from them, but walked and talked with them. He taught them many things about the Kingdom to which they were going, and it was as though grace flowed from His lips and sweet ointments and spices were diffused wherever He went. How thankfully Much-Afraid would have stayed there for the rest of her life; she would have cared no more about reaching the High Places, had it not been that she still walked on crooked feet, still had a twisted mouth, still had a fearing heart.

# Destiny's Leap

The anticipation of the leap into complete self-abandonment to Jesus carries with it more torment and terror than the leap of faith itself. All the fears from our sinful nature and all the enemy's lies are ignited to keep us from helplessly depending on God, who is our life! Yet to cast oneself down in abandonment to Jesus is the loveliest movement in all the world. In fact, our progress in the Christian life is in direct proportion to the degree we humble ourselves in complete, dependent abandonment upon Him. Our example in this case is John the Baptist, who said:

*"He must increase, but I must decrease—He must grow more prominent, I must grow less so"*
(Jn. 3:30 AMP).

Every time we lay aside what we want to do in our flesh and decide instead to let the Lord have His way through our self-giving, a few more links in the chains that bind us are broken. So instead of the annihilation we feared, we are released to live the life we were designed to live.

Lord Jesus, I want more of You and less of me. I choose to give myself to You.

It was not, however, that the sun always shone, even there on that borderland of the High Places. There were days of mist when all the gleaming peaks were completely blotted out by a curtain of cloud, so that if one had never seen them it would have been impossible to be sure that they really existed and were round about, quite close at hand, towering high above the mist and clouds into the clear blue sky above.

Every now and again, however, there would be a rent in the veil of mist, and then, as though framed in an open window, would appear a dazzling whiteness. For a moment one of the vanished peaks would gleam through the opening as if to say, "Be of good courage, we are all here, even though you cannot see us." Then the mist would swirl together again and the window in heaven would close.

On one such occasion the Shepherd said to Much-Afraid, "When you continue your journey there may be much mist and cloud. Perhaps it may even seem as though everything you have seen here of the High Places was just a dream, or the work of your own imagination. But you have seen reality and the mist which seems to swallow it up is the illusion.

"Believe steadfastly in what you have seen. Even if the way up to the High Places appears to be obscured and you are led to doubt whether you are following the right path, remember the promise, 'Thine ears shall hear a word behind thee, saying, This is the way, walk ye in it, when ye turn to the right hand and when ye turn to the left.' Always go forward along the path of obedience as far as you know it until I intervene, even if it seems to be leading you where you fear I could never mean you to go.

"Remember, Much-Afraid, what you have seen before the mist blotted it out. Never doubt that the High Places are there, towering up above you, and be quite sure that whatever happens I mean to bring you up there exactly as I have promised." As He finished speaking another rent appeared in the curtain

# Quiet Rest

*"He makes me lie down in green pastures;*
*He leads me beside quiet waters"*
(Ps. 23:2 NAS).

Is Jesus pulling you aside today to rest for a while in Him? If so, do not resist. After all, He understands our weaknesses more than we do. He knows what causes us to be over fatigued.

*"As a father loves and pities his children, so the*
*Lord loves and pities those who fear Him—with*
*reverence, worship and awe. For He knows our*
*frame; He [earnestly] remembers and imprints*
*[on His heart] that we are dust"*
(Ps. 103:13-14 AMP).

Concentrate upon His loveliness, His love poured out for us, His faithfulness, and how He always does everything right. Let Him minister refreshment, rest, and grace to you. Let what He speaks to you in this rest sustain you during the obscure times. Meditate on His words until their reality sustains you.

Dear Lord Jesus, thank You for understanding my weakness. I rest in Your love and grace.

of mist, and one of the peaks of the High Places framed in blue sky shone down on them.

Before the curtain closed again Much-Afraid stooped down and picked a few of the gentians growing near her feet as a reminder of what she had seen, for, said she to herself, "These actually grew on the lower slopes of the High Places and are an earnest that though the peaks may again become invisible they are there all the time."

On the last day they stayed there the Shepherd did a very wonderful thing. He took Much-Afraid apart by herself and carried her right up to the summit of one of the High Places—in the Kingdom of Love itself. He took her to a high peak, dazzling white, uplifted like a great throne with numberless other peaks grouped round about.

Up there on the mountaintop He was transfigured before her, and she knew Him then to be what she had dimly sensed all along—the King of Love Himself, King of the whole Realm of Love. He was clothed in a white garment glistening in its purity, but over it He wore a robe of purple and blue and scarlet studded with gold and precious gems. On His head He wore the crown royal, but as Much-Afraid bowed herself and knelt at His feet to worship, the face that looked down upon her was that of the Shepherd whom she had loved and followed from the very low places up to the heights. His eyes were still full of gentleness and tenderness but also of strength and power and authority.

Putting out His hand, without a word He lifted her up and led her to a place where on the topmost pinnacle of all they could look right out on the whole realm around them. Standing there beside Him and so happy as to be scarcely conscious of herself at all, Much-Afraid looked out over the Kingdom of Love. Far, far below were the valleys and the plains and the great sea and the desert. She even thought she could recognize the Valley of Humiliation itself, where she had lived so long and had first learned to know the Shepherd, but that seemed so long ago it was like remembering another existence altogether.

# Ecstasy Savored

What a joy it is to spend time with our Lord in our secret place! When we walk with Jesus in an awareness of His presence, whether it is in the ordinary affairs of life or in quiet times with Him in the secret place, He will choose times to let us "taste" and experience Him in a unique, special way. Such times are gifts He loves to bestow upon us when we are seeking only Him, and not a gift or experience. Cherish these times as an earnest or foretaste toward our full heritage.

*"O taste and see that the Lord [our God] is good!*
*Blessed—happy, fortunate [to be envied]—is the*
*man who trusts and takes refuge in Him"*
(Ps. 34:8 AMP).

I praise You, Lord Jesus, for the gifts that You give me today–whether they are small, like the breath I breathe; or large, like experiencing Your gentleness, tenderness, strength, power, or authority in a special way. Lord, I give myself to You that my self-consciousness might be swallowed up in God-consciousness. You are an awesome God with whom to share life.

All around her, in every direction, were the snowy peaks of the High Places. She could see that the bases of all these mountains were extremely precipitous and that higher up they were all clothed with forests, then the green slopes of the higher alps and then the snow. Wherever she looked, the slopes at that season of the year were covered with pure white flowers through whose half-transparent petals the sun shone, turning them to burning whiteness.

In the heart of each flower was a crown of pure gold. These white-robed hosts scented the slopes of the High Places with a perfume sweeter than any she had ever breathed before. All had their faces and golden crowns turned down the mountains as if looking at the valleys, multitudes upon multitudes of them, which no man could number, like "a great cloud of witnesses," all stooping forward to watch what was going on in the world below. Wherever the King and His companion walked, these white-robed flowers bowed beneath their feet and rose again, buoyant and unsullied, but exuding a perfume richer and sweeter than before.

On the utmost pinnacle to which He led her was an altar of pure gold, flashing in the sun with such splendor that she could not look at it but had to turn her eyes away at once, though she did perceive that a fire burned on it and a cloud of smoke perfumed with incense rose from it.

Then the King told her to kneel and with a pair of golden tongs brought a piece of burning coal from off the altar. Touching her with it He said, "Lo! this hath touched thy lips; and thine iniquity is taken away, and thy sin purged" (Isa. 6:7).

It seemed to her that a burning flame of fire too beautiful and too terrible to bear went through her whole being, and Much-Afraid lost consciousness and remembered no more.

When she recovered she found that the Shepherd was carrying her in His arms and they were back on the lower slopes of the borderland. The royal robes and the crown were gone, but something of the expression on His face remained, the look

# Sweet Surrender

The white-robed flowers growing on the High Places that were buoyant and unsullied after being walked on by the Shepherd and Much-Afraid, are perfect examples of what happens when we lay our lives down for Him. Instead of being damaged as we might fear, we rise again to exude a perfume richer and sweeter than before. Is there anything you are hesitant to lay down? Think about it for a moment. Then, with renewed commitment and yieldedness, come to your Lord and say:

You are my King—the King of love and of everything that is lovely.

Kneel before Him knowing that you are kneeling before the One who is gentle and tender, but also full of strength, power, and authority. Express to Him your desire to have burned or pressed out of you all that is not of Him. Hear Him say:

> "...Lo, this has touched your lips; your iniquity
> and guilt are taken away, and your sin is
> completely atoned for and forgiven"
> (Is. 6:7 AMP).

Thank Him for the reality of the experience when it pleases Him to bring it forth. Patiently wait for His timing.

of utmost authority and power. Above them towered the peaks, while everything below was shrouded in cloud and mist.

When He found that she was sufficiently recovered, the Shepherd took her by the hand, and they walked together down into the white mist and through a little wood where the trees were scarcely visible and there was no sound but drops of water splashing onto the ground. When in the middle of the wood a bird burst into song. They could not see it for the mist, but high and clear and indescribably sweet the bird sang and called the same series of little notes over and over again. They seemed to form a phrase constantly repeated, always with a higher chirrup at the end which sounded just like a little chuckling laugh. It seemed to Much-Afraid that this was the song the bird was singing:

> *He's gotten the victory, Hurrah!*
> *He's gotten the victory, Hurrah!*

The wood rang with the jubilant notes, and they both stood still among the dripping trees to listen.

"Much-Afraid," the Shepherd said, "you have had a glimpse of the Kingdom into which I am going to bring you. Tomorrow you and your companions start on the last part of your journey which will bring you thither."

Then with wonderful tenderness He spoke words which seemed too glorious to be true. "Thou hast a little strength and hast kept My word, and hast not denied My name...Behold I will make thine enemies to come and worship before thy feet, and to know that I have loved thee. Behold, I come quickly: Hold fast that which thou hast, that no man take thy crown, and she that overcometh will I make a pillar in the temple of My God, and she shall go no more out: and I will write upon her the name of My God...I will write upon her My new name" (Rev. 3:8-12).

It was then that Much-Afraid took courage to ask Him something which she had never dared ask before. With her hand

# Victory Chorus

"He's gotten the victory, Hurrah!" Can you sing or shout this phrase today? Before you answer, meditate upon what God says to us:

*"But thanks be to God, Who gives us the victory—making us conquerors—through our Lord Jesus Christ"*
(1 Cor. 15:57 AMP).

*"Yet amid all these things we are more than conquerors and gain a surpassing victory through Him Who loved us"*
(Rom. 8:37 AMP).

How can we be "more than conquerors"? Could it be that when we fight in a battle and win, we are said to be a conqueror? But in this case, Jesus has fought the battle and won, and given the victory to us! Wow! The enemy has no chance among us, for we already have the victory in Jesus. Can you, in light of this knowledge, sing the phrase today, "He's gotten the victory, Hurrah!" Make it your victory chorus.

held in His she said, "My Lord, may I ask one thing? Is the time at last soon coming when You will fulfill the promise that You gave me?"

He said very gently, yet with great joy, "Yes—the time is not long now. Dare to begin to be happy. If you will go forward in the way before you, you will soon receive the promise, and I will give you your heart's desire. It is not long now, Much-Afraid."

So they stood in the mist-filled wood, she trembling with hope and unable to say a word, worshiping and wondering if she had seen a vision, or if this thing had really happened. Upon His face was a look which she would not have understood even if she had seen it, but she was too dazed with happiness even to look at Him. High over the dripping trees the little bird still sang his jubilant song, "He's gotten the victory," and then in a burst of trills and chuckles, "Hurrah! Hurrah! Hurrah!"

A little later they were down in the meadows where Sorrow and her sister were waiting for their return. It was time to go forward on the journey, but after the Shepherd had blessed them and was turning to go His way again, Suffering and Sorrow suddenly knelt before Him and asked softly, "Lord, what place is this where we have been resting and refreshing ourselves during these past days?"

He answered very quietly, "This is the place to which I bring My beloved, that they may be anointed in readiness for their burial."

Much-Afraid did not hear these words, for she was walking a little ahead, repeating over and over again, "He said, 'Dare to begin to be happy, for the time is not long now, and I will give you your heart's desire.'"

# Humble Anointing

Which of the following words or phrases would you like to be true of you?

> "...thou hast a little strength, and hast kept My word, and hast not denied My name. ...behold, I will make [your enemies] to come and worship before thy feet, and to know that I have loved thee. ...Behold, I come quickly: hold that fast which thou hast, that no man take thy crown. Him that overcometh will I make a pillar in the temple of My God, and he shall go no more out: and I will write upon him the name of My God...and I will write upon him My new name"
> (Rev. 3:8-9; 11-12 KJV).

Prepare for anointing for burial.

> "Mary therefore took a pound of very costly perfume of pure nard, and anointed the feet of Jesus, and wiped His feet with her hair; and the house was filled with the fragrance of the perfume"
> (Jn. 12:3 NAS).

The Father used Mary to anoint Jesus for His burial. Now you give yourself to Jesus and ask Him to anoint you in any way He chooses. Request that your ministry to others be symbolic of your pouring our your life as oil upon His feet and wiping them with your hair, causing a rich fragrance for His glory.

# CHAPTER 15

# The Floods

The path they followed did not go straight up to the heights but sloped gently up the mountainside. The mist still shrouded everything, and indeed grew a little thicker. All three walked in silence, occupied with different thoughts. Much-Afraid was thinking of the promise the Shepherd so recently had given her, "Behold, I come quickly...and will give thee thy heart's desire." Suffering and Sorrow perhaps were thinking of the answer they had received to the question asked of Him at parting. Whether or not this was so there was no indication, for they walked in complete silence, though the help they gave their lame companion was, had she noticed it, even more gentle and untiring than before.

Toward evening they came to another log cabin standing at the side of the path with the Shepherd's secret mark inscribed upon the door, so they knew that they were to rest there for the night.

Once inside they noticed that someone must have been there quite recently, for a fire was burning brightly on the hearth and a kettle of water was singing on the hob. The table, too, was laid for three, and a supply of bread and fruit upon it. Evidently their arrival had been expected and these kindly preparations made, but of the one who had thus gone in the way before them there was no sign. They washed themselves and then sat down at the table, gave thanks, and ate of

# True Desire

In silence draw near to Jesus, allowing Him to collect, sift, and filter your emotions and thoughts. Consider these words:

*"Behold, I come quickly..."*
(Rev. 3:11 KJV).

*"...He shall give thee the desires of thine heart"*
(Ps. 37:4 KJV).

What do these words ignite within you? Have the things of the world been put in their proper perspective so you are anxious for Him to come quickly? If so, rejoice. Are there things you still want to have or experience before He returns for you? If so, release those things up to Him. What are the desires of your heart? Take time to wade through the debris and search for the true desires of your heart. Now thank Him for His timely and complete preparations for you for each and every occasion and situation in your life, that these desires might be fulfilled. Do not be surprised, though, if He works differently than you expect and you don't recognize His hand at first.

My Lord, I release my life to You. Thank You that the rest You have provided absorbs my weariness!

the prepared meal. Then, being weary, they lay down to rest and immediately fell asleep.

How long she had slept Much-Afraid could not tell, but she woke suddenly while it was still quite dark. Her companions slumbered peacefully beside her, but she knew that someone had called her. She waited in silence, then a Voice said: "Much-Afraid."

"Behold me, here I am, my Lord," she answered.

"Much-Afraid," said the Voice, "take now the promise you received when I called you to follow Me to the High Places, and take the natural longing for human love which you found already growing in your heart when I planted My own love there and go up into the mountains to the place that I shall show you. Offer them there as a Burnt Offering unto Me."

There was a long silence before Much-Afraid's trembling voice spoke through the darkness.

"My Lord—am I understanding you right?"

"Yes," answered the Voice. "Come now to the entrance of the hut and I will show you where you are to go."

Without waking the two beside her, she rose silently, opened the door of the hut, and stepped outside. Everything was still shrouded in mist, and the mountains were completely invisible, swallowed up in darkness and cloud. As she looked, the mist parted in one place and a little window appeared through which the moon and one star shone brightly. Just below them was a white peak, glimmering palely. At its foot was the rocky ledge over which the great waterfall leaped and rushed down to the slopes below. Only the lip of rock over which it poured itself was visible, all below being shrouded in the mist.

Then came the Voice, "That is the appointed place."

Much-Afraid looked, and replied, "Yes, Lord. Behold me—I am Thy handmaiden, I will do according to Thy word."

She did not lie down again, but stood at the door of the hut waiting for daybreak. It seemed to her that the voice of the fall now filled the whole night and was thundering through her

# "Yes, Lord"

When Jesus speaks to you, how do you answer? Do you say, in effect, "What do You want?"—waiting to hear His request before giving your answer. Or do you respond like Samuel:

> "And the Lord came, and stood, and called as at other times, Samuel! Samuel! Then Samuel answered, Speak, Lord, for Your servant is listening"
> (1 Sam. 3:10 AMP).

When we say, "Lord," that should automatically mean "yes" to any request He has for us. By the very act of calling Him "Lord," we are saying that He is in charge and that we are eager to listen and obey with our hearts fully surrendered to Him. "No, Lord," is a contradiction. Practice saying "Yes, Lord," all day today. Practice so you can answer like Mary:

> "...Behold I am the handmaiden of the Lord; let it be done to me according to what you have said..."
> (Lk. 1:38 AMP).

Step out today and say "yes" to Him.

trembling heart, reverberating and shouting through every part and repeating again and again, "Take now the promise that I gave you, and the natural human love in your heart, and offer them for a burnt offering."

With the first glimmer of dawn she bent over her sleeping companions and said, "We must start at once. I have received commandment to go up to the place where the great fall pours itself over the precipice."

They rose immediately, and after hurriedly eating a meal to strengthen themselves, they started on their way. The path led straight up the mountainside toward the thunderous voice of the fall, though everything was still shrouded in mist and cloud and the fall itself remained invisible.

As the hours passed they continued to climb, though the path was now steeper than ever before. In the distance thunder began to roll and flashes of lightning rent the veil of mist. Suddenly, higher up on the path, they heard the sound of running feet, slipping and scraping on the rocks and stones. They stopped and pressed themselves closely to one side of the narrow path to allow the runners to pass, then out of the ghostly mist appeared first Fear, then Bitterness, followed by Resentment, Pride, and Self-Pity.

They were running as though for their lives, and as they reached the three women they shouted, "Back! Turn back at once! The avalanches are falling ahead, and the whole mountainside is shaking as though it will fall too. Run for your lives!"

Without waiting for an answer, they clattered roughly past and fled down the mountainside.

"What are we to do?" asked Suffering and Sorrow, apparently at a loss for the very first time. "Shall we turn back to the hut and wait until the avalanches and the storm are over?"

"No," said Much-Afraid in a low, steady voice, speaking for the first time since she had called them to rise and follow her.

# Critical Choice

God uses others in our lives to comfort, instruct, and intercede, but when the final hour of decision comes, we and we alone must make the critical choices in our lives. The Lord gives the necessary insights, pulls back just enough of the mist of life to show us His will, and then waits for our response.

*"If any man is willing to do His will, he shall know of the teaching, whether it is of God, or whether I speak from Myself"*
(Jn. 7:17 NAS).

Jesus Himself knew when the time had come for Him to leave this world and return to the Father. It was a time of hard choices. Nevertheless, He responded,

*"For the Lord God helps Me, therefore, I am not disgraced; therefore, I have set My face like flint, and I know that I shall not be ashamed"*
(Is. 50:7 NAS).

There was no thought of turning back for Jesus. What about you? Who is there for you to turn to other than Him? It's time for you to decide.

"No, we must not turn back. I have received a commandment to go up to the place where the great fall pours over the rock."

Then the Voice spoke close at hand. "There is a place prepared for you here beside the path. Wait there until the storm is over."

In the rocky wall beside them was a little cave so low that it could be entered only if they stooped right down, and with just enough room for them to crouch inside. Side by side, they sat huddled together, then all of a sudden the storm burst over them in frightful fury. The mountains reverberated with thunder and with the sound of falling rocks and great avalanches. The lightning flashed incessantly and ran along the ground in sizzling flames.

Then the rains descended and the floods came, and the winds blew and beat upon the mountains until everything around them seemed to be shivering and quaking and falling. Flood waters rushed down the steep cliffs and a torrent poured over the rocks which projected over the cave so that the whole entrance was closed with a waterfall, but not a single drop fell inside the cave where the three sat together on the ground.

After they had been there for some time and the storm, far from abating, seemed to be increasing in strength, Much-Afraid silently put her hand in her bosom and drew out the leather bag which she always carried. Emptying the little heap of stones and pebbles into her lap, she looked at them. They were the memorial stones from all the altars which she had built along the way, from the time that she stood beside the Shepherd at the pool and allowed Him to plant the thorn in her heart and all along the journey until that moment of crouching in a narrow cave upon which the whole mountain seemed to be ready to topple. Nothing was left to her but a command to offer up the promise on which she had staked her all, on the strength of which she had started on the journey.

# Unlimited Allegiance

*[handwritten: +++ Thank you my Father and my Lord. Thank you.]*

S aying "yes" to Jesus, no matter the cost, releases within us the strength and dignity that we long for.

*"She is clothed with strength and dignity;*
*she can laugh at the days to come"*
(Prov. 31:25 NIV).

Unlimited allegiance to Jesus enables us not only to laugh at our enemies, but also to see all of life lined up in His divine perspective. Also, when we obey our Lord's voice, no word or action formed against us can prosper. The deluge of destructive forces aimed at us will not be able to destroy us as the enemy intended. Instead, they will simply rid us of hostile elements lurking within the limits of our liberty and freedom.

*"Therefore everyone who hears these words of Mine,*
*and acts upon them, may be compared to a wise man,*
*who built his house upon the rock. And the rain*
*descended, and the floods came, and the winds blew,*
*and burst against that house; and yet it did not fall,*
*for it had been founded upon the rock"*
(Mt. 7:24-25 NAS).

L ord Jesus, I place my feet upon the path You have chosen for me today. Thank You for being the Rock beneath my feet. *[handwritten: Amen:]*

She looked at the little pile in her lap and asked herself dully, "Shall I throw them away? Were they not all worthless promises which He gave me on the way here?" Then with icy fingers she picked up the first stone and repeated the first words that He had spoken to her beside the pool. "I will make thy feet like hinds' feet and set thee upon thine High Places" (Hab. 3:19). She held the stone in her hand for a long time, then said slowly, "I have not received hinds' feet, but I am on higher places than ever I imagined possible, and if I die up here, what does it matter? I will not throw it away."

She put the stone back in the bag, picked up the next and repeated, "What I do thou knowest not now; but thou shalt know hereafter" (John 13:7); and she gave a little sob and said, "Half at least of that is true, and who knows whether the other half is true or not—but I will not throw it away."

Picking up the third stone, she quoted, "This is not unto death, but for the glory of God" (John 11:4). "Not unto death," she repeated, "even though He says, 'Offer the promise as a Burnt Offering'?" But she dropped the stone back into the bag and took the fourth. "Bread corn is bruised...but no one crushes it forever" (Isa. 28:28). "I cannot part with that," she said, replaced it in the bag, and took the fifth. "Cannot I do with you as the Potter? saith the Lord" (Jer. 18:6). "Yes," said she, and put it back into the bag.

Taking the sixth, she repeated, "O thou afflicted, tossed with tempest, and not comforted, behold, I will lay thy stones with fair colors..." (Isa. 54:11), then could go no farther but wept bitterly. "How could I part with that?" she asked herself, and she put it in the bag with the others, and took the seventh. "My sheep hear My voice, and they follow Me" (John 10:27). "Shall I not throw this one away?" she asked herself. "Have I really heard His voice, or have I been deceiving myself all the time?"

Then as she thought of His face when He gave her that promise she replaced it in the bag, saying, "I will keep it. How

# Exalted Name

Our Lord has exalted above all else His name and His Word. He always fulfills the promises in His Word.

*"For ever, O Lord, Your Word [stands firm as the heavens] is settled in Heaven"*
(Ps. 119:89 AMP).

What promise of the Lord has been sustaining you? What have you latched on to, clung to, and relied upon? Consider who made the promise.

*"You alone are the Lord. You made the heavens, even the highest heavens, and all their starry host, the earth and all that is on it, the seas and all that is in them. You give life to everything, and the multitudes of heaven worship You"*
(Neh. 9:6 NIV).

Lord, Your way of fulfilling Your Word is so much higher than my ways that I hold Your promises to me in an open hand. I do not want to be presumptuous, however, or offer You any suggestions. That would simply anticipate control.

He waits to strip us of everything except Himself. When that happens, His promises enhance Him, but never replace Him. Let Him and Him alone be your God!

can I let it go?" and took the eighth. "Now shalt thou see what I will do" (Ex. 6:1). Remembering the precipice which had seemed so terribly impossible and how He had brought her to the top, she put the stone with the others and took the ninth. "God is not a man, that He should lie...hath He said, and shall He not do it? or hath He spoken, and shall He not make it good?" (Num. 23:19)

For a very long time she sat trembling with that stone in her hand, but in the end she said, "I have already given the only answer possible when I told Him, 'If Thou canst, Thou mayest deceive me.'"

Then she dropped the icy-cold little pebble into the bag and took the tenth. "Thine ears shall hear a word behind thee, saying, 'This is the way, walk ye in it, when ye turn to the right hand, and when ye turn to the left'" (Isa. 30:21). At that she shuddered, but after a while added, "Thou hast a little strength, and hast not denied My name...Hold that fast which thou hast, that no man take thy crown" (Rev. 3:8,11).

Returning the tenth stone to the bag, after a long pause she picked up an ugly little stone lying on the floor of the cave and dropped it in beside the other ten, saying, "Though He slay me, yet will I trust in Him" (Job 13:15). Tying up the bag again, she said, "Though everything in the world should tell me that they are worthless—yet I cannot part with them," and put the bag once again in her bosom.

Sorrow and her sister had been sitting silently beside her watching intently as she went over the little heap of stones in her lap. Both gave a strange laugh, as though of relief and thankfulness, and said together, "The rain descended, and the floods came, and the winds blew, and beat upon the house; and it fell not: for it was founded upon a rock" (Matt. 7:25).

By this time, the rain had ceased, the cataract was no longer pouring over the rocks, and only a light mist remained. The rolling of the thunder and the roar of the avalanches were fading away into the distance, and as they looked out of the cave,

# Eternal Trust
✝✝✝

The enemy will attack us and try to make us think that we cannot hear the Lord's voice, that we cannot trust Jesus within us, or that we are losing our minds. If the enemy can destroy this vital link of communication, he's put a major "kink" in our life's umbilical cord with Jesus. Rebuke the enemy with this:

*"For God hath not given us the spirit of fear;*
*but of power, and of love, and of a sound mind"*
(2 Tim. 1:7 KJV).

Then gently sink down before God in a humility that confesses its nothingness. Wait before Him until your soul is quieted. Say to your Lord:

I don't know how You will work in my life, who You will use, or when You will show me Your ways, but I have no one other than You whom I can rely on, in either Heaven or earth.

*"Though He slay me, yet will I trust in Him"*
(Job 13:15a KJV).

My heart is abandoned to You. I desire to neither grab, grasp, or cling to anything except You. Thank You for Your care of my heart.

up from the depths beneath came through the wreaths of mist the clear, jubilant notes of a bird. It might have been brother to that which sang in the dripping woods at the foot of the High Places:

> *He's gotten the victory, Hurrah!*
> *He's gotten the victory, Hurrah!*

As the pure clear notes came floating up to them the icy coldness in the heart of Much-Afraid broke, then melted away. She pressed her hands convulsively against the little bag of stones as though it contained priceless treasure which she had thought lost, and said to her companions, "The storm is over. Now we can go on our way."

From that place on, it was very steep going, for the path now went straight up the mountainside, so straight and steep that often Much-Afraid could hardly do more than crawl forward on hands and knees. All along she had hoped that the higher she went and the nearer she got to the High Places, the stronger she would become and the less she would stumble, but it was quite otherwise.

The higher they went, the more conscious she was that her strength was leaving her, and the weaker she grew, the more she stumbled. She could not help dimly realizing that this was not the case with her companions. The higher they went, the more vigorous and strong they seemed to become, and this was good, because often they had almost to carry Much-Afraid, for she seemed utterly spent and exhausted. Because of this they made very slow progress indeed.

On the second day they came to a place where a little hollow in the mountainside formed a tiny plateau. Here a spring bubbled out of the cliff and trickled across the hollow and down the side of the mountain in a little waterfall. As they paused to rest, the Voice said to Much-Afraid, "Drink of the brook at the side of the way and be strengthened."

Stooping down at the spring where it bubbled up from between the rocks, she filled her mouth with the water, but as

# Divine Light

*✝✝✝.*

Lhe closer we get to Jesus, who is Light, the more our dirt is revealed. It is much like viewing a dimly lit room and concluding it is spotless. Then you turn on the lights and pull back the drapes and lo! The dust, stains, and cobwebs are exposed. Jesus said:

*"...I am the Light of the world. He who follows Me will not be walking in the dark, but will have the Light which is Life"*
(Jn. 8:12 AMP).

This Light also reveals those who truly serve Him. When we submit to His light, we prove that we have His heart!

*"For every wrongdoer hates (loathes, detests) the light and will not come out into the light, but shrinks from it, lest his works—his deeds, his activities, his conduct—be exposed and reproved. But he who practices truth—who does what is right—comes out into the light; so that his works may be plainly shown to be what they are, wrought with God—divinely prompted, done with God's help, in dependence upon Him"*
(Jn. 3:20-21 AMP).

Lhank You, Lord Jesus, that Your light has revealed some weaknesses in me. Instead of being discouraged though, I know this is proof that I am improving and drawing nearer to You. Show me all that You need to expose. *Amen.*

soon as she swallowed it she found it so burning and bitter that her stomach rejected it altogether and she was unable to retain it. She knelt by the spring, gasping for a moment, and then said very quietly and softly through the silence, "My Lord, it is not that I will not, but that I cannot drink of this cup."

"There is a tree growing beside this spring of Marah," answered the Voice. "Break off a piece of branch, and when you have cast it into the waters they will be sweetened."

Much-Afraid looked on the other side of the spring and saw a little stunted thorn tree with but one branch growing on either side of the splintered trunk, like the arms of a cross. They were covered all over with long, sharp spines.

Suffering stepped forward, broke off a piece of the thorn tree, and brought it to Much-Afraid, who took it from her hand and cast it into the water. On doing this she stooped her head again to drink. This time she found that the stinging, burning bitterness was gone, and though the water was not sweet, she could drink it easily. She drank thirstily and found that it must have contained curative properties, for almost at once she was wonderfully refreshed and strengthened. Then she picked up her twelfth and last stone there beside the water of Marah and put it into her bag.

After they had rested a little while she was able to resume the journey, and for a time was so much stronger that although the way was even steeper than before, she was not nearly so faint and exhausted. This greatly comforted her, for by that time she had only one desire in her heart, to reach the place appointed and fulfill the command which had been given her before her strength ebbed away altogether. On the third day, "they lifted up their eyes and saw the place afar off," the great rock cliff and the waterfall, and continuing up the rocky path, at midday they came through the shrouding mist to the place which had been appointed.

# Sweet Waters

Our sin-infested world carries with it bitter pain—pain so bitter that we would not be able to drink of it except our Lord laid down His life on the cross to sweeten the waters of life. As in the Israelites' exodus experience, the water at Marah was too "bitter" to drink until God showed Moses how to make it sweet.

*"Then he [Moses] cried out to the Lord, and the Lord showed him a tree; and he threw it into the waters, and the waters became sweet"*
(Ex. 15:25a NAS).

Sometimes during times of intense pain or stress, we may be immobilized or disoriented. We may feel that we are losing our equilibrium. However, at Marah He not only brings us into balance, but also ushers us into a new place of health, freedom, and liberty. And He does it—either directly or indirectly.

Thank You, Lord Jesus, for laying down Your life on the cross at Calvary that I might be brought into Your fullness. *Amen*

# CHAPTER 16

# Grave on the Mountains

The path led forward to the edge of a yawning chasm, then stopped dead. The gravelike gorge yawned before them in each direction as far as they could see, completely cutting off all further progress. It was so filled with cloud and mist that they could not see how deep it was, nor could they see across to the other side, but spread before them like a great gaping grave, waiting to swallow them up. For a moment Much-Afraid wondered whether this could be the place, after all, but as they halted on the edge of the canyon, they could plainly hear the sound of mighty, swirling waters, and she realized that they must be standing somewhere near the lip of the great fall and that this was indeed the place appointed.

Looking at her companions, she asked quietly, "What must we do now? Can we jump across to the other side?"

"No," they said, "it would be impossible."

"What, then, are we to do?" she asked.

"We must leap down into the canyon," was the answer.

"Of course," said Much-Afraid at once. "I did not realize at first, but that is the thing to do."

Then for the last time on that journey (though she did not know it at the time) she held out her hand to her two companions that they might help her. By this time she was so weak and exhausted that instead of taking her hands, they came close up to her and put their hands beneath her arms so that she leaned

258

# Glorious Appointment

The place that God appoints to bring forth His glory in our lives usually does not look like an appropriate place—at least, not from our perspective and expectations. For example, would Abraham have ever expected God to ask him to sacrifice the son for whom he had waited so long and through whom his descendents were to come? However, Abraham was able to look beyond his expectation and see the end from God's perspective:

> *"For he reasoned that God was able to raise [him] up even from among the dead. Indeed in the sense that Isaac was figuratively dead (potentially sacrificed), he did [actually] receive him back from the dead"*
> (Heb. 11:19 AMP).

Also, God will not waste anything in order to show us His will. He will use those people He has placed in our lives to give us perspective when our vision is cloudy and to aid us in knowing and doing His will.

Lord Jesus, I too want to worship You with my life by completely obeying You in every way, even when it does not seem reasonable, logical, or feasible. Help me to see things from Your perspective.

*yes Father and my Lord.*

with her full weight against them. Thus with Suffering and Sorrow supporting her, Much-Afraid cast herself down into the yawning grave.

The place into which they had thrown themselves was deep, and had she been alone she must have been badly hurt by the fall. However, her companions were so strong that the jump did not seem to harm them at all, and they bore her so easily between them and broke the fall so gently that she was no more than bruised and shaken. Then, because the canyon was so filled with mist and cloud that nothing was visible, they began to feel their way slowly forward and saw, looming up before them, a flat, oblong rock. On reaching it, they found it to be some kind of stone altar with the indistinct figure of someone standing behind it.

"This is the place," said Much-Afraid quietly. "This is where I am to make my offering." She went up to the altar and knelt down. "My Lord," she said softly through the mist. "Will You come to me now and help me to make my burnt offering as You have commanded me?"

But for the first time on all that journey there seemed to be no answer—no answer at all—and the Shepherd did not come.

She knelt there quite alone in the cold, clammy mist, beside the desolate altar in this valley of shadow, and into her mind came the words which Bitterness had flung at her long before when she walked the shores of loneliness: "Sooner or later, when He gets you up on the wild places of the mountains He will put you on some sort of a cross and abandon you to it."

It seemed that in a way Bitterness had been right, thought Much-Afraid to herself, only he had been too ignorant to know and she too foolish at that time to understand that in all the world only one thing really mattered, to do the will of the One she followed and loved, no matter what it involved or cost. Strangely enough, as she knelt there by the altar, seemingly abandoned at that last tremendous crisis, there was no sign or sound of the presence of her enemies.

# New Ways

Learning to let God and God alone be our God is a continual process of stripping away layers and forms. It is easy to become presumptuous and, without knowing it, start expecting God to work and to respond to us in the familiar ways of the past. Some of the early Jewish believers had to learn that lesson. They were so used to being the chosen people that they could not believe God would reveal Himself to the Gentiles. Peter responded to these people:

> " 'If God therefore gave to them the same gift
> as He gave to us also after believing in the
> Lord Jesus Christ, who was I that I could
> stand in God's way?' And when they heard this,
> they quieted down, and glorified God, saying,
> "Well then, God has granted to the Gentiles
> also the repentance that leads to life' "
> (Acts 11:17-18 NAS).

Show me, Lord Jesus, when I start putting You in a box or trying to control my life and others' lives with my expectations. Let me always be open and eagerly embracing the new ways Your Spirit is moving in my life. Thank You for Your faithfulness to me.

*yes.*

The grave up on the mountains is at the very edge of the High Places and beyond the reach of Pride and Bitterness and Resentment and Self-Pity, yes, and of Fear too, as though she were in another world altogether, for they can never cast themselves down into that grave. She knelt there feeling neither despair nor hope. She knew now without a shadow of doubt that there would be no Angel to call from heaven to say that the sacrifice need not be made, and this knowledge caused her neither dread nor shrinking.

She felt nothing but a great stillness in which only one desire remained, to do that which He had told her, simply because He had asked it of her. The cold, dull desolation which had filled her heart in the cave was gone completely; one flame burned there steadily, the flame of concentrated desire to do His will. Everything else had died down and fallen into ashes.

After she had waited for a little and still He had not come, she put out her hand and with one final effort of failing strength grasped the natural human love and desire growing in her heart and struggled to tear them out. At the first touch it was as though anguish pierced through her every nerve and fiber, and she knew with a pang almost of despair that the roots had wound and twined and thrust themselves into every part of her being. Though she put forth all her remaining strength in the most desperate effort to wrench them out, not a single rootlet stirred.

For the first time she felt something akin to fear and panic. She was not able to do this thing which He had asked of her. Having reached the altar at last, she was powerless to obey. Turning to those who had been her guides and helpers all the way up the mountains, she asked for their help, and for them to do what she could not for herself, to tear the plant out of her heart. For the first time Suffering and Sorrow shook their heads.

# Gentle Whisper

J esus said:

*"For I have come down from heaven, not to
do My own will, but the will of Him who sent Me"*
(Jn. 6:38 NAS).

When the issue of whose will we intend to accomplish—
His, ours, or others'—is settled, the major battle is over. In
this posture of abandonment to Him—the abandonment of
our wills—a stillness and peace penetrates our beings. In
the stillness we can hear God's voice and direction, just
as Elijah experienced on the mountain.

*"…Then a great and powerful wind tore the mountains
apart and shattered the rocks before the Lord, but the
Lord was not in the wind. After the wind there was an
earthquake, but the Lord was not in the earthquake. After
the earthquake came a fire, but the Lord was not in the
fire. And after the fire came a gentle whisper. When Elijah
heard it, he pulled his cloak over his face and went out
and stood at the mouth of the cave. Then a voice said
to him, 'What are you doing here, Elijah?' "*
(1 Kings 19:11-13 NIV).

When we decide to follow God's will only, everything else
dies down and falls into ashes.

L ord Jesus, let the flames of concentrated desire to do Your will burn steadily in my heart.

*Yes.*

"We have done all that we can for you," they answered, "but this we cannot do."

At that the indistinct figure behind the altar stepped forward and said quietly, "I am the priest of this altar—I will take it out of your heart if you wish."

Much-Afraid turned toward him instantly. "Oh, thank you," she said. "I beg you to do so."

He came and stood beside her, his form indistinct and blurred by the mist, and then she continued entreatingly, "I am a very great coward. I am afraid that the pain may cause me to try to resist you. Will you bind me to the altar in some way so that I cannot move? I would not like to be found struggling while the will of my Lord is done."

There was complete silence in the cloud-filled canyon for a moment or two, then the priest answered, "It is well said. I will bind you to the altar." Then he bound her hand and foot.

When he had finished, Much-Afraid lifted her face toward the High Places which were quite invisible and spoke quietly through the mist. "My Lord, behold me—here I am, in the place Thou didst send me to—doing the thing Thou didst tell me to do, for where Thou diest, will I die, and there will I be buried; the Lord do so to me, and more also, if aught but death part Thee and me" (Ruth 1:17).

Still there was silence, a silence as of the grave, for indeed she was in the grave of her own hopes and still without the promised hinds' feet, still outside the High Places with even the promise to be laid down on the altar. This was the place to which the long, heartbreaking journey had led her. Yet just once more before she laid it down on the altar, Much-Afraid repeated the glorious promise which had been the cause of her starting for the High Places. "The Lord God is my strength, and He will make my feet like hinds' feet and He will make me to walk upon mine High Places. To the chief singer on my stringed instruments" (Hab. 3:19).

# Self Sacrificed

Have you ever thought, "I want to do God's will more than anything in life, but I am so afraid that I cannot trust myself to do the right thing under extreme duress." Thank God that when we take our position to do His will, He takes over where our strength and ability ends. We can give ourselves to Him ahead of time, trusting Him to bind us to the altar with His cords of love.

*"The Lord is God, Who has shown and given us light—He has illuminated us [with grace, freedom and joy]. Decorate the festival with leafy boughs and bind the sacrifices to be offered with thick cords [all over the priest's court, right up] to the horns of the altar"*
(Ps. 118:27 AMP).

Lord Jesus, I give myself to You so You can completely accomplish Your will in and through me. I would not like to be found struggling while Your will is being done. Please bind me to the altar of Your will.

The priest put forth a hand of steel, right into her heart. There was a sound of rending and tearing, and the human love, with all its myriad rootlets and fibers, came forth.

He held it for a moment and then said, "Yes, it was ripe for removal, the time had come. There is not a rootlet torn or missing."

When he had said this he cast it down on the altar and spread his hands above it. There came a flash of fire which seemed to rend the altar; after that, nothing but ashes remained, either of the love itself, which had been so deeply planted in her heart, or of the suffering and sorrow which had been her companions on that long, strange journey. A sense of utter, overwhelming rest and peace engulfed Much-Afraid. At last, the offering had been made and there was nothing left to be done. When the priest had unbound her she leaned forward over the ashes on the altar and said with complete thanksgiving, "It is finished."

Then, utterly exhausted, she fell asleep.

# Choice Harvest

When we start dealing with a problem, the first step is usually to will the right choice. Then, gradually, we begin to choose His way. (We must choose, however. Others can have input into our lives, but the final choice is ours.) As we continue to choose His way, there comes an appointed time when our Lord brings forth the harvest and He removes the final rootlets and fibers that have tormented and bound us. Then we delight to do His will with complete peace and unspeakable joy.

*"For You have delivered my life from death, yes, and my feet from falling, that I may walk before God in the light of life and of the living"*
(Ps. 56:13 AMP).

Praise to You my God, my Lord, my all in all. You are an awesome God, and mighty to be praised and exalted. Thank You for the privilege of presenting my body, myself, to You as a living sacrifice.

# Part Two

*"Joy cometh in the morning"*
*(Psalm 30:5)*

## CHAPTER 17

# Healing Streams

When at last Much-Afraid awoke, the sun was high in the sky, and she looked out through the mouth of the cave in which she found herself lying. Everything was shimmering in a blaze of radiant sunshine which burnished every object with glory. She lay still a little longer, collecting her thoughts and trying to understand where she was.

The rocky cave into which the sunbeams were pouring was warm and quiet and drenched with the sweet perfume of spikenard, frankincense, and myrrh. This perfume she gradually realized was emanating from the wrappings which covered her. She gently pushed back the folds, sat up, and looked about her. Then the memory of all that had happened returned to her.

She and her two companions had come to a cloud-filled canyon high up on the mountains and to an altar of sacrifice, and the priest had wrenched out of her heart her flower of human love and burned it on the altar. On remembering that, she glanced down at her breast and saw it was covered with a cloth soaked in the spices whose perfume stole out and filled the cave with sweetness. She pushed the cloth aside a little curiously and was astonished to find no trance of a wound—not even a scar, nor was there any hint of pain or aching or stiffness anywhere in her body.

# Consecrated Creature

Turn to the Lord Jesus today, basking in His all-encompassing love and radiant glory. Quiet your soul before Him and marvel that He calls you holy. The old you has died, and the new you is holy.

*"Therefore if any man is in Christ, he is a new creature; the old things passed away; behold, new things have come"*
(2 Cor. 5:17 NAS).

*"...to those consecrated and purified and made holy in Christ Jesus, [who are] selected and called to be saints (God's people) together with all those who in any place call upon and give honor to the name of our Lord Jesus Christ..."*
(1 Cor. 1:2 AMP).

Jesus demonstrated His love. He did not just say, "I love you"; He laid down His life to prove and purchase your life.

Walking in Your love, my Lord, turns all pain into a sweet, perfumed aroma. Let my life, likewise, be a sweet perfume in Your nostrils.

Rising quietly, she went outside, then stood still and looked about her. The canyon, which had been so shrouded in mist that nothing had been distinguishable, now shimmered in the golden sunlight. Soft, verdant grass grew everywhere, starred with gentians and other little jewel-like flowers of every variety. There were banks of sweet-smelling thyme, moss, and myrtle along the sides of the rocky walls, and everything sparkled with dew.

In the center of the canyon, at a little distance from the cave, was the long stone altar to which she had been bound, but in the sunlight she saw that the flowers and mosses grew all about it and clothed its sides with verdure. Little birds hopped about here and there, scattering the dewdrops off the grasses and chirping merrily as they preened their plumage.

One was perched on the altar itself, its little throat throbbing as it trilled forth a song of joy, but the most beautiful and wonderful thing of all was that out from under the rock altar there gushed a great "river of water, clear as crystal." It then flowed in a series of cascades and through rock pools right through the canyon till it came to a broad lip of rock, over which it poured with a noise of shouting and tumultuous gladness. She was at the very source of the great fall and knew now that it flowed from under the altar to which the priest had bound her.

For some time she stood looking about her, her heart leaping and thrilling with a growing joy which was beyond her understanding and a peace indescribably sweet which seemed to enfold her. She was quite alone in the canyon. There were no signs of her companions Sorrow and Suffering nor of the priest of the altar. The only things which breathed and moved in the canyon beside herself were the cheerful little chirping birds and the insects and butterflies flitting among the flowers. High overhead was a cloudless sky, against which the peaks of the High Places shone dazzlingly white.

The first thing she did, after she had taken in her surroundings, was to step toward the river which gushed out from under the

# Joy Reborn

It's amazing, my Lord, to see that in Your hands a place of sacrifice and dread is turned into a place of life and indescribable joy. Your death on the cross of Calvary looked like a place of loss for a period of time. But instead of death destroying You, Life came forth!

Much-Afraid's altar looked so dismal; however, it too became a place of celebration for not only her, but also for God's creation! The lovely, glimmering golden rays of sunlight, the blooming flowers, and the chirping birds all rejoiced around that altar.

*"The Rock! His work is perfect, for all His ways are just; a God of faithfulness and without injustice, righteous and upright is He"*
(Deut. 32:4 NAS).

I freely lay on the altar of the Rock today all that I have been hesitant to lay down in the past. Let Your waters of living water flow freely through me, my Lord. *Yes.*

altar. It drew her irresistibly. She stooped down when she got to the bank and dabbled her fingers in the crystal water. It was icy cold, but it sent a shock of ecstasy tingling through her body, and without further delay she put off the white linen robe she was wearing and stepped into one of the rocky pools. Never had she experienced anything so delicious and exhilarating. It was like immersing herself in a stream of bubbling life. When at last she again stepped out of the pool she was immediately dry and tingling from head to foot with a sense of perfect well-being.

As she stood on the mossy bank by the pool she happened to glance down and noticed for the first time that her feet were no longer the crooked, ugly things which they always had been, but were "straight feet," perfectly formed, shining white against the soft green grass.

Then she remembered the healing streams of which the Shepherd had spoken, which gushed out of the ground on the High Places. Stepping straight back into the pool with a shock of sweetest pleasure and putting her head beneath the clear waters, she splashed them about her face. Then she found a little pool among the rocks, still and clear as a mirror. Kneeling down, she looked into its unruffled surface and saw her face quite clearly. It was true, the ugly, twisted mouth had vanished and the face she saw reflected back by the water was as relaxed and perfect as the face of a little child.

After that she began to wander about the canyon and noticed wild strawberries and blueberries and other small berries growing on the banks. She found a handful of these as refreshing and sustaining a meal as ever she had eaten.

Then she came to the lip of the rock cliff over which the river cast itself, and stood a long time watching the water as it leaped over the edge with the noise of its tumultuous joy drowning every other sound. She saw how the sun glorified the crystal waters as they went swirling downward and far below she saw the green alps where the Shepherd had led her and where they

# Exhilarated Heart

A s I draw near to You, my Lord, my heart is exhila-
rated by Your patient wooing, Your drawing me
to Yourself. I have foolishly turned to other sources in
my search to be satisfied. Thank You for consistently
showing me that You and You alone give life.

> *"And he shewed me a pure river of water of life,*
> *clear as crystal, proceeding out of the throne*
> *of God and of the Lamb"*
> (Rev. 22:1 KJV).

> *"Therefore with joy will you draw water*
> *from the wells of salvation"*
> (Is. 12:3 AMP).

Walking in an awareness of Your presence, my Lord, is
like being immersed in Your streams of bubbling life. I
choose today to live that way.

> *"Blessed—happy, fortunate [to be envied]—is the*
> *man whose strength is in You; in whose heart are*
> *the highways to Zion. Passing through the valley*
> *of weeping they make it a place of springs; the*
> *early rain also fills [the pools] with blessings"*
> (Ps. 84:5-6 AMP).

Thank You, Lord Jesus, for my journey through the
valley of weeping so You might break any destructive
patterns in my life, which releases me to enjoy the
pools of blessings. I delight to worship You and live
with You in the simplicity of childlike trust.

had stood at the foot of this same fall. She felt completely encompassed by peace, and a great inner quietness and contentment drowned every feeling of curiosity, loneliness and anticipation.

She did not think about the future at all. It was enough to be there in that quiet canyon, hidden away high up in the mountains with the river of life flowing beside her, and to rest and recover herself after the long journey. After a little she lay down on a mossy bank and slept, and when she woke again, bathed herself in the river. So the long, quiet day passed like a sweet dream while she rested and bathed and refreshed herself at intervals with the berries and then slept again.

When at last the shadows lengthened and the sun sank in the west and the snow peaks glowed glorious in rose and flame color she went back into the cave, laid herself down among the spice-perfumed coverings and slept as deeply and dreamlessly as she had the first night when the priest laid her there to rest.

# Encompassing Peace

*"He refreshes and restores my life—my self;*
*He leads me in the paths of righteousness…"*
(Ps. 23:3 AMP).

Snuggle up in Your Shepherd's arms, in that place of warmth and acceptance. Rest there until the things of the future disappear and the things of the past are swallowed up in Him who is your all in all. Be encompassed by peace, a great inner quietness and contentment, as you focus on who your God is and who you are "in Him." Cooperate unreservedly in what He is doing in and through you.

*"You will guard him and keep him in perfect*
*and constant peace whose mind [both its inclination*
*and its character] is stayed on You, because he commits*
*himself to You, leans on You and hopes confidently in You"*
(Is. 26:3 AMP).

*"The Lord will give [unyielding and impenetrable]*
*strength to His people; the Lord will bless*
*His people with peace"*
(Ps. 29:11 AMP).

Dear Lord, You are indeed a Life Giver. I thank You, Jehovah, my Redeemer, for being my Shepherd.

# CHAPTER 18

# Hinds' Feet

On the third day, while it was still almost dark, she woke suddenly, and sprang to her feet with a shock of joy tingling through her. She had not heard her name called, had not even been conscious of a voice, yet she knew that she had been called. Some mysterious, poignantly sweet summons had reached her, a summons which she knew instinctively she had been awaiting ever since she woke up for the first time in the cave. She stepped outside into the fragrant summer night. The morning star hung low in the sky, and in the east the first glimmer of dawn appeared. From somewhere close at hand a solitary bird uttered one clear, sweet note and a light breeze stirred over the grasses. Otherwise there was no sound save the voice of the great waterfall.

Then it came again—tingling through her—a call ringing down from some high place above. Standing there in the pale dawn, she looked eagerly around. Every nerve in her body surged with desire to respond to the call, and she felt her feet and legs tingling with an almost irresistible urge to go bounding up the mountains, but where was the way out of the canyon? The walls seemed to rise smooth and almost perpendicular on all sides, except at the end which was blocked by the waterfall.

Then, as she stood straining every nerve to find a possible means of exit, up from a nearby mossy bank sprang a mountain hart with the hind close behind him, just as she had seen them at the foot of the great Precipice of Injury. As she watched,

# Deep Calling

*"Deep calls to deep at the sound of Thy waterfalls;*
*all Thy breakers and Thy waves have rolled over me"*
(Ps. 42:7 NAS).

Remember all the times you laid down your will for His will? There were times it seemed you would surely break under the strain. Yet you were propelled forward in spite of the obstacles and detours. That was the "deep calling to the deep." When His waves of love and acceptance, when His waves of letting you know that you are of great value, totally forgiven, and complete in Him rolls over you, they break all the bondages of the past. His everlasting weight of glory makes those painful afflictions seem momentary and light.

*"And He raised us up together with Him and made*
*us sit down together—giving us joint seating with*
*Him—in the heavenly sphere [by virtue of our being]*
*in Christ Jesus, the Messiah, the Anointed One"*
(Eph. 2:6 AMP).

Ask Jesus to open up this mystery to you in a practical way. Then thank Him that you are secure, loved, and treasured. Be encouraged to risk responding to the call of the "deep"–your mysterious, poignant, sweet summons from Him.

the hart sprang onto the altar of rock, and from there with a great leap he reached a projecting ledge on the wall on the farther side of the ravine. Then, closely followed by the hind, he began springing up the great wall of the canyon.

Much-Afraid did not hesitate one instant. In a moment she was on the rock altar herself, the next, with a flying leap, she, too, reached the ledge on the wall. Then, using the same footholds as the hart and the hind, leaping and springing in a perfect ecstasy of delight, she followed them up the cliff, the hooves of the deer ringing on the rocks before her like little silver hammers.

In a moment or two all three were at the top of the canyon, and she was leaping up the mountainside toward the peak above, from which the summons had come. The rosy light in the east brightened, the snow on the summits of the mountains caught the glow and flushed like fire, and as she skipped and jumped from rock to rock excitedly the first sunbeams streamed over the mountaintop. He was there—standing on the peak— just as she had known He would be, strong and grand and glorious in the beauty of the sunrise, holding out both hands and calling to her with a great laugh, "You—with the hinds' feet— jump over here."

She gave one last flying spring, caught His hands and landed beside Him on the topmost peak of the mountain. Around them in every direction towered other and greater ranges of snow mountains, whose summits soared into the sky higher than her sight could follow them. He was crowned, and dressed in royal robes, just as she had seen Him once before when He had carried her up to the High Places, and had touched her with the live coal from off the golden Altar of Love. Then His face had been stern in its majesty and gravity, now it was alight with glory of joy which excelled anything which she had ever imagined.

"At last," He said, as she knelt speechless at His feet, "at last you are here and the 'night of weeping is over and joy comes to you in the morning.' " Then, lifting her up, He continued, "This is the time when you are to receive the fulfillment

278

# Finished Work

Just as Much-Afraid used the rock altar to leap up to the High Places, so must we keep the cross of Calvary as our anchor and springboard.

> *"But far be it from me to glory [in anything or any one] except in the cross of our Lord Jesus Christ, the Messiah, through Whom the world has been crucified to me, and I to the world!"*
> (Gal. 6:14 AMP)

Both the rock altar and the cross represent the finished work of the Shepherd, the Lord Jesus Christ. However, is there anything in you that you feel will never be completed? Lift it up to Him and see Him reaching to receive it. Know that one day, when you least expect it, the mist will roll back and the rosy light in the east will dance upon the snow-capped mountain peaks of your life.

> *"And I am convinced and sure of this very thing, that He Who began a good work in you will continue until the day of Jesus Christ—right up to the time of His return—developing [that good work] and perfecting and bringing it to full completion in you"*
> (Phil. 1:6 AMP). *Amen.*

of the promises. Never am I to call you Much-Afraid again." At that He laughed again and said, "I will write upon her a new name, the name of her God. The Lord God is a sun and shield: the Lord will give grace and glory: no good thing will He withhold from them that walk uprightly" (Psa. 84:11). "This is your new name," He declared. "From henceforth you are Grace and Glory."

Still she could not speak, but stood silent with joy and thanksgiving and awe and wonder.

Then He went on, "Now for the flower of Love and for the promise that when it blooms you will be loved in return."

Grace and Glory spoke for the first time. "My Lord and King," she said softly, "there is no flower of Love to bloom in my heart. It was burned to ashes on the altar at Thy command."

"No flower of Love?" He repeated, and laughed again so gently and joyfully that she could hardly bear it. "That is strange, Grace and Glory. How, then, did you get here? You are right on the High Places, in the Kingdom of Love itself. Open your heart and let us see what is there."

At His word she laid bare her heart, and out came the sweetest perfume she had ever breathed and filled all the air around them with its fragrance. There in her heart was a plant whose shape and form could not be seen because it was covered all over with pure white, almost transparent blooms, from which the fragrance poured forth.

Grace and Glory gave a little gasp of wonder and thankfulness. "How did it get there, my Lord and King?" she exclaimed.

"Why, I planted it there Myself," was His laughing answer. "Surely you remember, down there by the sheep pool in the Valley of Humiliation, on the day that you promised to go with Me to the High Places. It is the flower from the thorn-shaped seed."

"Then, my Lord, what was the plant which the priest tore out of my heart when I was bound to the altar?"

# New Name

Did you know that one day you will receive a new name from Jesus—a name that will perfectly describe the marvelous life journey you have traveled? Yes, it's true!

*"...To him who overcomes (who conquers)... I will give him a white stone, with a new name engraved on the stone which no one knows or understands except he who receives it"*
(Rev. 2:17 AMP).

Won't it be exciting to find out what your name is? Won't you be glad that you decided to obey Him? As we work toward receiving this new name, each step of obedience to Jesus, empowered by His Spirit, opens us up to know and receive His love.

*"Whoever has My commands and obeys them, he is the one who loves Me. He who loves Me will be loved by My Father, and I too will love him and show Myself to him"*
(Jn. 14:21 NIV).

O my Lord, You do not withhold any good thing from those who walk with You. Open my ears to hear and my heart to respond in obedience to each leading of Your Spirit, that my new name might accurately describe my new life.

"Do you remember, Grace and Glory, when you looked into your heart beside the pool, and found that My kind of love was not there at all—only the plant of Longing-to-be-loved?"

She nodded wonderingly.

"That was the natural human love which I tore out from your heart when the time was ripe and it was loose enough to be uprooted altogether so that the real Love could grow there alone and fill your whole heart."

"You tore it out!" she repeated slowly and wonderingly, and then, "O my Lord and King, were You the priest? Were You there all the time, when I thought You had forsaken me?"

He bowed His head and she took His hands in hers, the scarred hands which had sown the thorn-shaped seed in her heart, and the hands with the grasp of steel which had torn out that love which had been the cause of all her pain, and kissed them while tears of joy fell on them.

"And now for the promise," said He, "that when Love flowers in your heart you shall be loved again." Taking her hand in His, He said, "Behold I have set My love upon thee and thou art Mine...yea, I have loved thee with an everlasting love: therefore with loving-kindness have I drawn thee" (Jer. 31:3). After that He said, "Give Me the bag of stones of remembrance that you have gathered on your journey, Grace and Glory."

She took it out and passed it to Him and then He bade her hold out her hands. On doing so, He opened the little purse and emptied the contents into her hands. Then she gasped again with bewilderment and delight, for instead of the common, ugly stones she had gathered from the altars along the way, there fell into her hands a heap of glorious, sparkling jewels, very precious and very beautiful. As she stood there, half-dazzled by the glory of the flashing gems, she saw in His hand a circlet of pure gold.

"O thou who wast afflicted, tossed with tempest and not comforted," He said, "behold I lay thy stones with fair colors."

# Overcoming Believer

Have you ever reasoned within yourself, "Some will overcome, but I'm afraid that I am not in that group. I'll never make it." Listen to the truth from God's lips:

*"For everyone born of God overcomes the world. This is the victory that has overcome the world, even our faith. Who is it that overcomes the world? Only he who believes that Jesus is the Son of God"*
(1 John 5:4-5 NIV).

Thank You for planting the desire to know and respond to You in my heart, Lord Jesus.

Your heart is like a garden that needs care. As you allow Him to take care of the "little" daily things He shows you from your heart, it looses the soil so He can lift out, at the right time, the plants that are not of Him. He can then uproot what needs to be removed, with all its myriad rootlets and fibers, thus allowing His love to grow and bloom freely. Of course, we too can aid in the gardening of our hearts. The Lord's Word says:

*"Guard your own heart, look straight ahead at your own path, and keep your own feet from evil"*
(Prov. 4:23, 25-27, my paraphrase).

Lord Jesus, help me to guard my heart. Let me not be discouraged, but always remember that in You I have overcome and gained the victory.

First He picked out of her hand one of the biggest and most beautiful of the stones—a sapphire, shining like the pavement of heaven, and set it in the center of the golden circlet. Then, taking a fiery, blood-red ruby, He set it on one side of the sapphire and an emerald on the other. After that He took the other stones—twelve in all—and arranged them on the circlet, then set it upon her head.

At that moment Grace and Glory remembered the cave in which she had sheltered from the floods, and how nearly she had succumbed to the temptation to discard as worthless those stones which now shone with glory and splendor in the crown upon her head. She remembered, too, the words which had sounded in her ears and had restrained her, "Hold fast that thou hast, that no man take thy crown." Supposing she had thrown them away, had discarded her trust in His promises, had gone back on her surrenders to His will? There could have been no jewels now to His praise and glory, and no crown for her to wear.

She marveled at the grace and love and tenderness and patience which had led and trained and guarded and kept poor faltering Much-Afraid, which had not allowed her to turn back, and which now changed all her trials into glory. Then she heard Him speaking again and this time the smile on His face was almost more joyful than before.

"Hearken, O daughter, and consider, and incline thine ear; forget also thine own people, and thy father's house; so shall the King greatly desire thy beauty: for He is thy Lord; and worship thou Him....The King's daughter is all glorious within. She shall be brought unto the King in clothing of wrought gold, in raiment of needlework. The virgins, her companions that follow her, shall be brought unto thee. With gladness and rejoicing shall they be brought: they shall enter into the King's palace" (Psa. 45:10-15). Then He added, "Now that you are to live with Me here on the High Places, to go where I go, and to share My work in the valley below, it is fitting, Grace and Glory, that you

# Bejeweled Treasure

As you wait before the Lord, ask Him to bring to your mind the things in your life that could be described as storms or troubles. Then prayerfully read these words:

> "O you afflicted, storm-tossed and not comforted, behold, I will set your stones in fair colors—in antimony [to enhance their brilliance]—and lay your foundations with sapphires. And I will make your windows and pinnacles of [sparkling] agates or rubies, and your gates of [shining] carbuncles, and all the walls of your enclosures of precious stones"
> (Is. 54:11-12 AMP).

Are you being tempted to discard your trust in His promises? Are you flirting with the idea of rebelling against His will today? Ask Him to rearrange your expectations, correct any distorted way of thinking you have embraced, or show you His hand in an altogether new way. Remember too that the Lord does not waste anything in our lives. Instead, He uses everything as "raw material" to produce a loveliness beyond our highest prayers, desires, thoughts, hopes, or dreams—He turns our trials into an everlasting weight of glory.

Lord, ever remind me to continue holding on!

> "I am coming quickly; hold fast what you have, so that no one may rob you and deprive you of your crown"
> (Rev. 3:11 AMP).

should have companions and handmaidens, and I will bring them to you now."

At that Grace and Glory regarded Him earnestly, and there were almost tears in her eyes, for she remembered Suffering and Sorrow, the faithful companions whom He had given her before. It had been through their help and gentleness and patience she had been able to ascend the mountains to the High Places. All the time she had been with her Lord and King, receiving her new name, and being crowned with joy and glory, she had been thinking of them and wishing—yes, actually wishing and longing that they were there too, for why should she receive everything? They had endured the same journey, had supported and helped her, had been through the same trials and attacks of the enemy.

Now she was here and they were not. She opened her mouth to make her first request, to beg her Lord to let her keep the companions He had chosen in the beginning and who had brought her to the glory of the High Places. Before she could speak, however, He said with the same specially lovely smile, "Here are the handmaidens, Grace and Glory, whom I have chosen to be with you henceforth and forever."

Two radiant, shining figures stepped forward, the morning sunshine glittering on their snowy garments, making them dazzling to look at. They were taller and stronger than Grace and Glory, but it was the beauty of their faces and the love shining in their eyes which caught at her heart and made her almost tremble with joy and admiration. They came toward her, their faces shining with mirth and gladness, but they said not a word.

"Who are you?" asked Grace and Glory softly. "Will you tell me your names?"

Instead of answering they looked at one another and smiled, then held out their hands as though to take hers in their own. At that familiar gesture, Grace and Glory knew them and cried out with a joy which was almost more than she could bear.

# Answered Call

What concerns you today? Are you struggling with such thoughts as, "Does Jesus really care about me? Will things ever work out?" Jesus' heart is for you, and He is diligently working out the details of your life to bless you and bring Him glory.

*"And it shall be that before they call I will answer,*
*and while they are yet speaking I will hear"*
(Is. 65:24 AMP).

*"The Lord will perfect that which concerns me;*
*Your mercy and loving-kindness, O Lord, endure for*
*ever; forsake not the works of Your own hands"*
(Ps. 138:8 AMP).

What a faithful, loving God we are privileged to walk with. He delights to give us the desires of our hearts.

Thank You, my Lord, that You perform on my behalf and reward me by bringing to pass Your purposes for me. Thank You that it is You who completes them! Surely You do all things well–for me and for all those whom I love.

"Why! You are Suffering and Sorrow. Oh, welcome, welcome! I was longing to find you again."

They shook their heads. "Oh, no!" they laughed, "we are no more Suffering and Sorrow than you are Much-Afraid. Don't you know that everything that comes to the High Places is transformed? Since you brought us here with you, we are turned into Joy and Peace."

"Brought you here!" gasped Grace and Glory. "What an extraordinary way to express it! Why, from the first to last you dragged me here."

Again they shook their heads and smiled as they answered, "No, we could never have come here alone, Grace and Glory. Suffering and Sorrow may not enter the Kingdom of Love, but each time you accepted us and put your hands in ours we began to change. Had you turned back or rejected us, we never could have come here."

Looking at one another again, they laughed softly and said, "When first we saw you at the foot of the mountains, we felt a little depressed and despairing. You seemed so Much-Afraid of us, and shrank away and would not accept our help, and it looked so unlikely that any of us would ever get to the High Places. We told ourselves that we would have to remain Sorrow and Suffering always, but you see how graciously our Lord the King arranged for all of us, and you did bring us here. Now we are to be your companions and friends forever."

With that they came up to her, put their arms around her, and all three embraced and kissed one another with a love and thankfulness and joy beyond words to express. So with a new name, and united to the King and crowned with glory, Grace and Glory, accompanied by her companions and friends, came to the High Places and was led into the Kingdom of Love.

# Perfect Symphony

When we are willing to be vulnerable, transparent, and lovingly honest with those we journey with through life, God uses us in each others' lives to make us like Himself. We grow and learn together, and His work of completing His Body is brought forth.

> *"[Even] now I rejoice in the midst of my sufferings on your behalf. And in my own person I am making up whatever is still lacking and remains to be completed [on our part] of Christ's afflictions, for the sake of His body, which is the Church"*
> (Col. 1:24 AMP).

We can trust God's heart even when we cannot trace His ways. His desire is to take all the details of our lives that often seem dangling and disconnected and tie them together in a perfect symphony. Rejoice that He is taking you to that place in Him, even if you are not presently tasting it. Accept help from others in His Body. Enjoy how all of you are being changed to be like Him!

How awesome and fearfully glorious are Your works, Lord!

# CHAPTER 19

# High Places

Grace and Glory with her handmaidens Joy and Peace stayed up on the High Places for several weeks while all three explored the heights and learned many new lessons from the King. He led them Himself to many places, and explained to them as much as they were able to understand at that time. He also encouraged them to explore on their own, for there are always new and lovely discoveries to make up there on the High Places.

Even these High Places were not the highest of all. Others towered above them into the sky, where mortal eye could no longer follow them, and where only those who have finished their pilgrim life on earth are able to go. Grace and Glory and her friends were on the lowest, the "beginners' slopes" in the Kingdom of Love, and these were the parts which they were to explore and enjoy at this time. From these slopes, too, they were able to look down on the valleys below, and from that new viewpoint gain an understanding of many things which had been puzzling and mysterious to them before. From beneath they had not been seen clearly, and even then only a small part had been visible.

The first thing, however, which they realized up there on the slopes of the Kingdom of Love was how much more there would be to see and learn and understand when the King took them higher on future occasions. The glorious view which they now enjoyed was but small in comparison with all that lay beyond, and would be visible only from yet higher places above.

# Complete Creation

Consider your walk with Jesus, how you explore His ways and are encouraged by them. Doesn't it remind you of a baby chicken that has just pecked its way out of its shell? Reflect upon the most recent bondage or "shell" that, through His love, has been removed from your soul. Isn't the new range of freedom and liberty you now see wonderful?

> "...What eye has not seen, and ear has not heard, and
> has not entered into the heart of man, [all that,]
> God has prepared—made and keeps ready—for
> those who love Him [that is, for those who hold Him
> in affectionate reverence, promptly obeying Him and
> gratefully recognizing the benefits He has bestowed]"
> (1 Cor. 2:9 AMP).

Also, a little chick, as it sits there half in and half out of its shell, scrawny as it can be with its wet down, is still as much a chicken as it ever will be. True, it must grow and mature, but it is a complete chicken. That is the way you are "in Him."

> "And in Him you have been made complete"
> (Col. 2:10a NAS).

Thank You, Lord, that I have already been made complete. No performance can add to my completeness. Living from Your perspective is much more joyful. I look forward to exploring the untold regions You have before me!

It was now perfectly evident to them that there must be ranges upon ranges of which they had never dreamed while they were still down in the narrow valleys were their extraordinarily limited views. Sometimes, as she looked on the glorious panorama visible from these lowest slopes in the Kingdom of Love, she found herself blushing as she remembered some of the dogmatic statements which she and others had made in the depths of the valley about the High Places and the ranges of Truth. They had been able to see so little and were unconscious of what lay beyond and above. If that had been the case while down in the valley, how much more clearly, she now realized, that even up on those wonderful slopes she was only looking out on a tiny corner of the whole.

She never tired of looking from the glorious new viewpoint on the first slopes of the Kingdom of Love and seeing it all from a new perspective. What she could see and could take in almost intoxicated her with joy and thanksgiving, and sometimes even with inexpressible relief. Things which she had thought dark and terrible and which had made her tremble as she looked up from the Valley because they had seemed so alien to any part of the Realm of Love were now seen to be but parts of a great and wonderful whole. They were so altered and modified that as she saw what they extended into, she wondered at having been so blind and stupid at having had such false ideas about them.

She began to understand quite clearly that truth cannot be understood from books alone or by any written words, but only by personal growth and development in understanding, and that things written even in the Book of Books can be astonishingly misunderstood while one still lives on the low levels of spiritual experience and on the wrong side of the grave on the mountains.

She perceived that no one who finds herself up on the slopes of the Kingdom of Love can possibly dogmatize about what is seen there, because it is only then that she comprehends how small a part of the glorious whole she sees. All she can do is to

# Merciful Heart

When you find yourself beginning to judge or criticize another, or making a dogmatic statement about a situation, run into Jesus' arms or into your secret place with Him. Give Him your critical attitude and ask Him to keep your heart from becoming hard, vindictive, or cruel. Also keep in mind that you are guilty of the very same things you criticize another for. You see hypocrisy, fraud, and unreality in others because such things exist in your own heart.

*"Therefore you are without excuse, every man of you who passes judgment, for in that you judge another, you condemn yourself; for you who judge practice the same things"*
(Rom. 2:1 NAS).

*"... I warn every one among you not to estimate and think of himself more highly than he ought.... Never overestimate yourself or be wise in your own conceits"*
(Rom. 12:3,16c AMP).

My Lord, when I consider what is in my own heart, I can never despair of another. There is no evil that would not have been manifested in me except for Your grace. Remind me that Your Spirit is the only one in the position to truly judge. He alone knows all the facts and sees the whole picture. So let me always view others as You view me: through Your marvelous atonement.

gasp with wonder, awe, and thanksgiving, and to long with all her heart to go higher and to see and understand more.

Paradoxical as it may seem, as she gazed out on dazzling vistas, so glorious that she could not look at them steadily or grasp their magnificent sweep, she often thought that the prayer which best expressed her heart's desire was that of the blind man, "Lord, that I might receive my sight! Help me to open myself to more light. Help me to fuller understanding." Another thing which gave her continual joy was their unbroken communion with the King. Wherever He went she and Peace and Joy went too, springing behind Him with a delight which at times was almost hilarious, for He was teaching and training them to use their hinds' feet. Grace and Glory quickly saw, however, that He always chose the way most carefully, and restrained His own amazing strength and power, taking only such springs and bounds as they could manage too.

So graciously did He adapt Himself to what was possible to their newly acquired capacity that they scarcely recognized in the exhilaration of leaping and skipping like hinds on the mountains, that had He really extended His powers, they would have been left behind completely.

For Grace and Glory—who had been lame and limping all her life—the ecstasy of leaping about in this way and of bounding from rock to rock on the High Places as easily as the mountain roes, was so rapturous that she could hardly bear to cease from it even for rests. The King seemed to find great delight in encouraging this, and led her on and on, taking long and longer leaps, until at last she would be quite breathless. Then as they sat side by side on some new crag to which He had led her, while she rested He would point out some of the vistas to be seen from the new viewpoint.

One one of these occasions after they had been up on the High Places for several days, she flung herself down on the lichen and moss-covered crag to which He had led her, and, laughing and breathless, said, "Even hinds' feet seem to need a rest now and then!"

# Unbroken Communion

My Lord, I am beginning to grasp the life of the High Places—it is unbroken communion with You. Such companionship involves participating in what You are doing, which produces intoxicating joy. It also recognizes that You and You alone hold all things together and so must have first place.

> *"...all things have been created by Him and for Him. And He is before all things, and in Him all things hold together. He is also head of the body, the church; and He is the beginning, the first-born from the dead; so that He Himself might come to have first place in everything"*
> (Col. 1:16-18 NAS).

I gasp with wonder, awe, and thanksgiving at all that You have shown me, Lord. I long with all my heart to go higher and to see and understand more. Thank You that You have already walked this path I am on and that You have perfectly proportioned and set aside within me, through Your Spirit, everything I need.

"Grace and Glory," He answered, "do you think you understand now how I was able to make your feet like hinds' feet and to set you on these High Places?"

She drew closer to Him and looked earnestly in His face and asked, "How were you able to do this, my Lord and King?"

"Think back over the journey you made," He replied, "and tell me what lessons you learned on the way."

She was silent for a while as she reviewed the whole journey, which had seemed so terribly long and in some places so cruelly difficult and even impossible. She thought of the altars which she had built along the way; of the time when she had stood with Him at the trysting-place in the Valley, when He had called her to follow Him to the heights. She remembered the walk to the foot of the mountains; the first meeting with Suffering and Sorrow and of learning to accept their help; she recalled the shock of what had seemed such a heartbreaking detour down into the desert, and of the things which she had seen there.

Then their journey along the shores of Loneliness; the empty cove which the sea had filled to the brim; and then the agony of disappointment and frustration experienced in the wilderness when the path once again had turned away from the High Places. She remembered crossing the great sea-wall, walking through the woods and valleys until the rapturous moment when the path had turned back toward the mountains. Her thoughts turned to the Precipice of Injury, the Forests of Danger and Tribulation, the great storm during which they had sheltered in the hut. And then the mist—the endless mist, and the awful moment when the path suddenly led down into the Valley of Loss, and the nightmare abyss of horror into which she had looked when she had thought of turning back.

She recalled the descent down into the Valley of Loss and the peace she had found there before reascending to the heights in the aerial chairs, and of the days spent in that place where

# Unfailing Love

Lord Jesus, as I think back over my journey with You, I remember wondering, "Why can't You instantly make me like You?" If that had happened, I would have had a new me that I did not know living within my body. Your way is perfect. Gradually I have seen what I am like apart from You and I began relying less on myself and more on You. Thus I have fallen more and more in love with You and turned loose more and more of my trust in myself.

*"Oh, how great is Your goodness, which You have laid up for those who fear, revere and worship You.... Be strong and let your heart take courage, all you who wait and hope for and expect the Lord!"*
(Ps. 31:19,24 AMP)

I also realize, as we reminisce over our journey, that it is not what I do for You that is so important, but what You did for me and in me. I see how Your wonderful ways followed me.

*"Surely or only goodness, mercy and unfailing love shall follow me all the days of my life; and through the length of days the house of the Lord [and His presence] shall be my dwelling place"*
(Ps. 23:6 AMP).

she had been prepared for burial. Then that last agonizing ascent, and the cave where they sheltered from the floods and where she had been tempted to cast away the promises. Then the spring called Marah, and finally the mist-shrouded grave up among the peaks where she had been bound to the altar. How little she had imagined, when first she set out on that strange journey, what lay ahead of her and the things which she would be called upon to pass through. So for a long time she sat silent—remembering, wondering and thankful.

At last she put her hand in His and said softly, "My Lord, I will tell You what I learned."

"Tell Me," He answered gently.

"First," said she, "I learned that I must accept with joy all that You allowed to happen to me on the way and everything to which the path led me! That I was never to try to evade it but to accept it and lay down my own will on the altar and say, 'Behold me, I am Thy little handmaiden Acceptance-with-Joy.' "

He nodded without speaking, and she went on, "Then I learned that I must bear all that others were allowed to do against me and to forgive with no trace of bitterness and to say to Thee, 'Behold me—I am Thy little handmaiden Bearing-with-Love,' that I may receive power to bring good out of this evil."

Again He nodded, and she smiled still more sweetly and happily.

"The third thing that I learned was that You, my Lord, never regarded me as I actually was, lame and weak and crooked and cowardly. You saw me as I would be when You had done what You promised and had brought me to the High Places, when it could be truly said, 'There is none that walks with such a queenly ease, nor with such grace, as she.' You always treated me with the same love and graciousness as though I were a queen already and not wretched little Much-Afraid." Then she looked up into His face and for a little time could say no more,

# Loving Intent

Learning to accept or embrace with joy all that God allows to happen to us is a critical lesson that ushers us along in our maturity. Joseph is a good example of this. He accepted what happened to him and continued to faithfully serve the Lord throughout it. Years later he saw how God used the vileness of his brothers to develop his character and put him in a place where he could save an untold number of lives. Joseph could say to his brothers, after their father had died and they feared retribution from him:

*"As for you, you thought evil against me;*
*but God meant it for good"*
(Gen. 50:20a AMP).

For us today, living under the New Covenant, we see the simple, yet life-giving truth that Jesus is in control and that He alone gives the life our souls seek.

Thank You, my Lord, that I can be secure in Your choice and provision for my life. No one else can take away what You give to me. Likewise, I cannot get for myself what You have not given me. In this way I can depend only on You. How wonderful You are!

but at last she added, "My Lord, I cannot tell You how greatly I want to regard others in the same way."

A very lovely smile broke out on His face at that, but He still said nothing, only nodded for the third time and waited for her to continue.

"The fourth thing," said she with a radiant face, "was really the first I learned up here. Every circumstance in life, no matter how crooked and distorted and ugly it appears to be, if it is reacted to in love and forgiveness and obedience to Your will can be transformed.

"Therefore I begin to think, my Lord, You purposely allow us to be brought into contact with the bad and evil things that You want changed. Perhaps that is the very reason why we are here in this world, where sin and sorrow and suffering and evil abound, so that we may let You teach us so to react to them, that out of them we can create lovely qualities to live forever. That is the only really satisfactory way of dealing with evil, not simply binding it so that it cannot work harm, but whenever possible overcoming it with good."

At last He spoke. "You have learned well, Grace and Glory. Now I will add one thing more. It was these lessons which you have learned which enabled Me to change you from limping, crippled Much-Afraid into Grace and Glory with the hinds' feet. Now you are able to run, leaping on the mountains and able to follow Me wherever I go, so that we need never be parted again.

"So remember this; as long as you are willing to be Acceptance-with-Joy and Bearing-in-Love, you can never again become crippled, and you will be able to go wherever I lead you. You will be able to go down into the Valley of the world to work with Me there, for that is where the evil and sorrowful and ugly things are which need to be overcome.

"Accept and bear and obey the Law of Love, and nothing will be able to cripple your hinds' feet or to separate you from Me. This is the secret of the High Places, Grace and Glory, it

# Transforming Love

As we receive God's love to us through forgiveness of others and of ourselves, and as we see ourselves from His perspective, we are released to reach into the lives of others to care for their temporal and eternal destinies. When the first commandment of loving God with all our hearts, souls, minds, and strength is met, we can live out God's next most important command:

*"And a second is like it, You shall love your neighbor as [you do] yourself"*
(Mt. 22:39 AMP).

Do you know God's love today? Is there someone you have not forgiven–another or yourself? Every circumstance in life, no matter how crooked, distorted, and ugly it appears to be, if it is reacted to in love, forgiveness, and obedience to God's will, it can be transformed. It is not what happens that is so important, but how we react to it. Do we respond from His power and perspective, or from our own strength and perspective? Evil can be overcome only with good.

*"So then, those who suffer according to God's will should commit themselves to their faithful Creator and continue to do good"*
(1 Pet. 4:19 NIV).

Thank You, Lord Jesus, that I can not only face, but also embrace and walk through the ugly things of life and see You overcoming evil with good.

is the lovely and perfect law of the whole universe. It is this that makes the radiant joy of the Heavenly Places." Then He rose to His feet, drew her up beside Him, and said, "Now use your hinds' feet again, for I am going to lead you to another part of the mountain."

Off He went, "leaping on the mountains and skipping on the hills," with Grace and Glory following close behind and the beautiful figures of Peace and Joy springing at her side. As they went she sang this song:

> *Set me as a seal upon thine heart*
> *Thou Love more strong than death*
> *That I may feel through every part*
> *Thy burning, fiery breath.*
> *And then like wax held in the flame,*
> *May take the imprint of thy Name.*
>
> *Set me a seal upon thine arm,*
> *Thou Love that bursts the grave,*
> *Thy coals of fire can never harm,*
> *But only purge and save.*
> *Thou jealous Love, thou burning Flame,*
> *Oh, burn out all unlike thy Name.*
>
> *The floods can never drown thy Love,*
> *Nor weaken thy desire,*
> *The rains may deluge from above*
> *But never quench thy fire.*
> *Make soft my heart in thy strong flame,*
> *To take the imprint of thy Name.*

(Cant. 8:6)

# Faithful Doer

The High Places for us can be paralleled to the Promised Land, the land of Canaan, for the children of Israel. God parted the Red Sea so they could walk through on dry land. As we walk in awareness of His presence, completely dependent and surrendered to Him (walking on the dry land), He helps us to separate the vile (waters restrained on either side), and to enjoy the precious (His complete provision). There were indeed giants to be faced in the Promised Land, but God gave victory to the Israelites as they walked in obedience to His will.

*"Every place on which the sole of your foot treads,*
*I have given it to you, just as I spoke to Moses. ...*
*Only be strong and very courageous; be careful to do*
*according to all the law which Moses My servant*
*commanded you; do not turn from it to the right or to*
*the left, so that you may have success wherever you go"*
(Josh. 1:3,7 NAS).

Praise Him for His faithful work in your life. Freely release any and all thoughts and desires to Him to master and fulfill.

# CHAPTER 20

# Return to the Valley

The place to which the King of Love now brought them was a most beautiful valley among the peaks of the High Places. The whole of this sheltered spot was laid out in quiet gardens and orchards and vineyards. Here grew flowers of rarest beauty and lilies of every description. Here, too, were trees of spices and of many kinds of fruits, and nut trees, almonds and walnuts, and many other varieties which Grace and Glory had never seen before. Here the King's gardeners were always busy, pruning the trees, tending the plants and the vines, and preparing beds for new seedlings and tender shoots.

These the King Himself transplanted from uncongenial soil and conditions in the valleys below so that they might grow to perfection and bloom in that valley high above, ready to be planted in other parts of the Kingdom of Love, to beautify and adorn it wherever the King saw fit. They spent several delightful days watching the gardeners as they worked under the gracious supervision of the King Himself and accompanying Him as He walked in the vineyards, teaching and advising those who tended the vines.

One day, however, Grace and Glory with her two attendants walked to the end of the valley and found themselves on the very edge of the High Places, from which they could look right down into the Low Places far below. As they stood there they saw a long, green valley between two chains of mountains through which a river wound like a ribbon of light. Here and

# Marriage Feast

No matter what peaks of the High Places we tread upon, no matter what beautiful valleys we pass through, all of life in time and space climaxes with our Lord calling us to the marriage supper of the Lamb. On our journey we tasted of Him and saw that He is as humble as the beds of spices and the terraces of sweet flowers. His eyes are full of compassion, yet they pierce to the innermost depths of our hearts. His nail-pierced hands and feet forever display the scars, reminding us that He alone paid the price for us to be His Bride.

> " 'Let us rejoice and be glad and give the glory to Him,
> for the marriage of the Lamb has come and His bride
> has made herself ready.' And it was given to her to
> clothe herself in fine linen, bright and clean; for the
> fine linen is the righteous acts of the saints"
> (Rev. 19:7-8 NAS).

As we walk where He plants us in His presence, we are being clothed in fine linen, bright and clean.

How gracious You are, my Lord, to carefully plant me in soil in which I can reach perfection and bloom for Your glory.

there were patches of brown and red which seemed to be villages and dwelling places, surrounded with trees and gardens.

All of a sudden, Grace and Glory gave a queer little gasp, for she recognized the place. They were looking down into the Valley of Humiliation itself, the place where she had lived in misery for so long and from which the Shepherd had called her to the High Places.

Without a word she sat down on the grassy slope, and as she looked a multitude of thoughts filled her mind. Down there was the little white cottage where she had lived, and the pastures where the shepherds tended the King's flocks. There were the sheepfolds, and the stream where the flocks went to drink and where she had met the Shepherd for the first time. In that valley were all her fellow workers and the friends among whom she had lived and with whom she had enjoyed such happy fellowship.

Others she had known were there, too. Away on the outskirts of the village was the cottage where her Aunt Dismal Forebodings lived and where she had spent her miserable childhood with her cousins Gloomy and Spiteful and Craven Fear. As she thought of them and their wretched existence a pang of compassion and pain shot through her heart.

Poor Aunt Dismal, trying to hide the fact that her heart was broken by the unhappy marriages which her two daughters had made, and embittered by the shameful doings of her darling son. She saw the dwellings of her other relatives; the Manor House, where decrepit old Lord Fearing lived, tortured by his failing powers and his dread of approaching death. There was the house where Pride lived, and near it the homes of Bitterness and Resentment, and under those dark trees lived miserable Self-Pity. She recognized the dwelling places of those who had so harassed her on her journey to the High Places, and round about were the homes of other inhabitants of the Valley, people who hated or despised or rejected the Shepherd.

306

# Reliant Faith

While you rest in Jesus' presence, think back over your life. When and where are the times and places in which you felt the safest and most secure? When did you feel most protected? Let Him teach you and open up your understanding as you wait before Him. Do you hear Him whisper, "Do you dare to walk with Me, in that same security, in those areas where you do not feel as confident?" Consider Abraham. He left all he knew to follow a God he wasn't really familiar with. Yet because of his obedience, he became the father of many nations as well as the father of our faith!

*"For this reason it is by faith, that it might be in accordance with grace, in order that the promise may be certain to all the descendants, not only to those who are of the Law, but also to those who are of the faith of Abraham, who is the father of us all"* (Rom. 4:16 NAS).

Lord, I choose to go from the secure places into the insecure places with You. Thank You for the victory You bring!

As Grace and Glory sat looking down into the Valley the tears welled into her eyes and her heart throbbed with pain, two sensations which she had completely forgotten up there on the High Places.

Suddenly she discovered that her feelings toward her relatives and those who lived down there in the Valley had undergone a complete change, and she saw them in a new light. She had thought of them only as horrible enemies, but now she realized that they were just miserable beings such as she had been herself. They were indwelt and tormented by their different besetting sins and ugly natures, just as she had been by her fears. They were wretched slaves to the natures which gave them their names, and the more horrible the qualities which characterized them, the more misery they endured, and the more we should show them compassion.

She could scarcely bear the thought, yet for so many years she had not only feared but also condemned them, had actually "disdained their misery," telling herself it was their own fault. Yes, she, detestable, fear-enslaved Much-Afraid had actually dared to disdain them for the things which made them so wretched and ugly when she herself was equally wretched and enslaved. Instead of a fellow feeling of compassion and passionate desire that they might be delivered and transformed from the pride and resentment and bitterness which made them what they were, she had just detested and despised them.

When she thought of that she turned to Joy and Peace, who were sitting beside her, and cried out desperately, "Can nothing be done for them down there in the Valley? Must my Aunt Dismal be left unhelped, and poor Spiteful and Gloomy too, and those cousins who went so far with us on the way to the High Places, trying to turn us back! If the Shepherd could deliver me, Grace and Glory, from all my fears and sins, couldn't He deliver them also from the things which torment them?"

"Yes," said Joy (who had been Sorrow). "If He can turn Sorrow into Joy, Suffering into Peace, and Much-Afraid into Grace

# Compassion Extended

As we care for our own hearts before the Lord, dealing with what He shows us needs to be dealt with, He brings forth in us a change of attitude toward others. Since our own identities become established as we walk with Him, the fear we once had somehow becomes transformed into compassion. We want to reach out to those caught in the same traps. We feel this way because God

*"comforts us in all our affliction so that we may be able to comfort those who are in any affliction with the comfort with which we ourselves are comforted by God"*
(2 Cor. 1:4 NAS).

This change of attitude also results from our repentance.

*"Bring forth fruit that is consistent with repentance—let your lives prove your change of heart"*
(Mt. 3:8 AMP).

Who can you reach out to today?

My Lord, when I was overwhelmed by my predicament, You raised me up and showed me my potential. Now allow me to do this for others. Demonstrate Your compassion through me.

and Glory, how can we doubt that He could change Pride and Bitterness and Resentment and Self-Pity too, if they would but yield to Him and follow Him? And your Aunt Dismal could be changed into Praise and Thanksgiving, and poor Gloomy and Spiteful also. We cannot doubt that it could be done that they could be completely delivered from all the things which torment them."

"But," cried Grace and Glory, "how can they be persuaded to follow the Shepherd? At present they hate Him and won't go near Him."

Then Peace (who before had been Suffering) said quietly, "I have noticed that when people are brought into sorrow and suffering, or loss, or humiliation, or grief, or into some place of great need, they sometimes become ready to know the Shepherd and to seek His help. We know, for example, that your Aunt Dismal is desperately unhappy over the behavior of poor Craven Fear, and it may be that she would be ready now to turn to the Shepherd. Then poor Gloomy and Spiteful are so wretched that though they felt no need of the Shepherd before, it is very possible that now is the time to try to persuade them to seek His help."

"Yes!" exclaimed Grace and Glory, "I am sure you are right. Oh, if only we could go to them! If only there were some way of helping them to find what we have found."

At that very moment, close at hand, sounded the voice of the King. He came and sat down beside them, looked with them down the Valley so far below, and said gently to Grace and Glory, "Thou that dwellest in the gardens, the companions hearken to thy voice; cause Me to hear it" (Cant. 8:13).

Grace and Glory turned to Him and laid her hand upon His arm. "My Lord," she said, "we were talking about the people who live down there in the Valley of Humiliation. They are my relatives, you know, all of them. They are so wretched and miserable. What can we do for them, my Lord? They don't know anything about the joy of the High Places and the Kingdom of Love. There

# Broken Yokes

What a joy to know we can be delivered from all the things that torment us, and that others likewise can be delivered, if they would choose to yield to Jesus and follow Him. God's Word says:

*"[Rather,] is not this the fast that I have chosen:*
*to loose the bonds of wickedness, to undo the bands*
*of the yoke, to let the oppressed go free, and that*
*you break every [enslaving] yoke?"*
(Is. 58:6 AMP)

What "fast"—an abstinence from something God has put His finger upon—is He calling you to in order to break an enslaving yoke in your life or in the life of another? Remember to differentiate these yokes from some of the things we go through to enter into the Kingdom of God. Paul and Barnabas said:

*"...it is through many hardships and tribulations*
*we must enter the kingdom of God"*
(Acts 14:22 AMP).

Let the Holy Spirit direct you in breaking the yokes that enslave.

is my poor Aunt Dismal Forebodings. I lived with her for a long time, and know that she is utterly wretched."

"I know her," said the King quietly, "she is a most unhappy woman."

"And her daughter Gloomy," went on Grace and Glory, looking at Him entreatingly as she spoke. "She married Coward, the son of old Lord Fearing, very rich, but much older than herself and a miserably unhappy and selfish creature. I believe she has not known a moment's peace since. There was talk in the Valley before I came away, that he was likely to desert her."

"He has done so," answered the King quietly, "and she has returned to her mother in the cottage, a miserable and disillusioned woman with a broken heart."

"And her sister Spiteful. Poor, poor soul, with her sharp tongue which makes so many enemies and deprives her of friends. She married Timid-Skulking, and they are desperately poor, and have to live in one little rented room in the house of my cousin Bitterness and his wife. I cannot bear to think of their wretched condition while I live up here in the Kingdom of Love."

"They are wretched indeed," said the King, even more gently and compassionately than before. "They have just lost the little daughter who poor Spiteful had hoped would be such a comfort to them in their dreary circumstances."

"And then," continued Grace and Glory with just a hint of hesitation in her voice, "there is their brother Craven Fear." She did not look at the King as she spoke, but paused a moment, then went on hurriedly. "He is the most unhappy member of the whole family. He has broken his mother's heart; neither of his sisters will speak to him any more, and he goes skulking about the Valley hated by everyone."

"I know him," replied the King gravely, but with just a hint of a smile. "I know him well. You do not exaggerate when you speak of his wretchedness. I have had to interfere and chastise

# Breach Repaired

God's desire is that families be united, restored, and healed of broken, painful relationships. The last two verses in the Old Testament call for the repentance and restoration (represented by the prophet Elijah) of families, in order to hold back God's hand from striking the land with a curse.

*"See, I will send you the prophet Elijah before that great and dreadful day of the Lord comes. He will turn the hearts of the fathers to their children, and the hearts of the children to their fathers; or else I will come and strike the land with a curse"*
(Mal. 4:5-6 NIV).

Lord, use me as it pleases You in the lives of my family. When I see myself in my family, enable me not to withdraw or be angry, but to trust You for them and for myself. It is my desire to be a repairer of breaches and a restorer of ways. Help me to separate the precious from the vile and see things from Your perspective. I thank You for Your grace in these situations.

him many times to try and correct his bullying propensities. But 'though I have chastened him sore I have not given him over unto death.' "

"No, no!" cried Grace and Glory imploringly, "don't ever do that, my Lord! Oh, I beg You, find some way to rescue and deliver him from himself, as You delivered me."

He made no answer for a little while, only looked at her very kindly and with a look of great contentment and happiness on His face. At last He spoke. "I am more than willing to do what you suggest," said He. "But, Grace and Glory, these unhappy souls we are speaking about will not allow Me into their homes, nor even permit Me to speak to them. I need a voice to speak for Me, to persuade them to let Me help them."

"I see what you mean," she cried joyfully. "We will go down with You and speak to them and show what You have done for us and what You are willing and able to do for them."

"Do you think they will listen to you?" He asked, smiling at her very gently as He spoke.

"No, I don't think it's at all likely—at least, not at first," she answered. "I was not at all the sort of person to make them want to listen to me. I did not behave at all lovingly to them, but You will tell me what to say. You will teach me and I will say it for You.

"O my Lord, let us make haste, and go down there. When they see what You have done for me, when they see Peace and Joy, I do think in the end they will want You to help them too. It is because they have lied to themselves about You and have persuaded themselves that You cannot do them good that they resist You and turn from Your help, but we will plead with them. Especially now, my Lord, when they are so unhappy and so despised by others. Their very misery and loneliness and sorrow will make them more willing to listen to news of Your grace and of Your desire to help them."

# Restorative Words

Those closest to us are in a position to be the greatest source of blessing in our lives, but conversely, can cause more pain than others. Therefore, we often try to protect ourselves. Although self-protection is a normal reaction of the flesh, we must let

*"our inner selves wait [earnestly] for the Lord;*
*He is our help and our shield"*
(Ps. 33:20 AMP).

Perhaps there is someone in particular you have shielded yourself from, but who you long would come to know the abundant life that only Jesus can give. Have you been hesitant to speak with that person for fear of experiencing more pain? When you go with a heart of love and make yourself available to walk through the doors that Jesus opens, you can rest upon His Word in Luke 12:12:

*"For the Holy Spirit will teach you in that very*
*hour and moment what [you] ought to say"*
(AMP).

My Lord, I am available to You. Direct my path and tell me what to say to my loved one or to anyone else You have in mind.

"True," He agreed, "that is just what I think. This is indeed a specially favorable time for us to go down and try to help them."

He rose to His feet as He spoke. She sprang up too, and all four stood joyful and radiant on the edge of the High Places, ready to go leaping down to the Valley again. Then Grace and Glory saw that the great waterfall quite close at hand was leaping down to the Valley too, with the tumultuous, joyful noise of many waters, singing as they poured themselves down over the rock lip:

> *From the heights we leap and flow*
> *To the valleys down below,*
> *Sweetest urge and sweetest will,*
> *To go lower, lower still.*

Suddenly she understood. She was beholding a wondrous and glorious truth; "a great multitude whom no man could number" brought like herself by the King to the Kingdom of Love and to the High Places so that they could now pour out their lives in gladdest abandonment, leaping down with Him to the sorrowful, desolate places below, to share with others the life which they had received. She herself was only one drop among that glad, exultant throng of Self-givers, the followers of the King of Love, united with Him and with one another, each one equally blessed and beloved as herself. "For He loves each one of us," she said to herself, "as though there were only one to love."

The thought of being made one with the great fall of many waters filled her heart with ecstasy and with a rapturous joy beyond power to express. She, too, at last, was to go down with them, pouring herself forth in Love's abandonment of Self-giving. "He brought me to the heights just for this," she whispered to herself, and then looked at Him and nodded.

At that He began leaping and springing down the mountainside before them, bounding from rock to rock, always choosing, however, leaps which were within their power to follow, and sure footholds for less experienced feet. Behind Him

# Loving Ambassadors

Do you know that God loves each one of His children as though He has only that one to love? Yes, it is true! Grasp and receive such love from His heart to your heart. Bask in it. Then freely pour yourself out to others as the waters cast themselves down in glad abandonment from the heights of the waterfall to the sorrowful, desolate places below, bringing refreshment and good news. Make yourself available just as He made Himself available to us.

*"To the thirsty I [Myself] will give water without price from the fountain (springs) of the water of Life"*
(Rev. 21:6b AMP).

Consider yourself to be God's ambassador, the Lord's official representative, appointed and accredited to demonstrate His Kingdom to others.

*"Therefore, we are ambassadors for Christ, as though God were entreating through us; we beg you on behalf of Christ, be reconciled to God"*
(2 Cor. 5:20 NAS).

I pour myself forth in love's abandonment of self-giving, my Lord.

went Grace and Glory, with Joy and Peace beside her, leaping down, just as the waters leaped and sang beside them. They mingled their voices with the joyful music of the many waters, singing their own individual song:

> *Make haste, Beloved, be thou like an hart*
> *On mountains spicy sweet;*
> *And I, on those High Places where thou art,*
> *Will follow on hinds' feet;*
> *As close behind the hart, there leaps the roe,*
> *So where thou goest, I will surely go.*

That, as perhaps you know, is the last verse of the Song of Songs, which is Solomon's. But for Grace and Glory it was the beginning of a new song altogether.

# Sweet Companionship

J esus' first words to us are:

> *"Come to Me, all who are weary and heavy-laden,*
> *and I will give you rest. Take My yoke upon you,*
> *and learn from Me, for I am gentle and humble*
> *in heart; and you shall find rest for your souls.*
> *For My yoke is easy, and My load is light"*
> (Mt. 11:28-30 NAS).

Once we come, learn, and rest, His last words are:

> *"Go then and make disciples of all the nations,*
> *baptizing them into the name of the Father and*
> *of the Son and of the Holy Spirit; teaching them*
> *to observe everything that I have commanded you,*
> *and lo, I am with you all the days... to the [very]*
> *close and consummation of the age..."*
> (Mt. 28:19-20 AMP).

With unconcealed eagerness to share sweet companionship with Jesus, the One altogether lovely, say like Ruth:

> *"...whither thou goest, I will go; and where thou*
> *lodgest, I will lodge: thy people shall be my people,*
> *and thy God my God: where thou diest, will I die,*
> *and there will I be buried: the Lord do so to me,*
> *and more also, if ought but death part thee and me"*
> (Ruth 1:16-17 KJV).

# Be sure to ask for these wonderful items from our Hinds' Feet Collection:

## Hinds' Feet — A Woman's Devotional

The entire "Hinds' Feet" text by Hannah Hurnard with an encouraging daily devotional by Darien B. Cooper.

## The Shepherd of the High Places — A Devotional for Men

The entire "Hinds' Feet" text with a challenging daily devotional by Karl Duff. It will be released January 1, 1994.

## My Journey to the High Places

A diary/journal featuring charcoal sketches from the illustrated edition. It will be released the Spring of 1994.

## Coloring Books for Children

A collection of delightful coloring books featuring the Hinds' Feet characters and teaching important lessons about praying and trusting Jesus. They will be released the Spring of 1994.

## Hinds' Feet on High Places — Illustrated for Children

This is 128 pages of total delight. Carefully illustrated in full color, this volume brings this classic to life!